Evidence-Based Counselling and Psychological Therapies

Evidence-Based Counselling and Psychological Therapies assesses the impact of the international drive towards evidence-based health care on NHS policy and the provision of psychological services in the NHS.

An outstanding range of contributors provides an overview of evidence-based health care and the research methods that underpin it, demonstrating its effect on policy, provision, practitioners and patients. Their thought-provoking chapters look at a variety of relevant issues including:

- generating and implementing evidence
- cost-effectiveness
- practice guidelines
- practitioner research

Evidence-Based Counselling and Psychological Therapies is essential for mental health professionals and trainees concerned with this movement which is having, and will continue to have, a huge impact on the purchasing, provision and practice of health care.

Nancy Rowland is the Research & Development Facilitator at York NHS Trust and is Head of Communication/Dissemination at the NHS Centre for Reviews and Dissemination at the University of York. She is a member of the British Association for Counselling's Research & Evaluation Committee.

Stephen Goss is an Honorary Research Fellow at the University of Strathclyde, a Counsellor at Napier University and a qualified counselling supervisor. He is a member of the British Association for Counselling Practice Development Committee and Chair of their Research and Evaluation Committee.

Evidence-Based Counselling and Psychological Therapies

Research and applications

Edited by Nancy Rowland
and Stephen Goss

London and Philadelphia

First published 2000 by Routledge
11 New Fetter Lane, London EC4P 4EE

Simultaneously published in the USA and Canada
by Taylor & Francis Inc
325 Chestnut Street, 8th Floor, Philadelphia PA 19106

Routledge is an imprint of the Taylor & Francis Group

Typeset in Times by Keystroke, Jacaranda Lodge, Wolverhampton
Printed and bound in Great Britain by TJ International Ltd, Padstow, Cornwall

British Library Cataloguing in Publication Data
A catalogue record for this book is available from the British Library

Library of Congress Cataloging in Publication Data
Evidence-based counselling and psychological therapies : research and
applications / edited by Nancy Rowland and Stephen Goss.
        p.   cm.
    Includes bibliographical references and index.
    1. Psychotherapy–Outcome assessment–Great Britain. 2. Mental health
policy–Great Britain. 3. Evidence-based medicine–Great Britain.
4. National Health Service (Great Britain)–Administration. I. Rowland,
Nancy, 1954– II. Goss, Stephen, 1966–

RC480.75 .E95 2000
362.2'0941–dc21   00–021257

ISBN 0–415–20506–9 (hbk)
ISBN 0–415–20507–7 (pbk)

To my parents
Nancy Rowland

To Catriona, Andrew and Lynn
Stephen Goss

Contents

Boxes

Tables

Contributors

Mark Baker is the Medical Director of North Yorkshire Health Authority and Honorary Visiting Professor at the University of York. He was previously Regional Director of Research and Development for Yorkshire Regional Health Authority and Director of the National Research & Development Programme for Mental Health.

Michael Barkham is Professor of Clinical and Counselling Psychology and Director of the Psychological Therapies Research Centre at the University of Leeds. He has previously carried out controlled trials into the efficacy of contrasting psychotherapies and is part of a research group that has developed a new evaluation tool – the CORE System. He has an abiding interest in a range of research methodologies and their role in bridging the gap between research and practice.

Peter Bower is a psychologist and Research Fellow at the National Primary Care Research and Development Centre (NPCRDC) at the University of Manchester. He currently conducts research on the effectiveness of psychological therapies in primary care, the relationship between mental health specialists and primary care professionals, and the doctor–patient relationship in general practice.

John Cape is Head of Psychology and Psychotherapy Services, Camden and Islington Community Health Services NHS Trust. He convenes the National Counselling and Psychological Therapies Clinical Guidelines Steering Group, and is chair of the Management Board of the British Psychological Society Centre for Outcomes Research and Effectiveness.

Brian Ferguson is Professor of Health Economics at the Nuffield Institute for Health, University of Leeds and Assistant Director (Clinical Governance) for the North Yorkshire Health Authority. His research interests are primarily around the implementation of evidence-based health care and clinical governance, in particular the contribution that economics can make towards improving service delivery and creating appropriate incentive mechanisms. Other interests include the assessment of payback from NHS R&D investment, and the economic impact of organisational mergers.

Simon Gilbody currently holds a Medical Research Council fellowship in Health Services Research based at the NHS Centre for Reviews and Dissemination, University of York, where he is studying for his doctorate. He is involved in the conduct of systematic reviews in the sphere of mental health and is an Editor of the Cochrane Schizophrenia Group. He has first degrees in both medicine and psychology and is a practising psychiatrist, with membership of the Royal College of Psychiatrists.

Stephen Goss is Honorary Research Fellow at the University of Strathclyde, a counsellor at Napier University and a qualified counselling supervisor. His research interests focus primarily on the development of pluralist approaches to the evaluation of counselling and psychotherapy. He also has an interest in the uses and limitations of technology in counselling and psychotherapy. He is Chair of the Research and Evaluation Committee of the British Association for Counselling and is involved in the strategic development of research in counselling in the UK.

Michael King is a research and clinical psychiatrist whose chief interests are psychiatric epidemiology and health services research. He has a particular expertise in the conduct of randomised clinical trials of complex interventions in mental health. He has conducted several trials concerning brief psychotherapy in primary and secondary medical care.

Jos Kleijnen was registered a physician (University of Limburg, Maastricht, Netherlands) in 1987. He worked as a research fellow in the department of Epidemiology, University of Limburg from 1987–93, and his Ph.D. Dissertation 'Food supplements and their efficacy' (in 1991) contained many systematic reviews. He was registered as an epidemiologist in 1993, moving to Amsterdam in that year as a clinical epidemiologist in the department of Clinical Epidemiology and Biostatistics in the Academic Medical Centre where he stayed until 1998 and worked with clinicians on various clinical research projects. Jos established the Dutch Cochrane Centre in 1994 and helped to establish the Cochrane Peripheral Vascular Diseases Review Group in 1995, and was a member of the Cochrane Collaboration Steering Group from 1996–8. Currently he is Professor and Director of the NHS Centre for Reviews and Dissemination, University of York. His special interests are methodology of clinical research, systematic reviews, the role of placebo effects in randomised trials, screening and diagnostic test evaluations.

John McLeod is Professor of Counselling at the University of Abertay Dundee. His main interests are in the development of narrative-informed therapies and the role of research in improving counselling services.

Alan Maynard is Professor of Health Economics at the University of York and co-director of the York Health Policy Group. He was Founding Director of the Centre for Health Economics, University of York (1983–95) and is Founding Editor of the journal *Health Economics*. He has published extensively in academic and professional journals and has worked as a consultant for the World Bank, the World Health Organization and the UK Department for International Development. He is Chair of the York NHS Trust.

John Mellor-Clark is a Visiting Senior Research Fellow at the University of Leeds, and Manager of 'Quality Evaluation Services' specialising in the audit, evaluation and outcome benchmarking of psychological therapy treatments in NHS, educational and employment settings. He is a member of the BAC Research & Evaluation Committee.

Glenys Parry is Director of Research for Community Health Sheffield NHS Trust, Professor Associate in Health Care Psychology at the University of Sheffield and Visiting Professor, University College London. A clinical psychologist and cognitive analytic psychotherapist, she led the NHS Executive review of strategic policy on NHS psychotherapy services in England. She has published in the fields of mental health, life event stress, social support, psychotherapy research, policy and practice.

Nancy Rowland is the R&D Facilitator at York NHS Trust and Head of Communication/Dissemination at the NHS Centre for Reviews and Dissemination, University of York. Her research interests include the evaluation of counselling, and getting evidence into practice. She is a member of the British Association for Counselling's Research & Evaluation Committee.

Ian Russell has been Founding Professor of Health Sciences at the University of York since the beginning of 1995. Research and development in the NHS is a major interest of his new department. Ian was educated at Cambridge (graduating in Mathematics), Birmingham (Statistics) and Essex (Health Services Research). He has held academic appointments in the Universities of Newcastle upon Tyne (where he mainly researched into general practice), North Carolina (mainly into ambulatory care), Aberdeen (where he was Director of the Scottish Health Services Research Unit, and mainly researched into acute services), and Wales (where he was Director of Research and Development for NHS Wales). Ian's part-time appointments have included: Associate Director of Research and Development for NHS Northern and Yorkshire; Chair of the NHS Commissioning Group for Health Technology Assessment; and Deputy Chair of the Health Services Research Board of the Medical Research Council.

Amanda Sowden is currently Senior Research Fellow at the NHS Centre for Reviews and Dissemination, University of York. She is involved in the conduct of systematic reviews and in developing methods for undertaking them. She also has an interest in the implementation of evidence into practice, and professional behaviour change. She has a first degree and a Ph.D. in psychology.

Preface

Evidence-based practice is increasingly being adopted as a fundamental principle in mental health care (e.g. UK Mental Health National Service Framework, 1999). However, it is important to remember the primary aim of evidence-based practice, which is to enable clinicians and patients to identify and access the interventions that are most likely to achieve the desired outcomes.

Following the recognition that it was almost impossible for clinicians and their patients and clients to keep up-to-date with important clinical advances, evidence-based practice has developed as a set of strategies designed to harness the advances in clinical epidemiology (the basic science of clinical practice) and information technology (allowing rapid access to up-to-date and reliable information).

Some have expressed concern that, in our current preoccupation with quantitative evidence, the central importance of the relationship between the clinician and patient and their therapeutic alliance may be overlooked. Nowhere is this danger more important than in mental health care. In the area of counselling and psychological therapies, there is a rich and sophisticated body of research applicable to clinical practice. The application of the rigorous standards of evidence-based practice in this field can initially be rather sobering. As in other fields of health care, the available evidence is often rather unreliable and rarely unequivocal. However, as this timely and useful book shows, when properly integrated with clinical judgement, the techniques of evidence-based practice can help practitioners and patients decide jointly on the therapeutic approaches that are likely to be most helpful.

John Geddes MD MRCPsych
Senior Clinical Research Fellow and Honorary Consultant Psychiatrist
Director, Centre for Evidence-Based Mental Health
Editor, *Evidence-Based Mental Health*

Part 1

What is evidence-based health care?

Chapter 1

Evidence-based psychological therapies

Nancy Rowland and Stephen Goss

INTRODUCTION

Those who work in the NHS need no reminding that health care reform is an international epidemic which shows no sign of abating (Klein, 1995). Keeping up with and managing the changes that come about as a result of health care reform is an all too familiar part of the job. Health care reforms spawn policies which invariably affect the pattern and provision of services, the professional practice of those who work in the NHS, and patient care. Much policy change is understood through the experience of implementing it. However, it is important to understand the origins of a particular health care reform, its aims, methodologies, the organisation and structures which support it, and the policies that it engenders.

This book is written for those with an interest in counselling and psychological therapies in the NHS – the clinical psychologists, counsellors, nurses and other professionals who provide mental health care, and the managers and service co-ordinators who plan services and implement policies. We aim to assess the impact of the evidence-based health care movement on NHS policy and the provision of psychological therapies in the NHS, as well as discussing the implications for professional practice. It is essential for psychological therapists to be well informed about the evidence-based health care movement, to understand its rationale and the methodologies which underpin it, so as to gain a clearer understanding of how evidence-based health care (EBHC) affects policy, provision, professional practice and, above all, patients.

DEFINITIONS

It is impossible to write a book about psychological therapies without first explaining what we mean by them. For years, authors and practitioners have been taxed with the question of where counselling ends and psychotherapy begins, whether there are more similarities or differences between them and where psychology and behavioural therapies fit in. In this book, which includes contributions from a range of practitioners and researchers reflecting diverse therapeutic and theoretical orientations, we have used the phrase 'psychological therapies' as an umbrella term to refer to the broad range of psychological treatments, including psychotherapy, counselling, cognitive behavioural treatments and problem-solving approaches. Although the practitioners offering these interventions may differ, and the interventions themselves may diverge, psychological treatments offered by psychological therapists all attempt to bring about improvements in mental health – for the purposes of this book, the terms and treatments are interchangeable.

Another bone of contention in the mental health field is whether those who receive treatment are called patients or clients. Once again, in this book, the terms are used interchangeably.

In defining evidence-based health care, it is perhaps fair to start with evidence-based medicine, as the drive towards evidence-based health care started within the medical profession. Sackett *et al.* (1996) define evidence-based medicine (EBM) as the conscientious, explicit and judicious use of current best evidence in making decisions about the care of individual patients. The practice of evidence-based medicine means integrating individual clinical expertise with the best available external clinical evidence from systematic research (Sackett *et al.*, 1996). Thus, evidence-based health care (EBHC) is defined as the conscientious, explicit and judicious use of current best evidence in making decisions about any aspects of health care (Li Wan Po, 1998). Like psychological therapies, evidence-based health care is another umbrella term which includes evidence-based medicine, evidence-based nursing and evidence-based mental health, as well as evidence-based practice, evidence-based patient choice and so on. The list of terms is almost endless. Although there may be controversy about the various definitions, particularly in relation to the type of evidence which is admissible, which type of evidence is best and how inclusive the evidence ought to be (Li Wan Po, 1998), the definition of evidence-based health care, above, takes a neutral stance in these respects. We leave our contributors to debate the methodological issues in later chapters of the book.

OVERVIEW

This book is written in three parts. The first gives a broad overview of the evidence-based health care movement, including its origins, its aims and the policies and structures that embed it in the NHS. The second part focuses on the methods used to generate the evidence, and debates the strengths and weaknesses of research methods which contribute to our knowledge about psychological therapies. The third part deals with synthesising the evidence, through systematic reviews and the development of guidelines. Implementation – or the relationship of policy to practice – is one of the major themes of the book, and, we hope, is evident throughout.

WHAT IS EVIDENCE-BASED HEALTH CARE?

In Chapter 2, Mark Baker and Jos Kleijnen describe the revolution beginning in the fields of health research leading to the movement for evidence-based health care. They describe the NHS R&D strategy and the agencies which support it. The purpose of the R&D strategy is to build a knowledge base to inform all decisions made by NHS managers, clinicians and practitioners. The policy involves an information strategy to assemble and interpret the results of completed research and to draw conclusions, a research-commissioning strategy to pose and address important unanswered questions and an implementation strategy to transfer reliable research findings into everyday practice. Baker and Kleijnen describe how research is commissioned, produced and disseminated and how it is assessed and accessed. They also depict the infrastructures, such as the Cochrane Collaboration, the NHS Centre for Reviews and Dissemination, and the National Institute for Clinical Excellence, which support evidence-based health care. Their focus on the difficulties of getting evidence into practice is taken up by other authors throughout the book, and highlights the need to develop implementation strategies. We will look at this initiative from the practitioner perspective in the concluding chapter.

Baker and Kleijnen's chapter is both practical, in that it gives a range of information about the world-wide industry of EBHC, and political, in that it criticises aspects of current UK mental health policy. Suggestions are made on how to improve the management of mental health services and research into mental health problems. As the authors point out in their conclusion, government policy provides a framework to drive evidence-based health practice on a national basis, by linking the outputs of reliable research to recommendations for effective practice, by setting up a monitoring agency (Commission for Health Improvement) and a focus on health.

Brian Ferguson and Ian Russell begin Chapter 3 by developing a philosophy of evidence-based health care and by defining its goals and the principles that underpin it. Drawing on work from the NHS Directorate of the Welsh Office, they focus on the goals of health gain, people centredness and resource effectiveness. Thus they highlight the need for evidence about individual and population health, the values and preferences of patients, carers and staff, and the optimal use of a range of resources. Ferguson and Russell offer a new definition of evidence-based health care: 'the collaborative process of generating, synthesising and implementing rigorous and relevant evidence about the effectiveness, fairness and efficiency of all forms of health care'. Alan Maynard takes up the theme of fairness and efficiency in his chapter on economics-based health care.

Ferguson and Russell introduce the case for deriving evidence about psychological therapies through randomised trials, presaging the current methodological debate about the strengths and weakness of experimental and observational methods in the evaluation of psychological interventions. This debate reflects pressing concerns among researchers and practitioners in the field. In the second part of the book a range of contributors expand and expound upon the issues raised here by Ferguson and Russell.

The authors next outline the threats to evidence-based health care. Once again, they introduce the preoccupations of other contributors, all of whom voice concern about the difficulties of implementing evidence. Indeed, in acknowledging the efforts that have been made to improve the knowledge base, there is a growing body of opinion that suggests a halt should be put to gathering evidence, and that efforts should now be put solely into implementing what is already known. While Ferguson and Russell do not advocate such a radical step, they do describe some of the problems of implementation, including the need for a shift in culture in the NHS, its staff and its patients, and highlighting the lack of adequate information technology systems to produce valid and reliable audit data on clinical performance. The authors warn against the mechanistic tendencies of EBHC through guidelines development compared with the inherent uncertainties of clinical practice. In their concluding section, Ferguson and Russell review the national policy initiatives that encourage evidence-based health care, such as setting objectives for health improvement and the development of National Service Frameworks. They focus in detail on clinical governance, with its emphasis on quality and accountability across primary and secondary care, suggesting that the NHS has now incorporated evidence-based health care into the statutory process of clinical governance. The role of the Health Authority is important here. Health Authorities (HA) in England and Wales are responsible for co-ordinating clinical governance across all local NHS organisations, including the newly formed (April 1999) Primary Care Groups. In summary, local clinical governance arrangements oblige HAs to ensure that commissioning and provision of health care is based on the available evidence.

Chapter 4 focuses on economic issues. Alan Maynard proposes that practitioners reframe their approach to health care, which focuses on treating patients if there is a benefit to them, and to think about a different perspective: population health. This involves an emphasis on the health of the community, rather than on the health of the individual being treated. Maynard argues that economics-based health care (EcBHC) is the most appropriate form of EBHC, in that it forms a transparent and rational basis from which to determine resource allocation criteria and evidence of cost-effectiveness. Interventions that are cost-effective will be clinically effective – although the reverse is not always true – and purchasing clinically cost-effective health care maximises population health gain. Such a commissioning strategy would have the added advantage of reducing variability in service patterns, whether for psychological or other services.

Maynard suggests that as the social objective of the health care system is the maximisation of health gains from a finite budget, rationing should be carried out explicitly on the basis of cost-effectiveness, not mere clinical effectiveness. He advocates the use of guidelines based on evidence of cost-effectiveness to determine clinical practice and further suggests that this demands a shift away from the individual practitioner–patient relationship and the individual interests of the patients, to a focus on the social interest of economics-based health care. Maynard introduces the methods of economic evaluation and discusses the challenge to practitioners and managers of EcBHC guidelines. His chapter may raise some uncomfortable questions for practitioners.

In the final chapter of this section, Glenys Parry summarises many of the arguments made in previous chapters, giving an overview of evidence-based psychotherapy, and anticipates some of the methodological issues discussed in more detail in the second part of the book. Parry argues that using research to inform the practice of psychological therapies is important, necessary – and problematic. Parry describes models of evidence-based psychotherapy, emphasising collaboration between researchers, clinicians and those commissioning services. Marshalling the arguments which illustrate the need for evidence-based psychotherapy, Parry goes on to review the nature of the evidence base for psychological therapies and to assess the applicability of different kinds of research evidence to practice. This critical examination leads to a summary of the case against evidence-based psychotherapy. Translating evidence that is valid into clinically valid recommendations for practice is problematic. The chapter concludes with an exploration of how the best aspects of evidence-based practice in the psychotherapies can be achieved, whilst avoiding the worst of the problems.

Parry advocates the development of service relevant research, including a range of research methods (both quantitative and qualitative) and the utilisation of practice research networks (PRNs) to take this forward. PRNs are a relatively new concept – typically, they consist of several NHS departments whose members have agreed to gather and pool data relating to clinical outcomes, using the same set of measures, in order to enable analysis of national data sets. Such collaboration demands practitioner training in research methods and critical appraisal, along with an under-standing of guidelines development and implementation skills.

Like Maynard, Parry suggests that the development of an evidence base and the implementation of guidance demand collaboration and co-operation between researchers and clinicians. It is interesting to note that the Department of Health is currently prioritising research to discover how to involve patients and the users of health services in the development and provision of evidence-based health care.

GENERATING THE EVIDENCE

In the second section of the book, we turn to the research methods which contribute to the evidence base for the psychological therapies. Our aim, in reviewing a range of methods advocated by a range of practitioners, is to give an overview of the strengths and weaknesses of different methods, and to highlight the need for a pluralistic – or inclusive – approach.

Routine clinical practice should use the most rigorous methods to ensure that only safe, effective and economical treatments are given to patients. In Chapter 6, Peter Bower and Michael King consider one particular form of evaluation that has been accorded significant status in EBHC – some practitioners would say an over-reliance – the randomised controlled trial (RCT). Randomised controlled trials are the gold standard of evidence-based research because of their rigour. The first part of this chapter explores why RCTs are so important in the evaluation of treatments; the second part considers a wide range of issues specific to the use of RCTs in the evaluation of psychological therapy. According to Bower and King, if the challenge of evidence-based practice is to be met, mental health practitioners need to answer two questions: the first is 'Does it work?' and the second is 'Which works best?' Bower and King demonstrate the strengths and weaknesses of the RCT design and the use of experimental studies in the evaluation of psychological therapies in clinical settings. They explain methodological issues such as randomisation, blinding and control. Issues of internal and external validity, replicability and relevance, and explanatory versus pragmatic trials are explored. Acknowledging that RCTs should not be considered the only legitimate source of evidence for health services, they also review the strengths and limitations of observational studies but conclude that when seeking evidence of causal relationships, or unbiased comparisons of treatments, the RCT methodology is likely to be the method of choice in most circumstances. Psychological treatments need to be proven to be safe, acceptable and effective; RCTs – and perhaps controlled patient preference trials – have a key role to play in providing evidence of efficacy.

In Chapter 7, John McLeod argues that the question of effectiveness has preoccupied researchers and practitioners and that it appears to have become generally accepted that the best, or sometimes the only way to evaluate the effectiveness of psychotherapy is to apply measures before and after treatment. McLeod presents the case for using qualitative methods in evaluating the effectiveness of the psychological therapies. He suggests that the absence of qualitative methods has limited the usefulness of the results of research to date and that their inclusion would make a significant contribution to evidence-based health care policies. McLeod's critique of the problems involved in applying existing quantitative techniques in therapy outcome research is followed by a discussion of the benefits of qualitative outcome research.

Focusing on the limitations of the use of self-report measures in psychological therapies outcome research, McLeod advocates use of a range of qualitative research methods including individual interviews, focus groups, transcripts of therapy sessions, diaries and case notes, ethnographic participant observation and narrative responses, such as biographies and novels. The key here is description rather than comparison; meaning and relevance rather than statistical significance. McLeod suggests that when there are as many rigorous qualitative outcome studies as there are quantitative ones, we will be in a better position to make a fair assessment of the benefits arising from the utilisation of qualitative research methods.

The final chapter in this section is contributed by Michael Barkham and John Mellor-Clark. They, too, offer a brief critique of the failings of the RCT methodology in assessing psychological therapies and suggest that practice-based evidence should help determine evidence-based practice, along with the contributions of RCTs and qualitative methods. Like Parry, the authors suggest that therapists and researchers in practice research networks (PRNs) can collaborate to collect and analyse large bodies of effectiveness, rather than efficacy, data, and that such observational or audit data, while lacking the rigour of RCT methods, may be more clinically relevant than that gathered under experimental conditions. Barkham and Mellor-Clark touch upon the strengths of efficacy studies, those carried out with scientific rigour in optimum conditions, but highlight their limitations in terms of their lack of relevance and representativeness in clinical settings that can rarely, if ever, achieve such idealised conditions. However, they suggest that there should be a greater emphasis on the interface between efficacy and effectiveness studies, and describe models which attempt to link the two approaches.

Barkham and Mellor-Clark suggest that effectiveness data collected via PRNs should be audited using a 'quality evaluation' approach, which includes measures of appropriateness, accessibility, acceptability, equity, effectiveness and efficiency in service delivery. Arguing that outcomes should be rigorous (i.e., reliable and based on sound methodology) and relevant (i.e., meaningful and reflecting clinical reality), they prescribe the use of reliable measures which aim to identify clinically significant change. Barkham and Mellor-Clark conclude by outlining the need for a national effectiveness initiative, to mirror the national efficacy databases utilised for Cochrane reviews.

SYNTHESISING THE EVIDENCE

Quality and variability of health care provision and delivery is mirrored by quality and variability of health care research. In the third section of this book, Simon Gilbody and Amanda Sowden demonstrate the recent shift in the way in which research evidence relating to the effectiveness of health care interventions is summarised. Traditional reviews of health care research have tended to rely on the author's selection of papers, which not surprisingly have tended to reflect his or her own intellectual bias. It is no longer sufficient for an author to open the filing cabinet and pull out the papers which have gathered dust over the years, or to rely on summarising the results of trials with interesting, usually 'positive' results; such actions result in the production of a biased review. In Chapter 9, Gilbody and Sowden provide an introduction to systematic reviews, which, in contrast with traditional reviews, aim to ensure a rigorous and objective approach to evaluating and summarising research findings. The history and rationale of systematic reviews, their strengths, weaknesses – and abuses – are discussed, with special reference to their ability to inform rational decision-making in mental health care.

Two important sources of systematic reviews, those produced by the Cochrane Collaboration and those summarised on the Database of Abstracts of Reviews of Effectiveness (DARE), are used to illustrate the process of systematic reviewing and the diversity of the interventions which have been subjected to systematic review. Gilbody and Sowden end this chapter by discussing how health care professionals, policy-makers, patients and carers might use the findings of reviews. Suggesting that the report of any review should communicate its purpose, findings and implications in a clear and concise way, they stress the importance of practitioners' and patients' easy access to good quality research presented in ways that are likewise easy to translate into routine clinical practice and policy. As such, dissemination and the development of implementation strategies are viewed as crucial steps in achieving evidence-based practice.

Health research is one of the biggest global industries but its results are often inconclusive or conflicting, dissemination and uptake is often poor and the gap between research and practice is compounded by poorly presented findings which are difficult to translate into guidance for treating individual patients in clinical settings. Clinical practice guidelines are systematically developed statements designed to address this problem by informing practitioner and patient decisions about appropriate health care for specific clinical circumstances (Field and Lohr, 1990). In essence, guidelines are tools to assist clinical decision-making. Promoted as a way of improving clinical effectiveness and reducing variation in standards and outcomes of medical care, their development in relation to psychological therapies is relatively recent. None the less, they constitute an important initiative which should result in improvements in mental health services by drawing on best evidence. In Chapter 10, John Cape and Glenys Parry explain what guidelines are, their purpose, methods and quality criteria. Reflecting on psychological therapies and their provision, they note that while all psychotherapies have in common a systematic intervention, based on explicit psychological principles, to improve health, well-being or self efficacy through the medium of a personal relationship, beyond these commonalities, diversity reigns – in methods, theories, purposes, goals, client groups and practitioners – to the extent that practitioners have few, overarching principles. Given this degree of clinical pluralism, a common basis for psychotherapeutic practice in evidence of what is effective and shared, research derived understandings of process would appear to be desirable. While outlining the case against guidelines development, Cape and Parry suggest that clinical practice guidelines hold enormous promise in fostering an evidence-based approach to the psychological therapies. The authors discuss the strengths and weaknesses of clinical practice guidelines and chart their development in this field. Returning to a theme introduced in earlier chapters they focus on the implementation of guidelines as an important initiative in improving mental health services by drawing on best evidence to inform both practitioners and patients.

In the final chapter of the book, we look at the challenge of evidence-based health care for providers of psychological therapies and consider methods by which managers and practitioners can systematically attempt to incorporate the conscientious, explicit and judicious use of current best evidence in making decisions about both the care of individual patients, and the service as a whole. It is a challenge all professionals must accept.

REFERENCES

Field, M. and Lohr, K. (eds) (1990) Clinical practice guidelines; direction for a new program. Washington, DC: National Academy Press.

Klein, R. (1995) *The New Politics of the NHS* (3rd edn). London and New York: Longman.

Li Wan Po, A. (1998) *Dictionary of Evidence Based Medicine*. Abingdon: Radcliffe Medical Press.

Sackett, D., Richardson, W., Rosenberg, W. and Haynes, R. (1996) *Evidence Based Medicine*. London: Churchill Livingstone.

Chapter 2

The drive towards evidence-based health care

Mark Baker and Jos Kleijnen

INTRODUCTION

In 1991, the NHS set about introducing a set of radical reforms to its structures and ways of working (Dept. of Health, 1989). At the same time, a more discrete – but also more enduring – revolution was beginning in the fields of health research leading to the movement for evidence-based health care.

THE NHS R&D STRATEGY

For several decades, academics in the House of Lords had criticised the performance of successive governments in organising and utilising health research (House of Lords, 1988). The government responded in 1990 by establishing a new post of Director of Research and Development in the NHS, heralding a major reorganisation of research funded by the DoH and the NHS and spawning the movement of evidence-based health care in the UK and some flagship infrastructures which have become of international importance.

A knowledge-based NHS

The purpose of the NHS R&D strategy (Dept. of Health, 1991, 1993) was to build a knowledge base to inform all decisions made by NHS managers and clinicians. The strategy had three arms:

1   an information strategy to assemble and interpret the results of completed research and to draw conclusions;

2   a research commissioning strategy to pose and address important unanswered questions;
3   an implementation strategy to transfer reliable research findings into everyday practice.

The R&D information strategy

It was recognised that health research was one of the biggest global industries, but that the results were often conflicting and that reliable outputs were inaccessible to those who needed them. The initiatives were launched to address these deficiencies.

1   A unit (the UK Cochrane Centre – see pp. 19–21) was established in Oxford to co-ordinate the development of groups to assemble and interpret the results of research (mainly but not exclusively randomised controlled clinical trials), and to provide information for clinicians about effective therapies and their impact. There are now many Cochrane Centres world-wide and almost one hundred and fifty collaborative working groups.
2   Another unit (the NHS Centre for Reviews and Dissemination – see pp. 21–22) was established in York to assemble and interpret evidence on key health service issues of importance to commissioners of health care, especially Health Authorities.
3   An electronic register of relevant research (the National Research Register) was created to inform commissioners and providers of research and health researchers of research in progress in key areas and of the identity of major research teams.

The research commissioning strategy

At a national level, a research commissioning framework was established to formulate key research questions and programmes of research to answer those questions. These programmes adopted various perspectives such as disease areas, client groups, organisation and management of health services and new technologies. The products of this process included the NHS R&D programme in mental health – a £5m programme over five years (now completed) – and the NHS Health Technology Assessment programme (NHS Executive, 1997).

This national framework was supported and complemented by more responsive regional commissioning programmes. Later, a new funding system was introduced for the way in which the NHS supports research carried out by its staff (Dept. of Health, 1994).

The national framework has now been replaced by three themed commissioned programmes covering health technology assessment, organisation and delivery of health services and the emerging technologies.

The implementation strategy

This is the most difficult and least developed of the arms of the overall strategy. Divided responsibilities in the DoH and the intrinsic difficulties of securing changes in individual practices have delayed the development of the systematic dissemination of the outputs of research and their implementation into practice (Baker and Kirk, 1998). These are now being addressed by *The New NHS* White Paper (Dept. of Health, 1997). Efforts to get research evidence and guidance into practice may be assisted by the recent publication of an *Effective Health Care* bulletin, *Getting Evidence into Practice* (NHS Centre for Reviews and Dissemination, 1999).

Hopes and expectations of the R&D strategy

At its simplest, a knowledge-based health service occupies the moral high ground. In politics, this is not enough. The high level of political support, and funding, for the NHS R&D strategy during the early 1990s was at least partly based on the belief that evidence-based health care would reduce health care costs. This has proved to be the case in organisational issues such as the shift to day case surgery, but the opposite occurs with some new technologies such as thrombolytic therapy for acute myocardial infarction and the use of taxanes as a first-line therapy in ovarian cancer. In the final equation, evidence-based health care has some costs and some savings; only the patients are the universal beneficiaries.

Mental health highlights

The NHS R&D programme in mental health comprised thirty-two projects. They include a major programme of work on the mental health of the NHS workforce, a longitudinal study of quality of care in community-based institutions (residential and nursing homes) and some major randomised controlled trials in severe psychotic illness covering cognitive behavioural therapy and intensive outreach interventions. The NHS R&D programme also included a trial comparing the effectiveness of counselling, CBT and GP care for patients with depression in general practice (National Research Register Project: NO484008694). A second RCT comparing counselling with GP care was also funded (Simpson, personal communication, 1999). Active dissemination of the outputs of these studies is now being planned.

DoH policy and mental health services

It is a regrettable truism that politics cannot always wait for evidence. This is especially true in mental health policy in the UK. During the last decade, successive policy initiatives have been based on perception and have had a detrimental effect on mental health services and patients.

There has been a systematic misunderstanding of the needs of mental health services and those they serve. The chronic underfunding of community care services, the low status of mental health services in the NHS internal market, the underestimation of the need for acute psychiatric beds, the failure to protect the funds released from the closure of the asylums, and a general bias against community-based services in NHS measures of efficiency have contributed to create a sense of crisis in mental health. The media obsession with the dangers posed by severely mentally ill people in the community has stimulated unhelpful and misdirected policies such as a supervision register. The serious incident enquiries impose blame but do not produce benefits to services, they are unco-ordinated and not evidence-based. The care programme approach has not improved health or reduced risk but has increased hospitalisation. These issues must now be addressed.

THE NEW NHS WHITE PAPER

The new NHS provides a new context for the implementation of evidence-based health care. The NHS internal market is being replaced by networks of collaboration and collective approaches to commissioning. The new Primary Care Groups will have multi-agency membership (though led by GPs) and will have the improvement of health as their main goal. The new planning frameworks secured by Health Authorities (health improvement programmes) are also multi-agency and focused on health. A more broadly based means of assessing the performance of the NHS is also being developed, though early drafts remain biased against community-based services and largely ignore chronic illness. There is also a highly significant reference to the preferred organisational arrangement for mental health services being specialised NHS Trusts.

THE *OUR HEALTHIER NATION* GREEN PAPER

The consultation paper on public health, *Our Healthier Nation* (Dept. of Health, 1998a), renews and develops an earlier attempt at a national health strategy (Dept. of Health, 1992). Mental health is retained as a national priority, but suicide is also retained as an outcome measure despite the growing discord between self-harm and treatable mental illness (see NHS Centre for Reviews and Dissemination, 1998). A 'contract for health' is introduced as a framework for comprehensive responses to health needs. Further elucidation of this idea may produce the following domains for a comprehensive health strategy:

a *strategic themes*, such as public health needs and inequalities, the range and location of services, financial strategy, performance of services, and involving the public and users of services;

b *programmes of care*, including mental health and other national priorities such as cancer and heart disease;

c *the determinants of health* which may be influenced, such as social and economic factors, the environment, lifestyle and effective services;

d *targeted action* to address the root causes of ill health, to prevent illness and to treat illness and reduce its impact;

e *the responsible agencies*, such as national government, local organisations and individual citizens.

As with all complex systems, comprehensive and successful efforts will be required in each domain to achieve the optimal outcome.

GENERATING THE EVIDENCE

In 1981, the Department of Clinical Epidemiology and Biostatistics at McMaster University (Hamilton, Ontario, Canada) published a series of readers' guides for judging clinical articles on aetiology, diagnosis, prognosis and therapy of illnesses (McMaster University, 1981). Around that time, they developed the concept of evidence-based medicine. This concept has been further refined, and is currently a hot topic for all those involved in health care. Centres for evidence-based health care have been established, and a new series of users' guides to the medical literature is being published (Guyatt and Rennie, 1993). The journal *Evidence-Based Medicine* has been started, and the Cochrane Collaboration has been established with the aim of preparing, maintaining and assuring accessibility of systematic reviews of the effects of health care (Bero and Rennie, 1995).

There is now a whole range of journals and databases which help to keep health care workers up to date with the progress and practice of evidence-based health care. Some of these are listed in Box 2.1

Articles on evidence-based health care are not restricted to a few countries in the Western world; evidence-based health care is now a worldwide phenomenon. A search in the Medline and Embase databases (January–June, 1999) for articles which have the words 'evidence-based medicine' or 'evidence-based health care' in the title yielded no less than 159 references. The authors were based in twenty-one different countries, as shown in Box 2.2.

The users' guides to the medical literature published in the *Journal of the American Medical Association* (*JAMA*), and courses on 'How to practice evidence-based health care', help health care workers to obtain the necessary skills in critically appraising the literature.

EVIDENCE-BASED MEDICINE

Sackett *et al*. define evidence-based medicine as follows:

> the conscientious, explicit and judicious use of current best evidence in making decisions about the care of individual patients. The practice of Evidence-based Medicine means integrating individual clinical expertise with the best available external clinical evidence from systematic research. Good doctors use both individual clinical expertise and the best available external evidence, and neither alone is enough. Without clinical expertise, practice risks becoming tyrannised by evidence, for even excellent external evidence may be inapplicable to or inappropriate for an individual patient. Without best current evidence, practice risks becoming rapidly out of date, to the detriment of patients.
>
> (Sackett *et al*., 1996: 71–72)

The practice of evidence-based medicine is a process of five steps:

1   formation of clinical questions in such a way that they can be answered;
2   search for the best external evidence (which often does not consist of the results of randomised clinical trials or systematic reviews);

Box 2.1   Journals and databases

Evidence-Based Medicine
Evidence-Based Nursing
Evidence-Based Mental Health
Evidence-Based Cardiovascular Medicine
Evidence-Based Surgery
Evidence-Based Health Policy Making
ACP Journal Club
Bandolier
The Cochrane Library The systematic reviews published by the
   Cochrane Collaboration
Effective Health Care and *Effectiveness Matters* bulletins and
   The Database of Abstracts of Reviews of Effectiveness
   published by the NHS Centre for Reviews and
   Dissemination

Box 2.2   Articles, by country of origin

Country	Articles	Country	Articles	Country	Articles
USA	45	Denmark	5	Bahrain	1
UK	38	Switzerland	5	India	1
Italy	11	Australia	4	Japan	1
Germany	10	Canada	4	Mexico	1
Spain	10	Portugal	4	Netherlands	1
France	6	Hungary	3	Singapore	1
Belgium	5	Greece	2	Sweden	1

3   appraisal of that evidence for validity and importance;
4   application in clinical practice (integration of individual clinical
    expertise with the best available external clinical evidence); and
5   evaluation or performance.

Evidence-based medicine is not the same as rationing:

Some fear that Evidence-based Medicine will be hijacked by
purchasers and managers to cut the costs of health care. This would

not only be a misuse of Evidence-based Medicine but suggests a fundamental misunderstanding of its financial consequences. Doctors practising Evidence-based Medicine will identify and apply the most efficacious interventions to maximise the quality and quantity of life for individual patients; this may raise rather than lower the cost of their care.

(Sackett *et al.*, 1997: 4)

Further information about evidence-based medicine can be found on the World Wide Web pages of the Centre for Evidence-based Medicine in Oxford: http://www.cebmjr2.ox.ac.uk/. The Centre has been established in Oxford as the first of several centres around the country whose broad aim is to promote evidence-based health care and provide support and resources to anyone who wants to make use of them. Other related web sites with interesting information include:

http://www.jr2.ox.ac.uk/Bandolier/. and http://www.ihs.ox.ac.uk/casp/.

Centre for Evidence-based Mental Health

The objective of the Centre for Evidence-based Mental Health is promoting and supporting the teaching and practice of evidence-based mental health care. The centre intends to develop its web site into a detailed collection of tools to help health care professionals to develop their skills in practising evidence-based mental health. The tool-kit will be aimed at those providing training courses, as well as those who wish to work through some online tutorials. The web address is:

http://www.psychiatry.ox.ac.uk/cebmh/

It is at the Centre for Evidence-based Mental Health that the *Journal of Evidence-based Mental Health* is published. Its purpose is to alert clinicians working in the field of mental health to important and clinically relevant advances in treatment, diagnosis, aetiology, prognosis, outcome research, quality improvement, continuing education and economic evaluation. They do this by selecting original and review articles whose results are most likely to be accurate and clinically useful. The articles are then summarised in value added abstracts and a commentary by a clinical expert is added. The target audience is psychiatrists, psychologists, nurses, occupational therapists, pharmacists and other professionals whose clinical work can be enhanced by up-to-date knowledge of research in mental health.

Centre for Evidence-based Nursing

The Centre for Evidence-based Nursing works with nurses in practice, other researchers, nurse educators and managers to identify evidence-based practice through primary research and systematic reviews. It promotes the uptake of evidence into practice through education and implementation activities in areas of nursing where good evidence is available. The Centre is also researching factors which promote or impede the implementation of evidence-based practice. Their web site is: http://www.york.ac.uk/depts/hstd/centres/evidence/ev-intro.htm

The objectives are:

- to collaborate with nurse clinicians to identify research questions and undertake primary research;
- to undertake primary research in dissemination and implementation;
- to identify those areas where nurses most urgently require summarised evidence and to carry out systematic reviews;
- to support and encourage other nurses to undertake systematic reviews, particularly within the Cochrane Collaboration;
- to undertake targeted dissemination activities in areas where good evidence is available;
- to design, promote and deliver courses in the area of evidence-based nursing for nurses at pre- and post-registration and undergraduate/postgraduate levels.

The purpose of the journal *Evidence-Based Nursing* is to select from the health-related literature those articles reporting studies and reviews that warrant immediate attention by nurses attempting to keep up to date with important advances in their profession. These articles are summarised in 'value added' abstracts and commented on by clinical experts.

Cochrane Collaboration

Healthcare professionals, consumers, researchers and policy-makers are overwhelmed with unmanageable amounts of information. In an influential book published in 1972, Archie Cochrane, a British epidemiologist, drew attention to our great collective ignorance about the effects of health care. He recognised that people who want to make well-informed decisions about health care do not have ready access to reliable reviews of the available evidence.

The Cochrane Collaboration has developed in response to Cochrane's call for systematic, up-to-date reviews of all relevant randomised controlled trials of health care. The Cochrane Collaboration has evolved rapidly since it was inaugurated in 1993, but its basic objectives and principles have remained unchanged. It is an international organisation that aims to help people make well-informed decisions about health care by preparing, maintaining and ensuring the accessibility of systematic reviews of the effects of health care interventions. This is certainly in accordance with the aims of health care professionals who want to practise evidence-based medicine. The web site for the Cochrane Collaboration is: http://www.cochrane.de/cc/default.html

The UK Cochrane Centre facilitates in a variety of ways the work of UK contributors to the Cochrane Collaboration – for example by organising workshops for Cochrane reviewers, by co-ordinating handsearches of the general health care journals and by monitoring and assisting review groups searching specialist literature published in the UK.

There are a number of mental health groups in the Cochrane Collaboration. The *Cochrane Dementia and Cognitive Impairment Group* aims to contribute to the improvement of health care by producing high quality systematic reviews of the available evidence in dementia and cognitive decline. It seeks, trains and supports reviewers, handsearchers and collaborators to carry out systematic reviews and participates fully, with critical input, in the Cochrane Collaboration in pursuit of its aims.

The *Cochrane Depression, Anxiety and Neurosis Group* is concerned with the evaluation of health care relevant to mood disorders, anxiety disorders, somatoform disorders, chronic fatigue syndrome, dissociative disorders and eating disorders. The group considers clinically significant problems, such as deliberate self-harm and suicide attempt, which are often associated with these disorders. The scope of the group is wide, but excludes those aspects of mental health care covered by other Cochrane review groups.

The *Cochrane Drugs and Alcohol Group* produces and disseminates systematic reviews of all randomised controlled trials and controlled clinical trials that are describing an active intervention (including prevention, treatment and rehabilitation) aimed at reducing the potential for harm or the actual harm directly related to the use of different dependence-producing substances.

The *Cochrane Schizophrenia Group* is concerned with the evaluation of care relevant to those with non-affective, functional psychotic illness. The treatment of those with schizophrenia is a major focus of the group but the care of those suffering from unspecified 'chronic/severe' mental illnesses and non-organic, schizophrenia-like conditions is also of interest to this group. Evaluating the ways of managing problems associated with interventions for schizophrenia or chronic/severe mental illnesses, such as the side effects of medication, are also part of the scope of the group.

NHS Centre for Reviews and Dissemination

The NHS Centre for Reviews and Dissemination (CRD) aims to provide the NHS with high quality research evidence. The activities of CRD can be divided into three interrelated strands: reviews, dissemination and information.

CRD produces rigorous systematic reviews, both in-house and by commissioning and collaborating with other academic institutions. The reviews cover the effectiveness and cost-effectiveness of interventions and the organisation and delivery of health care across a broad range of topic areas such as prevention, health promotion, treatment and rehabilitation. In addition, the Centre carries out research into the methodology of undertaking systematic reviews. The Centre's output is peer reviewed by independent panels of experts and health service managers and clinicians to help ensure its accuracy and relevance to the NHS.

Reviews are identified from several sources for the Database of Abstracts of Reviews of Effectiveness (DARE), they are assessed by CRD reviewers and detailed abstracts are written for those which meet pre-defined quality criteria.

Reviews are disseminated to a wide range of professional and lay audiences using a variety of printed and electronic media. The main paper-based dissemination outputs are the *Effectiveness Matters (EM)* and the *Effective Health Care (EHC)* bulletins. These summate the results of systematic reviews and are distributed to over 55,000 people throughout the UK. CRD also has a report series which is used to publish full systematic reviews and other associated research. Active steps are taken to ensure wide coverage of the results of the reviews in both the lay and professional press, as well as publication in relevant peer reviewed scientific journals. Examples of *Effective Health Care* bulletins on mental health are *Deliberate Self Harm* and *Mental Health Promotion in High Risk Groups.*

CRD also supports individuals, organisations and projects that have a role in getting the findings of research adopted into practice. In addition, CRD undertakes research relevant to the dissemination and implementation of results of health-related research.

The information team co-ordinates the production of a number of databases: these include DARE, the NHS Economic Evaluation Database, a database of Health Technology Assessment research (HTA) and an ongoing reviews database. Some are available free on the Internet and others appear on the *Cochrane Library* and the National Research Register (NRR).

The Information Service offers a telephone enquiry service, through which policy-makers and health care professionals can ask for information on available reviews, cost-effectiveness studies and sources of information on clinical effectiveness. The information staff also design and perform the literature searches, order the publications and provide advice on recording studies for CRD's systematic reviews. The information team are involved in primary research, including the development of highly sensitive search strategies.

The Centre is helping to raise the general standard of reviews of health research through educational activity, and, by supporting and co-ordinating others, carrying out reviews for the NHS. CRD has published guidelines for those carrying out or commissioning reviews (NHS Centre for Reviews and Dissemination, 1996). The Information Service offers training in searching the CRD databases and the *Cochrane Library* to interested groups in the NHS and beyond.

The NHS Centre for Reviews and Dissemination supplies a wealth of information both on paper and on its World Wide Web site (http://www.york.ac.uk/inst/crd).

MANAGEMENT AND IMPLEMENTATION

'The new NHS' introduced a new quality framework into the NHS. This has been described in more detail in a consultation paper, *A First Class Service* (Dept. of Health, 1998b). The framework comprises mechanisms to drive evidence-based practice on a national basis, local implementation systems and a monitoring strategy with teeth.

Driving evidence-based practice

A National Institute of Clinical Excellence (NICE) has been established to co-ordinate existing work on the development of evidence-based guidelines and best practice. Building on the outputs of the R&D strategy, the Institute will appraise the available evidence, agree guidance and disseminate it systematically to the NHS and its staff. It will, directly or indirectly, take over the work of government-funded initiatives such as Effective Health Care bulletins, prescribing advice, the National Centre for Clinical Audit and others. The Institute will take over the national confidential enquiries, including that into homicide and suicide by people with a mental illness.

A further initiative is the preparation of National Service Frameworks to provide an evidence-based description of major services which cross sectors. The prototype is the Calman/Hine report on commissioning cancer services (Dept. of Health, 1995) and new frameworks for 1999/2000 focus on adult mental health and ischaemic heart disease. Thereafter there will be one new framework each year.

Implementing evidence-based practice

Successive governments have been disturbed by major service failures in national screening programmes, mental health services and paediatric cardiac surgery. While strong responsive action has followed, not always evidence-based, the government wants to see anticipatory action to prevent these failures. This is the origin of clinical governance, a framework of accountability (of NHS organisations) for continuous improvement in service quality and safeguarding high standards of care by creating an environment in which excellence can flourish. It will apply to NHS Trusts and to general practices through Primary Care Groups. The key elements of clinical governance are:

a   NHS Trust chief executives and primary care group/Trust chairs are ultimately responsible and accountable for the quality of services provided. Formal reporting of quality assessment will be made regularly and in the public domain.

b   Comprehensive quality improvement programmes are required which include participation by all hospital doctors in local and national audits, ensuring that clinical standards of National Service Frameworks and the recommendations of the National Institute for Clinical Excellence are implemented.

c   Systematic assessment of individual and organisational clinical service risks and risk-reduction programmes.

d   Procedures to identify and remedy poor performance in all professionals.

Clinical governance will be supported by a lifelong learning approach to continuous professional development and by an, as yet, undefined strengthening of regulation of the professions and their performance. For now, professional self-regulation survives but is on trial.

Monitoring evidence-based health care

The overall performance of the NHS will be assessed through a six-pronged framework. The performance indicators are:

1   Improvements in the health of the population.
2   Fair, and equal according to need, access to health services regardless of where people live, their social status, their race, age or gender.
3   The effectiveness and appropriateness of health care, including evidence-based care and shorter waiting times.
4   The efficiency of NHS services in terms of unit costs, the productivity of staff and the utilisation of buildings and equipment.
5   The experience of patients and their carers of the quality of staff, environment, information and of the service as a whole.
6   The health outcomes of NHS care, such as reducing risk factors, reducing premature deaths and the complications of treatment and improving the quality of life.

Key data on comparative performance will be published.

Monitoring compliance

To strengthen monitoring, a new Commission for Health Improvement (CHI) will be set up. The Commission will have responsibilities similar to those which OFSTED has for schools. It will organise regular visits to all NHS organisations and may be called in to investigate specific problem areas. The Commission will especially examine clinical governance arrangements, including the implementation of National Service Frameworks and guidelines disseminated by the National Institute for Clinical Excellence. It is suggested that the Commission may take over the co-ordination of serious incident enquiries, including those involving mental health patients and people with severe personality disorder who commit homicide or suicide. A new National Survey of Patient and User Experience will be held annually to assess public confidence in the NHS and to compare local areas. The results of the Survey will be published on a national and local basis.

Evidence-based public health

To take forward the national priorities proposed in *Our Healthier Nation* (mental health, cancer, heart disease and stroke, accidents and the 'contract for health' approach), the UK Cochrane Centre and the NHS Centre for Reviews and Dissemination assembled an evidence base to inform action to help achieve the national targets for improved health outcomes. The results of this work formed an important part of the White Paper on public health *Saving Lives: Our Healthier Nation* published in 1999.

There are hopeful signs that this review will influence the more perverse policies affecting mental health services and call into question the continuation of those services which may have a harmful effect, such as anticipatory counselling for the witnesses of disasters (Wessely *et al.*, 1997).

Improving the management of mental health services

Mental health services are managed by various types of NHS Trust configuration; integrated 'whole district' Trusts, specialist mental health Trusts (usually combined with learning difficulties) and combined mental health and community services Trusts. Evidence (Sainsbury Centre, 1998) suggests that mental health services are not well served by integrated Trusts where acute general hospitals dominate, but are not compromised by combination with other community-based services. The seniority of mental health services managers, and the proportion of their time spent on mental health issues, is lower in integrated Trusts. It is unlikely that there will be a political instruction to dissolve integrated Trusts, but local proposals to do so will generally be supported whereas proposals to create integrated Trusts will be rejected. It is important that Trust Boards with responsibility for mental health have an understanding of the issues affecting these services and have a clear focus on the needs of mental health patients. Psychology services may find themselves increasingly split between mental health and general acute hospital services.

PAST, PRESENT AND FUTURE

The NHS R&D Strategy has had many successes in commissioning relevant research and improving information about research outputs. It has, however, been slow to develop a training strategy for researchers, to involve consumers in its work and in disseminating its outputs to users. Divisions in departmental responsibilities and an absence of incentives to change professional practice have contrived to restrict the efforts at implementing the results of research.

World-wide, there is a huge amount of research into mental health. However, a recent review of the clinical trials in schizophrenia showed that the trials were generally of poor quality leading to bias in favour of the intervention. Most trials were of single drugs and were funded by the pharmaceutical industry, involved patient follow up of no more than six weeks and used outcome measures which were of no relevance to patients or clinicians (Thornley and Adams, 1998). Trials of psychological therapies are also liable to criticism in terms of quality, duration of follow up and generalisability to everyday clinical services. Much tighter standards are required for the funding and ethical approval of clinical trials; experiments on humans which are unlikely to advance knowledge or benefit patients are intrinsically unethical.

Conversely, a *First Class Service* provides a strong new framework linking the outputs from reliable research to recommendations for effective practice, a system for enforcement and a focus on health. It is a challenge the professions must accept.

REFERENCES

Baker, M.R. and Kirk, S. (1998) *Research and Development for the NHS* (2nd edn). Oxford: Radcliffe Medical Press.

Bero, L. and Rennie, D. (1995) The Cochrane Collaboration. Preparing, maintaining and disseminating systematic reviews of the effects of health care. *Journal of the American Medical Association*, 274: 1935–1938.

Cochrane, A.L. (1972) *Effectiveness and Efficiency. Random Reflections on Health Services*. London: Nuffield Provincial Hospitals Trust.

Department of Health (1989) *Working for Patients*. London.

Department of Health (1991) *Research for Health*. London.

Department of Health (1992) *Health of the Nation*. London.

Department of Health (1993) *Research for Health*. London.

Department of Health (1994) *Supporting Research and Development in the NHS* (the Culyer Report). London.

Department of Health (1995) *Commissioning Cancer Services. The Report of the Expert Advisory Group on Cancer* (The Calman–Hine Report). London.

Department of Health (1997) *The New NHS Modern, Dependable*. London.

Department of Health (1998a) *Our Healthier Nation*. London.

Department of Health (1998b) *A First Class Service: Quality in the New NHS*. London.

Department of Health (1999) *Saving Lives: Our Healthier Nation*. London.

Guyatt, G.H. and Rennie, D. (1993) Users' guides to the medical literature. *Journal of the American Medical Association*, 270: 2096–2097.

House of Lords (1988) *Report of the Select Committee on Science and Technology into Priorities in Medical Research*. London: HMSO.

McMaster University (1981) Department of Epidemiology and Biostatistics. How to read clinical journals. 1: Why to read them and how to start reading them critically. *Canadian Medical Association Journal*, 124: 555–558.

NHS Centre for Reviews and Dissemination (1996) *Undertaking Systematic Reviews of Research on Effectiveness: CRD Guidelines for those Carrying Out or Commissioning Reviews*. CRD Report 4. York: University of York.

NHS Centre for Reviews and Dissemination (1998) *Effective Health Care: Deliberate Self Harm*. Vol. 4 No. 6 York: University of York.

NHS Centre for Reviews and Dissemination (1999) *Effective Health Care: Getting Evidence into Practice*. Vol. 5 No. 1 York: University of York.

NHS Executive (1997) *Annual Report of the NHS Health Technology Assessment Programme 1997*, London: Department of Health.

Sackett, D.L., Rosenberg, W.M.C., Gray, J.A.M., Haynes, R.B. and Richardson, W.S. (1996) Evidence-based medicine: what it is and what it isn't. *British Medical Journal*, 312: 71–72.

Sackett, D.L., Richardson, W.S., Rosenberg, W. and Haynes, R.B. (1997) *Evidence-based Medicine. How to Practice and Teach EBM*. New York: Churchill Livingstone.

Sainsbury Centre for Mental Health (1998) *Laying the Foundations*. London.

Simpson, S. (1999) Personal communication.

Thornley, B. and Adams, C. (1998) Content and quality of 2000 controlled trials in schizophrenia over 50 years. *British Medical Journal*, 317: 1181–1184.

Wessely, S., Rose S. and Bisson, J. (1997) *Systematic Review of Brief Psychological Interventions/Debriefing for the Treatment of Immediate Post Trauma Related Symptoms and the Prevention of Post Traumatic Stress Disorder*. Cochrane Library. Issue 2. Oxford.

Chapter 3

Towards evidence-based health care

Brian Ferguson and Ian Russell

INTRODUCTION

In this chapter we first develop a *philosophy* of evidence-based health care (EBHC). We argue that the evidence needed to improve health care takes three main forms. First, we need evidence about the health of patients and the general population, and how these can be improved; second, we need evidence about the values and preferences of patients, carers and NHS staff, and how these may be taken into account; finally, we need evidence about the optimal use of resources – NHS resources, the personal resources of patients and their carers, and other resources within our society. We suggest that rigorous evidence about effectiveness (health gain), fairness (people centredness) and efficiency (resource effectiveness) is essential in seeking better care.

The *practice* of EBHC has three main components: generating evidence; seeking and combining (or 'synthesising') all evidence, new and old; and disseminating and using (or 'implementing') the resulting synthesis. The second part of this book, and the second part of our chapter, focuses on generating evidence. We make the case for deriving evidence about psychotherapy through randomised trials, a case discussed in detail by Bower and King in Chapter 6.

In the third section we combine the philosophy and practice of evidence-based health care to show how EBHC relates to two major developments described in the previous chapter – the NHS Research and Development Programme and 'evidence-based medicine'. The final section addresses the implementation of EBHC from the perspective of a Health Authority.

EVIDENCE-BASED HEALTH CARE

What is it?

The National Health Service engenders widespread affection and respect – across the United Kingdom and beyond. Nevertheless there have been few serious attempts to define its goals and thus derive the principles that should underpin it. The NHS in Wales undertook one of the most coherent of these attempts during the early 1990s. Over a period of five years the NHS Directorate of the Welsh Office (1989, 1992a) defined and developed three strategic goals:

1 *Health gain*: 'the NHS in Wales aims to maximise the health status of the people of Wales within available resources'.
2 *People-centredness*: 'the NHS in Wales values people as individuals and aims to manage services to this end'.
3 *Resource effectiveness*: 'the NHS in Wales aims to achieve the most cost-effective balance in its use of available resources'.

These strategic goals explicitly underpinned developments in health policy and management over this period. As a result they gained a broad measure of support across the NHS in Wales. They soon gave rise to a series of 'protocols for investment in health gain' covering topics like cancers, cardiovascular disease, respiratory disease, and maternal and child health. These protocols represented an early step in identifying and collating 'knowledge' (a term that later gave way to 'evidence') as a basis for good health care. Later the strategic goals underpinned the development of an R&D strategy designed to strengthen the knowledge base of health care (NHS Directorate, 1992b; NHS Wales Office of Research and Development, 1994).

In developing this strategy the NHS Wales Office of Research and Development invoked the seminal work of Professor Archie Cochrane (who had spent most of his professional career in Wales) on effectiveness and efficiency in health care. His key theme may be paraphrased thus (Cochrane, [1972] 1989):

The development of good health care needs hard evidence, preferably from randomised trials, that the use of each therapy either alters the natural history of the condition or otherwise benefits many patients at a reasonable cost.

So rigorous evidence about effectiveness (synonym for 'health gain'), fairness (related to 'people-centredness') and efficiency (synonym for 'resource effectiveness') is essential in seeking better care.

Building on this experience in Wales we offer a new definition of 'evidence-based health care': 'the collaborative process of generating, synthesising, and implementing rigorous and relevant evidence about the effectiveness, fairness and efficiency of all forms of health care'.

GENERATING EVIDENCE FOR PSYCHOTHERAPY: TO RANDOMISE OR NOT TO RANDOMISE?

There is one issue that has dominated debate amongst health researchers and practitioners: how best to generate the evidence – to randomise or not to randomise? As can be inferred from the quote above, Cochrane ([1972] 1989) was an ardent advocate of randomised trials for all forms of health care. In this section we argue the case for randomisation. Consider for example the issue of evaluating the best form of psychological intervention for alcohol problems. In the USA, Project MATCH recently reported on their (randomised) comparison of three manual-guided psychological treatments for these problems: Cognitive Behavioural Therapy (Kadden et al., 1992); Twelve-Step Facilitation (Nowinski et al., 1992); and Motivational Enhancement Therapy (MET) – a 'brief' intervention lasting four sessions rather than twelve (Miller et al., 1992). There was no difference on average between these treatments in either of the principal outcome measures – clients' percentage of days abstinent or their number of drinks per drinking day (Project MATCH Research Group, 1997). Thus the less expensive MET is the most cost-effective of these three therapies, at least in the USA.

The newer Social Behavioural Network Therapy (SBNT) is based on the philosophy that people with drinking problems have the best chance of good outcomes when they have the support of 'social networks' of one or more people willing to help them to abstain from or reduce drinking (Galanter, 1993). The UK Alcohol Treatment Trial (UKATT) is currently comparing an enhanced and Anglicised version of SBNT with an Anglicised version of MET, using both drinking outcomes as in MATCH and more general outcomes relating to clients' quality of life (UKATT, 1998). The designers of UKATT recently faced the issue of how best to compare these two therapies. Suppose they had chosen an observational study comparing the outcomes of clients in Birmingham treated by SBNT with those of clients in Newcastle upon Tyne treated by MET. There are many differences between Birmingham and Newcastle, not only in the epidemiology of drinking problems but also in the structure of the alcohol treatment services and the characteristics of the clients who use them. Furthermore SBNT was Anglicised in Birmingham and MET in Newcastle. Hence it would have been impossible to attribute any significant difference in outcome between SBNT and MET clients to the difference in therapy rather than to the inevitable differences in the characteristics of clients or their therapists (Russell, 1983).

While accepting the intrinsic weakness of the observational approach, many critics of randomised trials argue that quasi-experimental research designs (Cook and Campbell, 1979) can ameliorate, if not resolve, the fundamental problem of attributing differences in outcome to their true cause. In health services research and development the most common of the rigorous forms of quasi-experiment is the controlled before-and-after study. In evaluating alternative therapies for alcohol problems, for example in UKATT, this design would be feasible if the standard therapy delivered by services in Birmingham changed from MET to SBNT, while that in Newcastle remained MET throughout. Such a design would compare clients treated before and after the change in Birmingham, controlled by clients in Newcastle treated before and after the date of the change in Birmingham. While the risk of bias in such a study is certainly less than in the previous observational design, this risk is very difficult, if not impossible, to eliminate (Russell, 1983). In this example there would be many potential sources of bias. For example the change of standard therapy is likely to lead to a change in the characteristics of patients referred for treatment, reflecting the brief nature of the old therapy and the social nature of the new therapy. This would be difficult to detect and even more difficult to correct with confidence in statistical analysis.

In contrast randomisation protects against selection bias in health care evaluation. Its other main advantage, less well known, is that it provides a sound mathematical basis for subsequent analysis. Even so there are many practical obstacles to randomisation. Professor Raymond Illsley expressed one of the more common objections at the time when he was Chairman of the Scottish Health Services Research Committee. He argued that randomised trials were seldom feasible in health services research (Illsley, 1982). Since he was excluding drug trials, he was right at the time. Stimulated by the NHS R&D Programme, however, the number of trials in health services research has been increasing ever since (e.g. Standing Group on Health Technology, 1998). In particular UKATT has followed the example of MATCH in adopting a randomised trial design.

Thus Illsley's objection no longer holds, even in a complex field like psychotherapy.

EBHC and the NHS Research and Development Programme

Generating, synthesising and implementing evidence: in this section we focus on how evidence is developed and managed under the auspices of the NHS Research and Development (R&D) Programme and how Health Authorities attempt implementation. In 1988 the report of the House of Lords Select Committee on Science and Technology recommended the establishment of R&D within the NHS. In 1991 the NHS appointed a Director of R&D and established central and regional directorates to support this role. These directorates were charged with identifying and prioritising the needs of the NHS for evidence. They were also given funds and responsibility for commissioning research to meet these needs. The funds come from a levy on HAs equivalent to 1.5 per cent of the total expenditure on the NHS. These funds are divided into two major budgets – Budget 1 (82 per cent of the total) to support research within NHS Trusts, and Budget 2 to support central and regional research programmes (18 per cent).

There are now three central programmes – one established programme of Health Technology Assessment (HTA), and two new programmes covering Service Delivery & Organisation (SDO) and New & Emerging Technologies. Over the past four years the HTA programme has commissioned research projects to address a wide range of topics. Almost all of these projects have addressed the issue of effectiveness and most have addressed the issue of efficiency (Tolley and Rowland, 1995). The findings of these projects are now flowing into the NHS to inform decisions focusing on the clinical- and cost-effectiveness of health technologies. While the two emerging programmes will also address these issues, we hope that the SDO programme will break new ground by addressing the neglected issue of equity. In these and many other ways, described by Baker and Kleijnen in Chapter 2, the NHS R&D Programme has contributed to the growth of EBHC within the NHS.

Evidence-based medicine or evidence-based health care?

The other major development that has contributed to the growth of EBHC is the introduction into the UK of 'evidence-based medicine' (EBM), also described in the previous chapter. Sackett *et al.* defined EBM as 'the conscientious, explicit and judicious use of current best evidence in making decisions about the care of individual patients' (Sackett *et al.*, 1996: 71). EBM was characterised as 'the integration of individual clinical expertise with the best available external clinical evidence from systematic research' (Sackett *et al.*, 1996: 71).

EBM has many strengths. First, it creates a context in which the contribution of health services R&D is clearer to individual clinicians. Second, it invokes skills in problem formulation, information retrieval, critical appraisal and performance monitoring. Third, it engenders healthy scepticism towards current practice. Finally, there is (limited) evidence that it is effective in changing that practice.

Before we can exploit these strengths, however, we need to recognise the weaknesses of EBM. First, its explicit focus on individual clinical practice neglects issues like fairness to other patients and efficient resource allocation within the NHS. Second, even within an individual consultation the emphasis on clinical evidence plays down patients' preferences and the costs of alternative treatments. Third, it can lead clinicians to put more weight on individual studies than on systematic literature reviews. Finally, it emphasises clinical judgement over more rigorous techniques like decision analysis.

Getting the best out of both EBM and the NHS R&D Programme demands an inclusive philosophy, such as that espoused by EBHC. It can be argued that EBHC is a more appropriate goal than EBM, since it emphasises that evidence-based practice is the responsibility of all health care professions. Moreover, the principles of EBHC are more relevant to policy-making and resource allocation at all levels of the NHS, including relationships between HAs, Primary Care Groups and NHS Trusts.

Before we discuss the implementation of EBHC, however, we assess potential threats to EBHC.

THREATS TO EVIDENCE-BASED HEALTH CARE

First, the implementation of EBHC in general, and clinical governance in particular, requires a major shift of culture. This will take skill and time to achieve. Policy initiatives to improve quality are more likely to succeed if they offer positive incentives. For example the 1990 general practitioner (GP) contract used financial incentives to improve child immunisation rates (Ritchie *et al.*, 1992). Berwick (1998: 58) has argued that the key to clinical improvement lies not in performance assessment alone but in the learning that it stimulates. Indeed he noted that NHS organisations have an incentive to 'bury evidence on their errors, instead of studying it in the service of improvement. Thus EBHC should avoid threatening clinicians whose performance appears to be weak. Assessment could stimulate improvement if it were connected to curiosity within a culture of learning.' So a culture of enquiry and lifelong learning is crucial for EBHC and the continuous improvement of health care.

Second, performance assessment requires valid and reliable information. The recent Health Service Circular about the new NHS information strategy recognises that 'the information requirements to support the National Framework for Assessing Performance (NFAP) and associated Health Authority indicators are well beyond the scope or reliability of currently established information flows' (NHS Executive, 1998a: para. 4.34). We hope that the NHS Executive can develop the IT systems needed to produce valid and reliable data on clinical performance in parallel with the culture shifts that are also needed.

Third, Birch (1997) argues that EBHC is inherently unfair. He claims that its focus on the average outcome of health care ignores the known variation in patients' ability to benefit from care. In particular, policies aimed only at health outcomes systematically favour those with better health. For example rich patients have benefited more than poor patients from recent improvements in coronary care. We share his concern that EBHC does not (yet) address the distribution of health benefits across different groups within society. However, the new definition of EBHC that we propose above explicitly includes the criterion of fairness. By itself that is not a complete answer to Birch's concern. It does, though, provide the means of making explicit the unfairness of evidence-based policies whenever those generating the evidence measure and record fairness. In short Birch's real quarrel is not with EBHC but with those who do not recognise the need for health care evaluation to generate evidence about fairness alongside effectiveness and efficiency.

Fourth, McKee and Clarke (1995: 101) warn against an enthusiastic, uncritical or mechanistic approach to EBHC. They are concerned that 'the most enthusiastic advocates for guidelines may have paid insufficient attention to the uncertainty inherent in clinical practice'. We agree that EBHC must recognise uncertainty. If the probabilities of success and the risks of adverse events can be estimated from the available evidence, EBHC must make these accessible. If not it must ensure that such weak evidence carries an appropriate warning.

Finally, Harrison (1998) warns that EBHC could encourage the rationing of scarce resources. He accepts that Cochrane championed the cause of effectiveness and efficiency in good faith. However, he sees a danger that quality of evidence could become a rationing criterion. This has socio-legal implications for HAs and Primary Care Groups, especially when evidence is encapsulated in clinical guidelines (Hurwitz, 1998). As health scientists, however, we prefer explicit rationing based on all the available evidence as opposed to the implicit rationing systems currently in operation.

Provided that the first two of these threats can be overcome, EBHC will make decision-making more explicit and reduce unacceptable variations in practice. The Health Authority now has a central role in overseeing clinical governance in primary and secondary care within the context of the Health Improvement Programme (HImP) (Ferguson, 1998). In fulfilling this role the Health Authority will have the support of national policies that have consistently stressed the need to improve the quality of health care and strengthen the basis for NHS decisions at all levels. In this final section, we focus on some of the policy initiatives that foster implementation.

IMPLEMENTING EVIDENCE-BASED HEALTH CARE

Policy initiatives

The development of the NHS R&D Programme has encouraged the government to press for health services to be based on sound evidence of clinical- and cost-effectiveness. For example, an NHS Executive Letter in 1996 asserted that improving the clinical effectiveness of health services would secure significant improvements in the health of the people of England. Another NHS Executive Letter in 1997 urged recipients 'to improve the cost-effectiveness of services throughout the NHS and thereby secure the greatest health gain from the resources available'. The White Paper on the 'new NHS' (Secretary of State for Health, 1997) led to the creation of a National Institute of Clinical Excellence (NICE) to promote clinical- and cost-effectiveness by producing clinical guidelines. It also initiated the development of evidence-based National Service Frameworks to derive and disseminate evidence on the cost-effectiveness of care for key conditions.

Clinical governance

The 1997 White Paper also introduced 'clinical governance' as a new means of ensuring accountability for the quality of health care in all settings. This aligns managerial and clinical objectives in improving quality. The subsequent White Paper on 'quality in the NHS' (NHS Executive, 1998b) reinforced this message. Clinical governance would provide 'a framework through which NHS organisations are accountable for continuously improving the quality of their services' (p. 3). The government is reinforcing this emphasis on quality through a clear NHS Performance Assessment Framework (NHS Executive, 1999a). Its aims include reducing unacceptable variations in the provision of health care and identifying 'poor clinical performance' at an early stage.

Fortunately the development of clinical governance is not entirely new. Many Trusts and HAs have already integrated some or all of clinical audit, clinical guidelines, continuous professional development, R&D and risk management, usually under the auspices of clinical effectiveness initiatives. However, clinical governance reinforces the need for quality assurance to be given the same weight as issues like financial probity. Some argue that quality has always been at the forefront of NHS activity. However, recent crises (e.g. NHS Executive South Thames, 1997) illustrate how serious problems can go unnoticed in the absence of systems to tackle or even identify them.

All NHS organisations are now responsible for the development and implementation of clinical governance and thus evidence-based health care. We focus on the role of the Health Authority as the body that co-ordinates clinical governance across all local NHS organisations. In particular the accountability of Primary Care Groups (PCGs) requires that the Health Authority oversee clinical governance in primary care. Although the arrangements for Trusts give a lesser role to the Health Authority, there are four ways in which it contributes to clinical governance in secondary care:

1   The decisions of PCGs to commission from Trusts are made within the framework of the HImP, for which the Health Authority is responsible.
2   Longer-term agreements between PCGs and Trusts reflect the general approach to quality and performance assessment within the HImP.
3   Clinical guidelines are to be implemented consistently across PCGs and Trusts, with the active involvement of both primary care teams and key Trust clinicians.

4   Although the Commission for Health Improvement (CHI) will visit
    Trusts, the Health Authority can contribute in several ways. First,
    it can work continuously and proactively with Trusts and PCGs to
    develop and implement clinical governance and evidence-based
    health care. Second, should problems arise, the Health Authority
    can alert CHI through the NHS Regional Office about concerns with
    local Trusts. Third, Trusts, HAs and PCGs are likely to work together
    to resolve problems identified by CHI (NHS Executive, 1998b: para.
    4.22).

The role of the Health Authority

The Health Authority is now responsible for planning with other
NHS organisations to meet local health needs. The plans to achieve these
targets will increasingly reflect the available evidence – in two ways. First,
the Health Authority will ensure that PCGs within their geographical
boundaries are using the same databases and drawing the same policy
conclusions from the available evidence. Take for example the provision
of counselling in primary care. There is emerging evidence about its
effectiveness as an intervention for patients suffering from depression
(King and Bower; Simpson and Corney; Hunot and Churchill: personal
communications, 1999). Hence HAs will find it difficult to support the
employment of practice-based counsellors in one PCG but not in another.
Thus there is a real incentive for the counselling profession to further
strengthen the evidence of its own effectiveness and efficiency.

Second, the Health Authority has a duty to ensure there are appropriate arrangements for clinical governance in all care settings. For
example it can ask: What arrangements ensure that clinicians are trained
to access evidence? How many *Effective Health Care* bulletins have
been adopted? Which clinical guidelines have been implemented? What
proportion of clinical audit projects are based on rigorous evidence?
And, ultimately, what proportion of these projects measure effects
on patients' health?

Thus HAs are accountable for ensuring measurable progress towards
specific health targets. In turn they hold PCGs accountable for commissioning health care and specifying quality criteria in service agreements
with providers. Whether they can hold PCGs responsible for their role as
providers is less clear while GPs remain independent contractors within
the NHS. In the meantime those responsible for clinical governance in
PCGs face the challenge of ensuring that all constituent general practices
provide consistently good care for their patients.

The NHS Executive (1999b) has summarised the HA's role in clinical governance as:

- setting priorities for local improvements in quality;
- deciding on actions and resources needed within the HImP to achieve these improvements;
- supporting and facilitating the local development of clinical governance, particularly in PCGs;
- identifying specialist services where clinical governance cannot be undertaken locally; and
- undertaking clinical governance of Health Authority functions.

This guidance also covers the roles of PCGs and Trusts. Each NHS organisation has to undertake four key implementation steps: establishing leadership and accountability arrangements; baseline assessment; action plan; and reporting arrangements. As we write NHS organisations are grappling with these steps. In particular, PCGs need support from HAs to undertake the baseline assessment. They need help with finding information on local health needs; identifying current priorities through the HImP and National Service Frameworks; building on existing clinical effectiveness systems; and assessing what is currently known about performance and quality.

In summary local clinical governance arrangements oblige HAs to ensure that the commissioning and provision of health care is based on the available evidence.

CONCLUSION

The NHS has now incorporated EBHC into the statutory process of clinical governance. Moreover, national policy initiatives are increasingly setting objectives for health improvement and performance assessment. The government's emphasis on reducing unjustified variations will also push the NHS to base decisions upon the available evidence. At the least this will require outlying individuals and organisations to justify their deviations from evidence-based norms.

As with all policy initiatives, there are dangers. When using evidence on clinical and cost-effectiveness, in particular when implementing clinical guidelines, the NHS must recognise the uncertainty inherent in clinical practice. Equally the introduction of clinical governance and the resulting progress towards EBHC must not stifle innovation. The key to success lies in setting these quality initiatives in the context of continuous learning by NHS clinicians and managers. This process must avoid any hint of attributing blame for poor performance. Instead there is an onus on all NHS organisations to share the available evidence and thereby improve patient care and the health of the population.

REFERENCES

Berwick, D.M. (1998) The NHS: feeling well and thriving at 75. *British Medical Journal*, 317: 57–61.

Birch, S. (1997) As a matter of fact: evidence-based decision-making unplugged. *Health Economics*, 6: 547–559.

Cochrane, A.L. ([1972] 1989) *Effectiveness and Efficiency: Random Reflections on Health Services*. London: British Medical Journal and Nuffield Provincial Hospitals Trust.

Cook, T.D. and Campbell, D.T. (1979) *Quasi-experimentation: Design and Analysis Issues for Field Settings*. Chicago: Rand McNally.

Ferguson, B.A. (1998) *Shaping up to Improve Health: The Strategic Leadership Role of the New Health Authority*. Discussion Paper 162. York: University of York, Centre for Health Economics.

Galanter, M. (1993) *Network Therapy for alcohol and Drug Abuse: A New Approach in Training*. New York: Basic Books.

Harrison, S. (1998) The politics of evidence-based medicine in the United Kingdom. *Policy and Politics*, 26: 15–31.

House of Lords Select Committee on Science and Technology (1988) *Priorities in Medical Research*. London: HMSO.

Hurwitz, B. (1998) *Clinical Guidelines and the Law: Negligence, Discretion and Judgment*. Abingdon: Radcliffe Medical Press.

Illsley, R. (1982). Research and the NHS. *Health Bulletin*, 40: 54–57.

Kadden, R.M., Carroll, K. and Donovan, D.M. (eds) (1992) *Cognitive Behavioural Coping Skills Therapy Manual: A Clinical Research Guide for Therapists Treating Individuals with Alcohol Abuse and Dependence*. Project MATCH Monograph 3. Rockville, Md.: National Institute on Alcohol Abuse and Alcoholism.

McKee, M. and Clarke, A. (1995) Guidelines, enthusiasms, uncertainty and the limits to purchasing. *British Medical Journal*, 310:101–104.

Miller, W.R., Zweben, A., DiClemente, C.C. and Rychtarik, R.G. (1992) *Motivational Enhancement Therapy Manual: A Clinical Research Guide for Therapists Treating Individuals with Alcohol Abuse and Dependence*. Project MATCH Monograph 2. Rockville, Md.: National Institute on Alcohol Abuse and Alcoholism.

NHS Directorate (1989) *Strategic Intent and Direction for the NHS in Wales*. Cardiff: Welsh Office.

NHS Directorate (1992a) *Caring for the Future*. Cardiff: Welsh Office.

NHS Directorate (1992b) *Sharpening the Focus: Research and Development Framework for NHS Wales*. Cardiff: Welsh Office.

NHS Executive (1996) *Improving the Effectiveness of Clinical Services*. EL(96)110. London: Department of Health.

NHS Executive (1997) *Priorities and Planning Guidance for the NHS in 1998–99*. EL(97)39. London: Department of Health.

NHS Executive (1998a) *Information for Health: An Information Strategy for the Modern NHS*. HSC 1998/168. London: Department of Health.

NHS Executive (1998b) *A First Class Service: Quality in the New NHS*. London: Department of Health.

NHS Executive (1999a) *The NHS Performance Assessment Framework*. HSC 1999/078. London: Department of Health.

NHS Executive (1999b) *Clinical Governance in the New NHS*. HSC 1999/065. London: Department of Health.

NHS Executive South Thames (1997) *Review of Cervical Cancer Screening Services at Kent and Canterbury Hospitals*. London: Department of Health.

NHS Wales Office of Research and Development (1994) *Strengthening the Knowledge Base of Health Care: The NHS Wales R&D Programme*. Cardiff: WORD (mimeo).

Nowinski, J., Baker, S. and Carroll, K. (1992) *Twelve Step Facilitation Manual: A Clinical Research Guide for Therapists Treating Individuals with Alcohol Abuse and Dependence*. Project MATCH Monograph 1. Rockville, Md.: National Institute on Alcohol Abuse and Alcoholism.

Project MATCH Research Group (1997) Matching alcoholism treatments to client heterogeneity: Project MATCH post-treatment drinking outcomes. *Journal of Studies on Alcohol*, 58: 7–29.

Ritchie, L.D., Bisset, A.F., Russell, D., Leslie, V. and Thomson, I. (1992) Primary and preschool immunisation in Grampian: progress and the 1990 contract. *British Medical Journal*, 304: 816–819.

Russell, I.T. (1983) The evaluation of computerised tomography: a review of research methods, in A.J. Culyer and B. Horsberger (eds) *Economic and Medical Evaluation of Health Care Technologies*. Berlin: Springer-Verlag.

Sackett, D.L., Rosenberg, W.M.C., Gray, J.A.M., Haynes, R.B. and Richardson, W.S. (1996) Evidence-based medicine: what it is and what it is not. *British Medical Journal*, 312: 71–72.

Sackett, D.L., Richardson, W.S., Rosenberg, W.M.C. and Haynes, R.B. (1997) *Evidence-based Medicine: How to Practice and Teach EBM*. Edinburgh: Churchill Livingstone.

Secretary of State for Health (1997) *The New NHS – Modern, Dependable*. London: Department of Health.

Standing Group on Health Technology (1998) *Report*. London: Department of Health.

Tolley, K. and Rowland, N. (1995) *Evaluating the Cost-effectiveness of Counselling in Health Care*. London: Routledge.

UK Alcohol Treatment Trial (UKATT) (1998) *Research Protocol*. Newcastle upon Tyne: Centre for Alcohol and Drug Studies.

Chapter 4

Economics issues

Alan Maynard

INTRODUCTION

What criteria should be used to determine patient access to care in the National Health Service? The answer to this question determines the principles under which purchasers should commission health care. Unfortunately Health Authorities and Primary Care Groups (the latest incarnation of general practice fund holding) 'do their own thing'. They generate resource allocation criteria often implicitly and inform their choices with all too little recourse to the evidence base. Unsurprisingly, the natural consequence of such practices is that the service patterns, be they for psychological or other services, vary and patient access to health care is determined by postcode rather than by their ability to benefit or some other criterion.

In this chapter the alternative access criteria are explored, the consequent requirements for the evidence base then being analysed. Finally, the policy implications of moving to economics-based health care (the appropriate form of evidence-based health care) are discussed.

RATIONING HEALTH CARE

One of the many paradoxes inherent in the NHS is that politicians claim that rationing does not exist in the Service whilst providers, be they clinicians, psychologists, nurses or counsellors, practise rationing every day of their working lives. Furthermore, whilst denying the existence of rationing, politicians continually reform health care systems with the aim of improving efficiency; that is, the way in which scarce health services are rationed amongst competing patients. Thus, at once, they deny the issue and seek to improve rationing in practice.

Rationing takes place when patients are denied services which are of benefit to them and which they want. Often professionals fail to inform patients about interventions of value (i.e. providers' rationing). Alternatively they use the queue and make patients wait. Again this is the providers rationing care: patients demand health and delegate decisions about their demands for health care to GPs, consultants and other practitioners. It is these providers, not patients, who create waiting lists and who, because of their failure to agree and implement practice guidelines, generate unequal access to care, both beneficial and wasteful.

What criteria should determine patient access to care? The essence of the NHS is a decision to cease to use willingness and ability to pay (the 'market mechanism') and instead allocate care on the basis of need. But what is need? Need can be a demand or supply side concept; that is, patients can demand care because they believe it is of benefit, or providers can supply care because they believe it will benefit their patients. Thus allocation on the basis of need involves measurement of ability to benefit.

The individual ethic of the professional is set in the context of the practitioner–patient relationship and a professional requirement to treat if there is benefit to the patient. This clinical effectiveness/evidence-based health care approach to resource allocation is one option. The public health physician and the economist offer another perspective: the social or opportunity cost approach. With NHS resources limited (£45 billion), the social objective of the Service should be to maximise improvements in population health by allocating resources on the basis of cost-effectiveness. A decision to treat one patient is a decision not to treat another. If population health gains are to be maximised, care has to be targeted (or rationed) by providers so that it is given to those patients who can gain most per unit of cost (the cost-effectiveness approach).

A simple example can illustrate the conflicts involved in purchasing choices based on clinical- and cost-effectiveness information. Imagine there is a group of patients suffering from depression (condition Y) and there are two ways of treating them: therapy A (anti-depressant medication) and therapy B (counselling).

1   therapy A (anti-depressants) produces three years of good quality life (or quality adjusted life years: QALYs);
therapy B (counselling) produces nine QALYs.

A clinician bound by the Hippocratic oath and motivated by the *individual ethic* of doing the best for his or her patient, would adopt therapy B (counselling), which gives the greatest clinical benefit.

2   if therapy A costs £300, the cost per QALY is £100.
if therapy B costs £1,800, the cost per QALY is £200.
or, put differently, therapy B (counselling) produces six more QALYs than therapy A (anti-depressants) and costs £1,500 more; the incremental (or marginal) cost per QALY of counselling is £250.

An evidence-based purchaser, looking to maximise the *population health* impact of his budget, would select the cost-effective option of therapy A – the prescription of drugs.

To reinforce this issue, let's assume that a government decided to pursue a health gain policy objective for the treatment of depression (condition Y) of 100 QALYs. The use of therapy B (counselling) to achieve this target would cost £20,000, whilst the use of therapy A (anti-depressants) would cost £10,000. Therapy B (counselling) is inefficient – its use wastes £10,000 which could be used to create additional QALYs with the funding of other therapies.

In some circumstances the therapy with the superior clinical effectiveness may also be cost-effective – i.e., provide greatest effectiveness for lowest cost. However, for instance in the treatment of the mentally ill, community care may be superior to hospital care in terms of effectiveness, but may not be cost-effective: the institutional care may give less effect at less cost. Clinical effectiveness is a necessary but not a sufficient criterion for selecting treatment. All interventions which are cost-effective will be clinically effective – but the reverse is not always the case.

Such considerations are germane in relation to the development of clinical governance and the creation in England of the National Institute for Clinical Excellence (NICE) and the Commission for Health Improvement (CHI) (Secretary of State, 1997). The former is to create guidelines to inform, at least, and maybe determine clinical practice. CHI exists to ensure that doctors do not 'monkey about' and produce poor quality care like that which led to the deaths of twenty-nine children in Bristol. It will presumably take the NICE guidelines and compare practice with them at the local Trust level and in Primary Care Groups.

In summary, access to health care can be determined by the market mechanism and/or non-market means. The market deprives those who are unable to pay: thus over 40 million US citizens with no insurance have reduced access to their health care system. In many European countries, Canada, Australasia and parts of the US system (e.g. Medicare and the Veterans Administration) access to care is not determined by ability to pay.

Often the alternative rationing mechanism, need, is poorly defined. Here it is argued that if the social objective of the health care system is the maximisation of health gains from a finite budget, rationing should be carried out on the basis of cost-effectiveness, and not mere clinical effectiveness.

Such a resource allocation rule offers two obvious challenges. First, the professions – all of them – have to collaborate in the construction of practice guidelines which are based on cost-effectiveness and are established for integrated packages of care for patient episodes. A team approach, so evident in the provision of care, has to be extended to the development and use of guidelines.

The second challenge is that such guidelines, based on cost-effectiveness and integrated packages of care would change usual clinical practice. The latter emphasises the practitioner–patient relationship and the individual interests of the patient, not the social interest of economics-based health care.

These challenges have been obvious and ignored for decades. Thus A.L. Cochrane argued that

> allocations of funds are nearly always based on the opinions of senior consultants, but, more and more, requests for additional facilities will be based on detached arguments with 'hard' evidence as to the gain to be expected from the patients' angle and the cost. Few could possibly object to this.
>
> (Cochrane, 1972: 82)

Cochrane also expressed the opinion that this economic approach would require significant administrative (i.e. managerial) changes. This underplays the issue nicely: such an approach requires a revolution in the training, continuing education, re-accreditation and management of all clinical professions.

IMPROVING THE EVIDENCE BASE

If the health care system is to be managed to maximise population health from a fixed budget, what techniques are available to move towards the rationing of health care in relation to the evidence base? There are two issues of importance: economic evaluation methods and the role of incentives, financial and non-financial, in inducing clinical teams to practise economics-based health care (EcBHC).

Techniques of economic evaluation

The literature setting out the nature of economic evaluation was initially published over twenty years ago (Williams, 1972, 1974). Williams set out a checklist of questions which, he suggested, should be used to interrogate any economic study (Box 4.1). This checklist has been developed and 'repackaged' many times since (e.g. Drummond *et al.*, 1987; Maynard, 1990). Currently the basic texts in this area are Jefferson *et al.* (1996) (introductory) and two 'standard' practitioners' texts: Gold *et al.* (1996) and Drummond *et al.* (1997).

This literature demonstrates the evolution of the practice of economic evaluation. There are five approaches, and these are set out in Table 4.1.

Table 4.1 Types of economic investigation of health care

	Measurement of costs of the alternatives	Measurement of benefits of the alternatives
Disease costing or social cost calculation	£	None
Cost minimisation analysis (CMA)	£	Assumed equal
Cost-effectiveness analysis (CEA)	£	Specific units of effect (e.g. life years gained or mental health improvements)
Cost utility analysis (CUA)	£	Generic units of effect (e.g. quality adjusted life years or QALYs)
Cost–benefit analysis (CBA)	£	£

Disease costing or social cost calculation

This first category is not an evaluation but merely a 'bean counting' exercise. The purpose of this type of study is to identify, measure and value the resource consequences of an illness (e.g. schizophrenia) or a health problem (e.g. alcohol and tobacco use). Such valuations of different illnesses can be used by pharmaceutical companies for marketing new products but they are useless for purchasers. Purchasers need to know

Box 4.1   The Williams checklist for interrogating economic evaluation

1 What precisely is the question which the study was trying to answer?
2 What is the question that it has actually answered?
3 What are the assumed objectives of the activity studied?
4 By what measures are these represented?
5 How are they weighted?
6 Do they enable us to tell whether the objectives are being attained?
7 What range of options was considered?
8 What other options might there have been?
9 Were they rejected, or not considered, for good reasons?
10 Would their inclusion have been likely to change the results?
11 Is anyone likely to be affected who has not been considered in the analysis?
12 If so, why are they excluded?
13 Does the notion of cost go wider or deeper than the expenditure of the agency concerned?
14 If not, is it clear that these expenditures cover all the resources used and accurately represent their value if released for other uses?
15 If so, is the line drawn so as to include all potential beneficiaries and losers and are resources costed at their value in their best alternative use?
16 Is the differential timing of the items in the streams of benefits and costs suitably taken care of (for example by discounting, and, if so, at what rate)?
17 Where there is uncertainty, or there are known margins of error, is it made clear how sensitive the outcome is to these elements?
18 Are the results, on balance, good enough for the job in hand?
19 Has anyone else done better?

Source: Williams (1974).

'the bang for the buck' from new products. This type of work creates a 'guestimate' of the resource consequences of an illness (guestimate because the epidemiology of the disease is usually incomplete and the cost data 'fashioned' from limited sources) but fails to inform decision-makers about whether a particular treatment gives more or less benefit for the £ spent at the margin than another treatment. Whilst pharmaceutical companies love to fund such studies, health care decision-makers should regard them as 'stories' of little consequence for resource allocation purposes.

Cost minimisation analysis

Cost minimisation analysis (CMA) is rarely a good practice because it is based on the assumption that the effects of the two alternatives being evaluated are identical. This is rarely the case. A nice example of this was a study twenty years ago of two interventions for varicose veins (Piachaud and Weddell, 1972): surgery versus injection, compression therapy. The researchers reviewed the literature, concluded the alternatives had similar effects, costed each therapy and concluded that the compression therapy, because it was the cheaper, was the preferred intervention. Subsequent to the publication of the study, clinical evidence of the superiority of surgery became available, thus nullifying the study's conclusions (Beresford *et al.*, 1978). This example demonstrates how economic evaluation is dependent not only on the economic analysis of the costs but also on the reliability of the available clinical evidence about health benefits.

Cost-effectiveness analysis

The next approach to economic evaluation is cost-effectiveness analysis (CEA). This involves the costing of the two alternatives being evaluated and the selection of a 'measure of effect'. CEA was developed by the US Pentagon in the Korean War and they used 'body count' as the measure of effect and then costed alternative ways of killing their opponents, e.g. bombing, artillery, infantry advances (with and without tanks), napalm and combinations thereof.

This grim example facilitated the development of the technique, with effect now more commonly being measured in terms of lives saved, years of life saved and clinical effects such as reduction in blood pressure and reduction in cholesterol. The obvious limitation of CEA is that such measures are therapy specific, facilitating choices *within* a therapeutic area, i.e. CEA can be used to identify the best way of treating chronic renal failure (lives saved by dialysis or transplant) but it does not facilitate choices *between* therapies (e.g. renal failure and cardiology) as the 'end point' effects may be different.

Cost utility analysis

To mitigate this problem, another technique, cost utility analysis (CUA), was developed in the 1980s. This approach involves the costing of the alternatives and the measure of the effects in terms of a generic measure which can be used to compare interventions across therapeutic areas. The generic measure used initially was the quality adjusted life year, or QALY (e.g. Williams, 1985). Evaluations using this technique can produce 'league tables' of therapies ranked in terms of the cost of producing one year of good quality life or QALY (Maynard, 1990). This approach has been criticised because of the uncertain validity of some of the measurement techniques (for reviews see Gold *et al.*, 1996 and Drummond *et al.*, 1997). Pragmatists such as Williams (see Culyer and Maynard, 1997) argue that perfection is unattainable and this approach is explicit and useful for informing choices between competing therapies.

Cost–benefit analysis

The final type of economic evaluation is cost–benefit analysis (CBA). This approach involves the identification, measurement and valuation in money terms of all the relevant costs and benefits associated with the alternative therapies. This is an ambitious agenda, e.g. valuing the pain and distress avoided in monetary terms. However, economists have invested much effort in doing this by approaches such as willingness to pay and conjoint analysis. Such techniques, in differing ways, seek to elicit valuations from individuals. Many examples of this work are available in the literature (e.g. the journal, *Health Economics*, and standard textbooks such as Gold *et al.*, 1996 and Drummond *et al.*, 1997).

Economic evaluation can be carried out in a variety of ways and the selection of method depends on the question being investigated and the resources available for analysis. The quality of evaluations is often disappointing in relation to the criteria set using guidelines of good practice derived from Williams (Box 4.1). Economic studies can be accessed as part of the Cochrane Library. The NHS Centre for Reviews and Dissemination (CRD) has a database called NHS Economic Evaluation Database (NHSeed) which is accessible on the Internet (http://www.york.ac.uk/

inst/crd). Another database organised by the Office of Health Economics (OHE) (funded by the Association of the British Pharmaceutical Industry) contains 14,000 articles. The NHS-CRD and the OHE (Health Economic Evaluation Database: HEED) review the articles in their databases and, whilst the former is free, the latter costs £5,000 for commercial purchasers, £2,000 for non-commercial buyers and £1,000 for academics (available from the OHE in London).

Researchers and policy-makers are advised to search these databases to determine not only the identity of relevant studies but also an assessment of their strengths and weaknesses in terms of the quality of their design, execution and reporting.

The major funder of clinical and economic trials (perhaps as much as 90 per cent of the total work) is the pharmaceutical industry. Their concern is to meet safety, efficacy and quality requirements, and acquire, from the regulatory authorities, product licences (i.e. permission to sell their product to the NHS). These trials may identify efficacy (i.e. effect, sometimes in comparison to placebo) but rarely provide information about relative effectiveness (i.e. effect in general use compared to an alternative, competing intervention). Evaluations of psychological therapies tend not to attract funding from pharmaceutical companies.

Economic evaluation can be carried out in one of two ways. First, it can be designed as an integral part of a prospective randomised clinical trial where, in addition to measuring effect (with end-points related to enhancements in the length and quality of life), the cost to society of the alternatives is identified, measured and valued. This approach is costly and may take years to complete but, if done well, can produce good quality data. However, an obvious limitation is that costs and effects in carefully designed and executed trials may differ from these characteristics in long-term use.

An alternative is modelling, i.e. taking the available data from often limited and partial trials and analysing possible alternative scenarios. The challenge with this work is to ensure transparency for, without this, much modelling may be difficult to evaluate and contain errors and biases (Maynard and Cookson, 1998).

Biases can be introduced into models innocently by a failure to review systematically the data drawn from other studies and incorporated into the model. Much research is very poor, with clinicians and economists wasting R&D resources by failing to keep to guidelines of good evaluative practice (e.g. Box 4.1). For example, non steroidal anti-inflammatory drugs (NSAIDs) are widely used. However, the evidence base about their clinical effect is poor. Gøtzche (1989: 54) reviewed 196 published trials of NSAIDs and concluded:

> Doubtful or invalid statements were found in 76% of the conclusions or abstracts. Bias consistently favoured the new drug in 81 trials, and the control in only 1 trial.

Rochon *et al.* (1994: 157), after reviewing the same therapeutic area, concluded that:

> With such an unsatisfactory knowledge base about the clinical effectiveness of NSAIDs, any economic evaluation must inevitably be fraught with difficulty.

Often judgements about the efficiency of competing interventions are based on bad science or no science. Thus practitioners in psychosocial medicine should not accept uncritically the advocacy of colleagues elsewhere in the health service. Evaluation in surgery has been criticised and likened to 'comic opera' (Horton, 1996); 'experts' must be treated with caution.

Incentives to practice efficiently

Traditionally, medical practice has been driven by trust with little investment in accountability. Scepticism about the evidence base of much of health care (e.g. Cochrane, 1972), observation of wide variations in clinical practice and gradual observation of variations in 'success' (e.g. patient mortality after particular surgical procedures) have eroded trust and led to public demand for greater accountability.

The focus of current UK reform is 'clinical governance', both in primary care and hospital provision (Department of Health, 1998). Clinical governance has been defined as:

> a framework through which NHS organisations are accountable for continuously improving the quality of their services and safeguarding high standards of care by creating an environment in which excellence in clinical care will flourish.
>
> (Department of Health, 1998: 33)

This vague, almost meaningless statement presumably defines 'quality' and 'excellence' in relation to the cost-effectiveness of the procedures delivered to patients. However, this presumption has to be strong as the text and political utterances are ill-defined and ambiguous.

If NICE sets practice guidelines in relation to cost-effectiveness, and CHI reviews practice in relation to such guidelines, the pressure to practise efficiently may be enhanced considerably. However, such processes will also reveal deficits in knowledge which will require expensive programmes of continuing education and training.

The improved definition and management of the NHS contract, particularly the better management of job specifications, may also be used to enhance the impact of guidelines on clinical practice. This is likely to be both a local NHS effect and one influenced by the development of the regulatory role of the Royal Colleges and other professional bodies.

Finally, in relation to NHS pay of clinicians and all other practitioners, it is possible that reward will be more related to performance, not only of clinical tasks but also in relation to continuing training and education. With rapid changes in technology, sharper professional and financial rewards may be necessary to ensure that evidence, once translated into practice guidelines, is applied in practice.

Overview

Confusion continues as to whether quality in performance and the system of clinical governance is related to concepts of clinical effectiveness or cost-effectiveness. The government's proposals are ambiguous due to looseness of drafting and political rhetoric in presentation. If the role of the NHS is to use the limited budget of £45bn to create the maximum possible increase in population health, then quality means the pursuit of cost-effectiveness and the production by NICE of practice guidelines relating to economics-based health care (EcBHC). This is a major but unavoidable intellectual and practical challenge to practitioners and managers.

SOME FURTHER POLICY CONCLUSIONS

It is remarkable that practice guidelines produced by professional groups have largely ignored economic issues. Practitioners have sought the ideal: reducing risks regardless of opportunity cost. Such practice is illogical, inefficient and unethical: there is an optimum level of risk beyond which the cost of its reduction exceeds the benefits in terms of reduced risks for patients. Patients and providers should not expect to receive zero-risk care or policy: no society can afford such a nonsensical goal even if media hysteria induces public belief in its availability (such as during the BSE crisis). Investment in reducing risks must bear in mind costs and benefits, not just the pursuit of the latter regardless of what is forgone in terms of scarce resources.

Professional bodies have tended to ignore economic issues and, by so doing, encourage the inefficient (and unethical) use of resources. They now have to re-focus their efforts and in this work they will be encouraged by government and its agents, NICE and CHI.

The nicest challenge will be the translation of such efforts into systems of re-accreditation. Airline pilots are tested for competence every six months. Health care practitioners must expect similar routine testing over their careers as the public demand protection from inadequate and inappropriate practice.

The cost of creating EcBHC and developing professional regulatory arrangements will be large. Again much of the discussion about clinical governance, NICE and CHI, is in terms of superficial advocacy with little detail and practically no consideration of the cost of developing the evidence base and improving practice. This failure to be realistic about the obstacles to the smooth development of these structures may lead to much frustration about an endeavour of great importance. The economic dimension to guideline creation, professional regulation and improved performance is central if uncomfortable for many practitioners who, too exclusively concerned about patient welfare, like to focus on benefits and believe costs are irrelevant. Such practice harms patients and does not facilitate improvements in population health.

REFERENCES

Beresford, S.A., Chant, A.D.B., Jones, H.O., Piachaud, D. and Weddell, J.M. (1978) Varicose veins: a comparison of surgery and injection-compression sclerotherapy. *Lancet*, 1 (29 April), 921–924.

Cochrane, A. (1971) *Effectiveness and Efficiency*. London: Nuffield Provincial Hospitals Trust.

Culyer, A.J. and Maynard A. (1997) *Being Reasonable About Health Economics: a collection of essays by Alan Williams*. London and Gloucester: Edward Elgar.

Department of Health (1998) *A First Class Service: Quality in the New NHS*. London: HMSO.

Drummond, M.F., Stoddart, G.L. and Torrance, G.W. (1987) *Methods for the Economic Evaluation of Health Care Programmes*. Oxford: Oxford University Press.

Drummond, M.F., O'Brien, B.J., Stoddart, G.L. and Torrance, G.W. (1997) *Methods for the Economic Evaluation of Health Care Programmes*, 2nd ed. Oxford: Oxford University Press.

Freemantle, N. and Maynard, A. (1994) Something rotten in the state of clinical and economic evaluations? *Health Economics*, 3: 63–67.

Gold, M.R., Siegel, J.E., Russell, L.M. and Weinstein, M.C. (1996) *Cost Effectiveness in Health and Medicine*, New York: Oxford University Press.

Gøtzche, P.C. (1989) Methodology and overt hidden bias in reports of 196 double-blind trials of nonsteroidal anti-inflammatory drugs. *Controlled Clinical Trials*, 10: 31–56.

Horton, R. (1996) Surgical research or comic opera: questions, but few answers. *Lancet*, 347 (9007): 984–985.

Jefferson, T., Mugford, M., Gray, A. and Demicheli, V. (1996) An exercise on the feasibility of carrying out secondary economic analyses. *Health Economics*, 5: 155–165.

Maynard, A. (1990) The design of future cost–benefit studies. *American Heart Journal*, 119 3(2): 761–765.

Maynard, A. (1991) Developing the health care market. *Economics Journal*, 101 (408): 1277–1286.

Maynard, A. and Cookson, R. (1998) Computer modelling: the need for careful evaluation and public audit. *Pharmacoeconomics*, 14 (suppl.2): 62–72.

Piachaud, D. and Weddell, J.M. (1972) The economics of treating varicose veins. *International Journal of Epidemiology*, 1: 287–294.

Rochon, P., Gurwitz, J., Simmis, R. *et al.* (1994) A study of manufacturer supported trials of nonsteroidal anti-inflammatory drugs in the treatment of arthritis. *Archives of Internal Medicine*, 154: 157–163.

Secretary of State (1997) *The New NHS: Modern, Dependable*. London: HMSO.

Williams, A. (1972) Cost benefit analysis: bastard science and/or insidious poison in the body politic. *Journal of Public Economics*, 1 (2): 199–225.

Williams, A. (1974) The cost benefit approach. *British Medical Bulletin*, 30 (3): 252–256.

Williams, A. (1985) Economics of coronary artery bypass grafting. *British Medical Journal*, 291: 1183–1188.

Chapter 5

Evidence-based psychotherapy

An overview

Glenys Parry

WHAT IS EVIDENCE-BASED PSYCHOTHERAPY?

Evidence-based psychotherapy is a concept of the 1990s that is far from self-explanatory – it needs exploration and critical review. In this chapter, I argue that using research to inform psychotherapy practice is important and necessary, yet problematic. Models of evidence-based psychotherapy are described, the nature of the evidence base for psychotherapy is reviewed and the applicability of different kinds of research evidence to practice is critically examined. The case against evidence-based psychotherapy is summarised. The chapter concludes with an exploration of how the most desirable aspects of evidence-based practice in the psychotherapies can be achieved whilst avoiding the worst of the problems.

First, it is necessary to define 'psychotherapy', since this deceptively simple term is used in so many different senses. In this chapter 'psychotherapy' refers to all formal and systematic psychological therapies, or 'talking treatments', which are offered by psychotherapeutically trained practitioners. In this sense, the term would include a formal series of counselling sessions offered by a trained counsellor in a primary care setting, but exclude informal counselling offered by the General Practitioner as part of a consultation. Cognitive behavioural, psychoanalytic, psychodynamic, humanistic-experiential, interpersonal, cognitive-analytic, rational-emotive, and systemic family therapies would all be examples. So would pragmatic, eclectic therapy based on pan-theoretical principles offered by a qualified psychologist or psychotherapist. However, the normal work of general psychiatrists, nurses and other mental health professionals is excluded from this definition, even if informed by one or more psychotherapeutic approach.

Since the early 1980s, there has been a major movement to promote better standards of health care interventions and to base health policy and management decisions on evidence of clinical effectiveness. This began in hospital medicine, where wide variations between the clinical practices of physicians, and their clinical outcomes, were observed, leading to doubts about the reliability of procedures for medical decision-making. The resulting movement in evidence-based medicine (EBM) was pioneered in McMaster University, Canada and was a logical extension of techniques of critical appraisal of the medical and scientific research literature. It aimed to help doctors make rational clinical decisions on the best available evidence. As Baker and Kleijnen illustrate in Chapter 2 it has now developed into a considerable industry, with a proliferation of books, journals, World Wide Web pages, CD-ROMs and internet discussion groups dedicated to pursuing this aim.

Evidence-based health care takes the logic of evidence-based medicine into broader multidisciplinary practice, into community health care, general practice and into purchasing decisions. It evaluates the effec- tiveness of health care interventions through a rigorous programme of health services research, conducted to high scientific standards, and disseminates the results of research in intelligible and useful forms to the organisations and individuals that need to know. In this way, the results of research are used to change clinical practice and the provision of health care. There is an emphasis here on cost-effectiveness and how to avoid wasteful, ineffective processes at the level of service delivery (Muir Gray, 1997).

A systematic attempt to ensure that research findings alter the practice of psychological therapies is now in progress, although a research-based approach to these therapies is not new. For example, the 'scientist- practitioner' paradigm in clinical psychology dates from the 1960s. Psychotherapists have been committed to testing theoretical and practical advances through research, particularly cognitive behavioural therapists and psychologists, whose commitment to research has been explicit from the outset. Psychotherapy research was one of the first fields to use meta-analytic methods to provide a quantitative summary of the effects found in large numbers of outcome studies (Smith and Glass, 1977).

Much more recent is the strategic movement to apply research findings to the full range of psychological therapy provision in the UK, as part of the movement in evidence-based health care. Diverse initiatives mark its progress. Parry (1992) reviewed evidence-based ways to improve psychotherapy services, and in 1994 a landmark conference was sponsored by the Mental Health Foundation on the research foundations of psychotherapy services (Aveline and Shapiro, 1995). In 1996, the first official policy statement on psychotherapy provision was published (the NHS Executive review of strategic policy on psychotherapy services in England: Department of Health, 1996), together with the research review which had been commissioned to inform it (Roth and Fonagy, 1996). These two documents set the agenda for evidence-based psychotherapy in the UK. Other texts related to the topic have started to appear. Examples include Davenhill and Patrick (1998), special issues of the journals *Clinical Psychology: Science and Practice* (1996) and *Psychotherapy Research* (1998) and, of course, the current volume. Integration of psychotherapy studies into mainstream journals in evidence-based psychiatry and mental health has been another signal of the *Zeitgeist*.

Both the NHS Psychotherapy review (1996) and Roth *et al*. (1996) propose the same model of evidence-based psychotherapy, which emphasises collaboration between researchers, clinicians and those commissioning services. This approach can be briefly summarised as follows:

- Psychotherapists continue to innovate and to develop new approaches, building on existing theory, knowledge and practice.
- Promising new therapies are formally researched to establish efficacy, but also field-tested in large samples in natural service systems.
- Both research evidence and clinical consensus inform clinical practice guidelines, in order to clarify where general statements can (or cannot) be made about best practice.
- Standards derived from research-based guidelines are set and clinical audit is used to check they are achieved.
- Skills deficits revealed by audit are addressed by training.
- Outcomes benchmarking may also have a role to play in improving patient care.

In addition to proposing this model, the NHS Executive review recommended that those responsible for commissioning psychological therapies should not fund services or procedures where there is clear empirical evidence that they are ineffective. It suggested that a commissioning strategy should drive forward the agenda of evidence-based practice by moving investment towards those psychology, counselling and psychotherapy services which meet five standards:

- they have adopted clinical guidelines for standard practice;
- the guidelines are informed by the findings of research and service evaluation;

- they specify the patient groups for which the service is appropriate;
- they monitor outcomes for innovative treatments;
- they audit key elements of standard practice.

Developments in the United States parallel those in the United Kingdom, but with significant differences because of the service context of 'managed care'. Here large health insurance companies employ health professionals and are also third party payers in fee-for-service therapy. Managed care has attempted to change clinician behaviour through the greater use of clinical protocols for reimbursement (Austad and Berman, 1991). These pressures have produced an emphasis in the US on 'empirically supported treatments', where criteria are set for which forms of psychotherapy have good evidence of efficacy (American Psychological Association Task Force on Psychological Intervention Guidelines, 1999; Chambless, 1996). This initiative was contentious (Elliott, 1998). Although it was supported by many researchers (Barlow, 1996; Crits-Christoph, 1996), others were highly critical (Garfield, 1996; Shapiro, 1996; Henry, 1998) on both scientific and pragmatic grounds.

It is important to note that the model of evidence-based psychotherapy that lists validated treatments was explicitly eschewed by the NHS Executive policy review. This was partly on the grounds that it goes beyond a reasonable use of research evidence, failing to take account of strong evidence that although therapy types and specific techniques have an influence on outcome, they do not account for much of the variance in outcome. However, for some, evidence-based psychotherapy implies that each separate psychotherapy type, with its theoretical base and specific set of techniques, is treated as if it were a drug. Like a pharmacological substance, each therapy would be tested against placebo or the standard treatment in a randomised clinical trial, in order to have its safety and efficacy established. The temptation to move in this direction remains a powerful one, despite the strong empirical evidence for common factors across psychotherapies and the comprehensive attack on the drug metaphor in psychotherapy research mounted by Stiles and Shapiro (1994).

One of the reasons the debate has become so acrimonious in the US is the link between treatment protocols and funding, specifically concurrent review of reimbursement undertaken by third party payers. Within the UK, the NHS has so far avoided the approach of making funding dependent on compliance with prescriptive treatment protocols. However, there is an explicit commitment to drive policy, make commissioning decisions and allocate resources on the basis of research evidence on what is clinically effective and cost-effective. This includes assessing evidence of need for a service or an intervention (basically defined in terms of people's capacity to benefit) and the measurable health gain for a given investment of revenue, sometimes expressed in terms of cost/utility ratios or £/quality adjusted life year (QALY). This is a prospect that provokes strong feelings. Some argue that ethically, generic measures of health benefit in relation to cost are essential in equitable and transparent allocation of limited public resources. Others are appalled at the prospect, equally convinced that there are no such easy utilitarian solutions to complex issues of power and value in the use of resources.

The need for evidence-based psychotherapy

The argument for basing psychotherapy provision on research evidence of what is most effective and cost-effective can be made on the following grounds:

- Psychotherapy is widely practised yet there is very little professional consensus on methods and indications for specific therapies, and wide variability in practice.
- Patients, often in severe distress, make a major investment of personal time and commitment to these therapies and have a right to know that they are safe and effective.
- There is inequity of access to these therapies across the UK, so that evidence is needed to make the case for appropriate levels of provision as part of national service frameworks.
- Although there is evidence, in broad terms, that psychological therapies are of benefit to patients, there is also evidence that patients can deteriorate if therapies are inappropriate or are carried out incompetently.
- Psychotherapy in the NHS represents a significant public funding investment and it is unethical to waste this funding in supporting ineffective treatments.
- Psychotherapy is still relatively weak and marginal in the health care system; research has an important role in establishing it as a bone fide treatment within mainstream health services.

On these grounds, it is possible to summarise the features of a health care system where evidence-based practice in the psychotherapies is well established, as follows:

- Psychotherapy research (of all types) would be funded at a credible level, systematically reviewed and summaries made available to therapists.
- Psychotherapists would be aware of research methods, major findings and the limitations of the evidence.
- Therapy practice guidelines, clinical audit and outcomes monitoring would be widely used as tools for improving standards.
- Case mix, procedures, evidence base and outcomes for services would be made explicit.
- Patients would be referred to the most appropriate service.

THE NATURE OF EVIDENCE: WHEN IS THE BEST THE ENEMY OF THE GOOD?

The application of psychotherapy research to individual practice is far from simple. As Roth and Fonagy (1996) point out, the aims and perspectives of researchers and clinicians fundamentally differ, and there are intrinsic tensions between the internal validity sought by researchers and the external, ecological validity essential to clinicians. The nature of evidence in these two worlds fundamentally differs. It is vital to formulate the problems in translating research-valid evidence into clinically valid recommendations.

Evidence about psychotherapy comes from many sources, including clinical case description, systematic observational studies, intensive study of psychotherapy process and process-outcome links, longitudinal studies of patient series, non-randomised outcome studies (e.g. case control studies) and randomised controlled trials. Controlled trials can be explanatory or pragmatic (Schwartz and Lellouch, 1967). An explanatory trial attempts to examine the impact of specific treatment elements on outcome, for example by comparing exposure treatment in agoraphobia with exposure plus cognitive therapy. A pragmatic trial is more concerned with the overall effectiveness of the intervention compared with usual treatment or no treatment.

Single-case studies and naturalistic service evaluations have greater external validity than experimental trials, and they certainly influence clinicians. Unfortunately, both are scientifically flawed. Often, those wanting to evaluate a treatment in a cohort of patients in their service do not allocate people randomly to a contrasting treatment. However, unless the treatment is unequivocally superior to alternatives – which is almost never the case – information about the relative efficacy of the treatment under test is needed. Roth and Parry (1997) give examples of misleadingly good results from uncontrolled evaluations, which were called into question when randomised controlled trials (RCTs) were reported.

Randomised controlled trials have been seen as the 'gold standard' for producing evidence of what is effective, when comparing the outcome of one form of treatment with another. The systematic appraisal of results from these trials is now an established feature in many areas of health care delivery and forms the basis of the international Cochrane Collaboration and the work of the NHS Centre for Reviews and Dissemination (1995).

Bower and King address the strengths and weaknesses of RCTs in Chapter 6 and Barkham and Mellor-Clark refer to naturalistic methodologies in Chapter 8. Practitioners are often critical of utilising RCT methodology to evaluate psychological therapies.

One of the commonest reasons psychotherapists are sceptical of the relevance of research to their practice is that, in the past, patients who enter research trials have not been representative of those seen in routine practice. Indeed, earlier behavioural research was not even conducted in clinical settings, but used 'analogue' methods with volunteer students. More recently, research has been conducted in clinical settings, but patient samples are usually diagnostically homogeneous in order to reduce an obvious source of outcome variance and some types of patient are very commonly excluded – for example, those with alcohol problems, personality disorder, psychosis or other co-existing conditions. This helps the internal validity of the research design, but reduces the external validity, since in most psychological therapy services referrals of complex problems and people with multiple diagnoses are common.

Current research trials go to some lengths to ensure that the treatment being carried out is standardised, both in terms of its duration and by using manuals that closely guide the procedures that the therapist carries out. This level of control enables researchers to make recommendations about which therapeutic techniques appear to have efficacy. However, outside the research setting, such adherence to a pure form of therapy is rare – real therapists aim for a balance between uniform application of therapy and making adaptive choices in order to maintain the integrity both of the treatment and the therapeutic alliance. There is always a degree of intrinsic tension between the individually tailored approach of the skilled clinician, and the more manual-based and formulaic applications seen in many research trials.

Randomisation removes any choice about which treatment a patient receives; in the clinic such choices are central to the initial stages of treatment. Though in clinical practice treatment allocation is rarely guided by empirical evidence (and is prone to error), there is a negotiated 'best fit' between expressed patient preference and assessed aptitude, the available treatments, the available therapists and the assessors' judgement of treatment of choice. The problem is that such processes are inaccessible to research using randomised designs.

The RCT is a vital tool in an evidence-based approach, but will never answer all research questions. These trials offer the best answer to questions on outcome rather than process, and efficacy rather than effectiveness. RCTs are one part of a research cycle; most appropriately they test the capabilities of a well-developed therapy after single case studies and before large-scale field trials.

Good efficacy evidence from randomised trials is now becoming available on a range of therapeutic methods, with the most common presenting problems such as depression and anxiety. For example, convergent evidence suggests that structured psychological treatments are helpful in treating depression, either as stand-alone therapy or in combination with medication (Roth and Fonagy, 1996; Mackay and Barkham, 1998; Schulberg *et al.*, 1998). This is in agreement with preliminary results from a Cochrane review of brief psychological treatments for depression (Hunot and Churchill, 1999). This review used a comprehensive search strategy to locate all randomised controlled trials or quasi-randomised controlled trials conducted in an out-patient setting, which compared explicit models of time-limited psychotherapy with one another, a placebo, or a treatment-as-usual control group, involving adult patients with a primary diagnosis of depression. Results from a meta-analysis of eleven trials give an odds ratio of 2.98 (95 per cent confidence interval 2.08–4.27) for all variants of psychotherapy compared with treatment as usual.

However, there are many gaps in the evidence base, for example in relation to longer-term therapies, psychoanalytic therapy, and many common problems, such as personality disorders. Obtaining good quality, replicated research findings on all therapeutic approaches across all diagnoses in their many complex combinations is a huge unfulfilled enterprise. Some would see it as practically impossible.

OTHER SOURCES OF EVIDENCE

Other research strategies complement the controlled trial. Two important sources of evidence are large sample surveys of psychotherapy recipients, and research on psychotherapeutic processes.

First, it seems essential to study psychotherapy as it is actually delivered, where the effects of self-selection and patient preference, therapist competence, service delivery milieu and referral pattern will all be present. Within the context of a comparative outcome trial, these are considered as confounding factors, but they are all vital to the actual results obtained in service delivery systems. This is an observational, descriptive exercise rather than an experimental one. An example of 'real world' evidence is the Consumer Reports survey reported by Seligman (1995). An American consumer organisation mailed 180,000 members with a questionnaire asking if 'at any time over the last three years you experienced stress or other emotional problems for which you sought help from any of the following: friends, relatives or a member of the clergy, a mental health professional or a support group'. There were 22,000 respondents, largely well-educated, middle-class people, of whom 2,900 had seen a mental health professional. The results showed that for this sample, the longer the therapy, the better the outcome, with this dose–response relationship shown for up to two years or more therapeutic contact. This sort of study has obvious methodological limitations but major advantages of realism, and the large sample allows some *post hoc* statistical reliability checks. The extent to which the methodological shortcomings undermine confidence in the validity of these findings is a matter of some debate (Mintz *et al.*, 1996; Brock *et al.*, 1996).

Qualitative research emphasises the negotiation and social construction of meanings (see McLeod, Chapter 7 this volume). It can also enhance and complement quantitative research, for example in explaining unexpected findings or exploring the meaning of process–outcome links. In psychotherapy research, intensive process analysis complements outcome research by examining the meaning of significant events in psychotherapy in contextual detail (Rice and Greenberg, 1984). For example, a number of studies show that the therapeutic alliance is the single most important predictor of psychotherapy outcome (Orlinsky *et al.*, 1994). The alliance is defined in terms of the bond between therapist and client, agreement on goals and agreement on tasks (Bordin, 1979). Intensive process analysis has been used to study ruptures in the therapeutic alliance, their links to patients' characteristic interactional patterns, and to develop and test a model of the skilful resolution of these problematic events (Safran *et al.*, 1990; Bennett *et al.*, 1999). The evidence gained in such studies is highly relevant to improving clinical practice and understanding the mechanisms of links between process and outcome.

One approach to gathering evidence which overcomes the problem of having to test every 'brand name' therapy aims to transcend specific therapeutic approaches. This research attempts to study psychological processes that are common to all successful psychotherapy. Research on the therapeutic alliance is one example of common factors research. Other important generic models include:

- the assimilation model – how painful material is warded off, then becomes accessible and worked through during therapy (Stiles *et al.*, 1990);
- Howard's (1993) phase model of psychotherapy – the concept of re-moralisation, remediation and rehabilitation in all successful therapies;
- studies of therapist competence (e.g. Shaw and Dobson, 1988);
- measurement of recurrent relationship themes in psychotherapy (Johnson *et al.* 1989; Luborsky and Crits-Christoph, 1997).

The case against evidence-based psychotherapy

Evidence-based medicine has generated considerable debate, with critics of EBM attacking the movement as arrogant, platitudinous, and biased in its claims. Miles *et al.* (1997: 83) accuse the advocates of EBM of committing two cardinal sins against clinical medicine, 'the barely concealed view that scientific data are an adequate basis for clinical decision making and the conviction that there can be absolute authority to identify and recommend the "best external evidence"'.

Evidence-based psychological therapies have, when taken seriously, produced equally strong negative reactions. In particular, the rhetoric of improving services can be seen as little more than a device to distract attention from the underlying purpose of cost containment. For example, Power (1998) draws attention to the intrinsic tensions between professional autonomy to control quality judgements and the managerial imperative to reduce public expenditure. Miller (1996) argues that the research evidence is insufficient to justify the managerial drive to replacing longer-term therapy with brief therapy. He sees brief therapy as a form of invisible rationing that compromises the client's best interests.

Objections to evidence-based psychotherapy fall into two categories. There is a root-and-branch rejection of the whole enterprise, a profound dislike of the values, assumptions and epistemological stance on which it is based. In holding this view one would, for example, reject the notion of psychiatric diagnosis, arguing that these medical terms, quasi disease entities, do not reflect the reality of complex psychological and cultural processes underlying mental distress. What is more, diagnoses conceal more than they reveal – the term 'anxiety disorder' is analogous to 'stomach pain' in its lack of explanatory power. The quantitative research enterprise itself depends on questionable 'measurement' of psychological states; indeed it reduces 'outcome' to that which can be measured, often over an arbitrary time scale. It cannot begin to address the complexities of psychological change, where a patient could feel worse symptomatically as part of a benign process of self-discovery. It also relies on statistical generalisations in large samples, which mask the reality of individual processes. In this radical view, quantitative research is fundamentally unsuited to reveal the important truths about psychotherapy. Yet such reductionist techniques give a misleading impression of precision and certainty, and by aping the research methods of power-holding biomedical elites assert a spurious authority for providing 'best evidence' of what 'works'. Some practitioners find the whole discourse relating to evidence-based psychotherapy so inimical to their world-view that they refuse to engage in it. For example, the author of one psychoanalytic critique of the NHS Executive psychotherapy review (1996) dismisses the terms of the discourse by interpreting the language of the document in terms of four 'primitive superego manifestations' (Taylor, 1998).

The second type of argument against the enterprise of evidence-based psychotherapy does not reject it so fundamentally, but sees it as fraught with difficulties and dangers. The genuine difficulties involved in establishing the evidential basis for individual clinical decisions has already been described. Many psychotherapists would argue that even state-of-the-art psychotherapy research has a long way to go before it is truly informative for individual clinical decisions. Take, for example, assessment of suicide risk. There is quite a respectable body of research on the precursors and predictors of completed suicide, but these are necessarily statistical associations and have very limited value in accurately predicting the likelihood of any individual attempting suicide. Another type of problem arises when transferring results from generalisations within group data to individual case decisions. In any group comparison between two therapies, although one treatment may be statistically superior to the other, there will be some individuals who do very well with the 'less effective' therapy. Unless we have very sound information about what characterises those individuals, it remains a matter of clinical judgement and experience who is likely to benefit from which approach. The hope of being able to specify the patient characteristics or aptitudes that will predict which type of therapy is most effective has not yet been realised. It is widely thought that the research designed to do this (Aptitude Treatment Interaction or ATI research) has not yet delivered on its promises (Shoham and Rohrbaugh, 1995).

It could also be argued that, as well as difficulties, there are dangers in taking an 'evidence-based' approach. The danger most often mentioned by clinicians is that funding decisions are going to be driven by research reviews and clinical practice guidelines. Research could even be used as a *post hoc* rationalisation for cutting services when the actual decision was driven by the requirement to reduce costs. Systematic reviews can only reflect findings for types of therapy which have been extensively researched, and, generally speaking, these have been the briefer, more structured and focal therapies, particularly (but not exclusively) cognitive behaviour therapy. Where research evidence is lacking for other approaches – for example, longer-term psychoanalytic work – it is easy to jump to the conclusion that such approaches are not supported by evidence. This could have disastrous consequences for those services, where funding could be withdrawn and potentially valuable and effective therapies lost to the NHS. Another danger is that by specifying 'standard treatments' and bringing practice into line with a narrow reading of research evidence, the capacity of psychotherapists to innovate and develop new approaches may be damaged.

ONE WAY FORWARD

The case against evidence-based psychotherapy is salutary – awareness of it enables the enterprise to proceed more cautiously but more securely. In this final section, I suggest we steer a pragmatic course between Scylla and Charybdis, by avoiding overzealous claims but not falling prey to methodological defeatism.

A sensible place to start seems to be with research questions and research designs. If we are pursuing research-based psychotherapy we must have service-relevant research. Improving the external validity of research designs will mitigate many of the intrinsic problems associated with clinical outcome trials. This means more pragmatic trials with clinically realistic samples and interventions, clinically meaningful comparison groups, analysis of 'intention to treat' samples, and greater awareness of the effects of patient preference (Aveline *et al.*, 1995; Bradley, 1997). Outcomes should be reported in terms of clinical as well as statistical significance (Jacobson, 1988).

As well as continuous improvement of the clinical relevance of RCTs, other research designs and paradigms should be reviewed and consensus reached on their implications for practice. These include large-scale field trials, service outcomes monitoring and studies which influence theory development, such as qualitative process research and tests of conceptual models.

Practice research networks (discussed further in Chapter 8) are valuable means to take this agenda forward, and these already exist. For example, in the UK the Society for Psychotherapy Research has a Northern England collaboration of NHS psychotherapy services co-ordinated through the University of Leeds Psychological Therapies Research Centre. The British Psychological Society's Clinical Outcomes Research and Effectiveness unit at University College London also co-ordinates a network in relation to patients with long-term severe mental health problems. Typically, a practice research network consists of NHS departments whose members have agreed to gather and pool data relating to clinical outcomes, using the same set of measures, in order to enable analysis of national data sets. Data are aggregated and anonymous, so that individual patient details are not identifiable. These networks help practitioners to take a research-based approach to exploring outcomes in their own services, sharing the findings, which can be compared with results obtained in more controlled experimental conditions. To the extent they allow high-quality clinical databases to be developed, practice research networks may provide an important source of valid and reliable evidence, an approach which is starting to bear fruit in other fields, such as surgery, obstetrics, haematology and oncology (Black, 1997).

A vital part of the change process in making psychotherapy more evidence-based is practitioner training. There are two ways in which training can be influenced by research. First, teaching on psychotherapy research methods and results could be incorporated into all psychotherapy training, which is not currently the case. Second, training itself could be more evidence-based.

There is a strong argument for a minimum standard of research competence to be agreed across all courses – competence in applying research evidence to practice as well as in doing research. For example, it could be argued that qualified practitioners of psychotherapy should be able to understand, in broad terms, the research evidence on the effectiveness of psychotherapies, and how their own approach stands in terms of this evidence. It would be helpful if practitioners had a basic and general (rather than advanced or specialist) understanding of research methods. Ideally, they would know how to read a research paper in the psychotherapy field and make a critical appraisal of its methods, the soundness of the conclusions and its applicability to clinical practice.

If there are difficulties in changing psychotherapy practice to reflect research evidence, how much more difficult it is to organise psychotherapy training on the basis of evidence. This is partly because of the dearth of good research on what constitutes competence in psychotherapy and the relationship of psychotherapy training and supervision to psychotherapy outcomes. However, there is some evidence. For example, research on the therapeutic alliance and therapist skill has important implications for how psychotherapists are trained and accredited. Training which uses targeted goals, specific feedback and guided practice in order to enable therapists to reach a stated criterion of competence is likely to be most effective (Luborsky, 1990a). Beutler *et al.* (1994) call for more rigorous and specific training methods than current supervision models provide, suggesting that competency-based training using therapy manuals may provide such an alternative. This method has been adopted to some extent in cognitive and behavioural therapy training (Bootzin and Ruggill, 1988; Dobson and Shaw, 1988; Dobson *et al.*, 1985; Shaw and Dobson, 1988). Although there are examples in psychodynamic therapy (Moss *et al.*, 1991; Strupp *et al.*, 1988) measures of specific psychodynamic competencies are not yet widely available. A research informed approach in psychoanalytic training is not, however, a pipe dream. For example, Bennett *et al.* (1999), using task analysis, developed a model of competence in resolving damaging transference/counter-transference enactments. Luborsky and Crits-Cristoph (1997) demonstrate how their research method of core conflictual role theme analysis can be used as a training tool.

Clinical practice guidelines are 'systematically developed statements to assist practitioner and patient decisions about appropriate health care for specific clinical circumstances' (Field and Lohr, 1990). When developed properly, they summarise current research evidence and clinical consensus on best practice in a given clinical situation, and can be a useful tool to help practitioners make clinical decisions. They are also useful as a jumping off point for audit, where practitioners set standards and monitor the extent to which they are achieving them. Guidelines have an important role to play, and are described and discussed in a later chapter (Cape and Parry, this volume).

To change practice, no one method will suffice. This was demonstrated by the Cochrane Collaboration on Effective Professional Practice (CCEPP), which systematically reviews the evidence for the effectiveness of interventions to change professional attitudes and behaviour (Oxman *et al.*, 1995). The reviewers found that clinical audit and feedback had a moderate effect on professional behaviour in the studies reported, but we can assume that the most widely used methods of audit are likely to have weaker effects than this, because many audits gather data but give insufficient feedback. Educational outreach is a method of influencing practice where clinicians receive a personal visit by the 'evidence-based health care representative', analogous to a drugs rep. in general practice. This seems to be a promising approach, rather more effective in influencing practitioners than clinical audit alone, but the characteristics of effective educational visits are not well understood. There is also some evidence for the value of working with opinion leaders, people who are nominated by their colleagues as educationally influential, although the reviewers found mixed effects and some difficulties in implementation. Computer support for clinician decision-making has some value, for example, in giving reminders for decisions on drug dosages, but on the other hand the evidence is relatively weak for computer-aided diagnosis. The review implies that there are no 'magic bullets' in implementing research findings, and that a range of different approaches are required to incorporate research evidence into routine clinical practice. Firth-Cozens (1997) explores how an evaluative culture can be developed in health organisations, by applying research evidence from studies of behaviour change – in organisational and health psychology, health promotion and marketing. She analyses forces that restrain the change towards evidence-based practice (such as high stress, resistance, insufficient time) and those which drive it forward (rewards, education, feedback, product champions, external and internal pressures).

All these techniques will need to be adapted to psychotherapy services if we are to see significant change. I am optimistic that this can be done. Despite the misgivings of some, there are large numbers of psychological therapists who are deeply committed to improving their services and who have a genuine interest in how research evidence can help them do it.

REFERENCES

American Psychological Association Task Force on Psychological Intervention Guidelines (1999) *Template for Developing Guidelines. Interventions for Mental Disorders and Psychosocial Aspects of Physical Disorders.* Washington, DC: American Psychological Association.

Austad, C.S. and Berman, W.H. (1991) Managed health care and the evolution of psychotherapy, in C.S. Austad and W.H. Berman (eds) *Psychotherapy in Managed Health Care.* Washington, DC: American Psychological Association, 3–18.

Aveline, M. and Shapiro, D.A. (1995) *Research Foundations for Psychotherapy Practice.* Chichester: Wiley.

Aveline, M., Shapiro, D.A., Parry, G. and Freeman, C.P.L. (1995) Building research foundations for psychotherapy practice, in M. Aveline and D.A. Shapiro (eds) *Research Foundations for Psychotherapy Practice*. Chichester: Wiley.

Barlow, D.H. (1996) The effectiveness of psychotherapy: science and policy. *Clinical Psychology: Science and Practice*, 3: 236–240.

Bennett, D., Parry, G. and Ryle, A. (1999) An Ideal Model for the Resolution of Alliance Threatening Transference Enactments. Submitted for publication.

Beutler, L.E., Machado, P.P.P. and Neufeldt, S.A. (1994) Therapist variables, in A.E. Bergin and S.L. Garfield (eds) *Handbook of Psychotherapy and Behavior Change* (4th edn). New York: Wiley, 229–269.

Black, N. (1997) Developing high quality clinical databases: the key to a new research paradigm. *British Medical Journal*, 315: 381–382.

Bootzin, R.R. and Ruggill, J.S. (1988) Training issues in behavior therapy. *Journal of Consulting and Clinical Psychology*, 56: 703–709.

Bordin, E.S. (1979) The generalisability of the concept of the working alliance. *Psychotherapy Theory, Research and Practice*, 16: 252–260.

Bradley, C. (1997) Psychological issues in clinical trial design. *Irish Journal of Psychology*, 18: 67–87.

Brock, T.C., Green, M.C., Reich, D.A. and Evans, L.M. (1996) The Consumer Reports study of psychotherapy: invalid is invalid. *American Psychologist*, 51: 1083–1084.

Chambless, D.L. (1996) In defense of dissemination of empirically supported psychological interventions. *Clinical Psychology: Science and Practice*, 3: 230–235.

Crits-Christoph, P. (1996) The dissemination of efficacious psychological treatments. *Clinical Psychology: Science and Practice*, 3: 260–263.

Davenhill, R. and Patrick, M. (1998) *Rethinking Clinical Audit: The Case of Psychotherapy Services in the NHS*. London: Routledge.

Department of Health (1996) *A Review of Strategic Policy on NHS Psychotherapy Services in England* (ed. G. Parry). London: NHS Executive.

Dobson, K.S. and Shaw, B.F. (1988) The use of treatment manuals in cognitive therapy: experience and issues. *Journal of Consulting and Clinical Psychology*, 56: 673–680.

Dobson, K.S., Shaw, B.F. and Vallis, T.M. (1985) Reliability of a measure of the quality of cognitive therapy. *British Journal of Clinical Psychology*, 24: 295–300.

Elliott, R. (1998) Editor's introduction: a guide to the empirically supported treatments controversy. *Psychotherapy Research*, 8: 115–125.

Field, M.J. and Lohr, K.N. (eds) (1990) *Clinical Practice Guidelines: Direction for a New Program*. Washington, DC: National Academy Press.

Firth-Cozens, J.A. (1997) Health promotion: changing behaviour towards evidence-based health care. *Quality in Health Care*, 6: 205–211.

Garfield, S.L. (1996) Some problems associated with 'validated' forms of psychotherapy. *Clinical Psychology: Science and Practice*, 3: 218–229.

Henry, W.P. (1998) Science, politics and the politics of science: the use and misuse of empirically validated treatment research. *Psychotherapy Research*, 8: 126–140.

Howard, K.I., Lueger, R., Maling, M. and Martinovitch, Z. (1993) A phase model of psychotherapy: causal mediation of outcome. *Journal of Consulting and Clinical Psychology*, 61: 678–685.

Hunot, V. and Churchill, R. (1999) Systematic review of brief psychological treatments for depression. Personal communication.

Jacobson, N.S. (1988) Defining clinically significant change. *Behavioral Assessment*, 10 (2):131–223.

Johnson, M.E., Popp, C., Schacht, T.E., Mellon, J. and Strupp, H.H. (1989) Converging evidence for identification of recurrent relationship themes: comparison of two methods. *Psychiatry*, 52: 275–288.

Luborsky, L. (1990) Theory and technique in dynamic psychotherapy – curative factors and training therapists to maximize them. *Psychotherapy and Psychosomatics*, 53: 50–57.

Luborsky, L. and Crits-Christoph, P. (1997) *Understanding Transference: The Core Conflictual Relationship Theme Method* (2nd edn). New York: Basic Books.

Mackay, H. and Barkham, M. (1998) Report to the National Counselling and Psychological Therapies Clinical Guidelines Development Group: Evidence from Published Reviews and Meta-analyses, 1990–98. Leeds: Psychological Therapies Research Centre, University of Leeds. Memo no. 369.

Miles, A., Bentley, P., Polychronis, A. and Grey, J. (1997) Evidence-based medicine: why all the fuss? This is why. *Journal of Evaluation in Clinical Practice*, 3: 83–86.

Miller, I.J. (1996) Time-limited brief therapy has gone too far: the result is invisible rationing. *Professional Psychology: Research and Practice*, 27: 567–576.

Mintz, J., Drake, R. and Crits-Christoph, P. (1996) The efficacy and effectiveness of psychotherapy: two paradigms, one science. *American Psychologist*, 51: 1084–1085.

Moss, S., Margison, F. and Godbert, K. (1991) The maintenance of psychotherapy skill acquisition: a two-year follow-up. *British Journal of Medical Psychology* 64: 233–236.

Muir Gray, J.A. (1997) *Evidence-based Healthcare. How to Make Health Policy and Management Decisions*. New York: Churchill Livingstone.

NHS Centre for Reviews and Dissemination (1996) *Undertaking Systematic Reviews of Research on Effectiveness*. York: University of York.

Orlinsky, D.E., Grawe, K. and Parks, B.K. (1994) Process and outcome in psychotherapy, in A.E. Bergin and S.L. Garfield (eds) *Handbook of Psychotherapy and Behavior Change* (4th edn). New York: Wiley, 270–376.

Oxam, A.D., Thomson, M.A., Davis, D.A. and Haynes, R.B. (1995) No magic bullets: a systematic review of 102 trials of interventions to improve professional practice. *Canadian Medical Association Journal*, 153: 1423–1431.

Parry, G. (1992) Improving psychotherapy services: applications of research, audit and evaluation. *British Journal of Clinical Psychology*, 31: 3–19.

Power, M. (1998) The audit fixation: some issues for psychotherapy, in R. Davenhill and M. Patrick (eds) *Rethinking Clinical Audit: The Case of Psychotherapy Services in the NHS*. London: Routledge, 23–37.

Rice, L.N. and Greenberg, L.S. (1984) *Patterns of Change: Intensive Analysis of Psychotherapy Process*. New York: Guilford Press.

Roth, A.D. and Fonagy, P. (1996) *What Works for Whom? A Critical Review of Psychotherapy Research*. New York: Guilford Press.

Roth, A.D., Fonagy, P. and Parry, G. (1996) Psychotherapy research, funding and evidence based practice, in A.D. Roth and P. Fonagy, *What Works for Whom? A Critical Review of Psychotherapy Research* New York: Guilford, 37–56.

Roth, A.D. and Parry, G. (1997) The implications of psychotherapy research for clinical practice and service development: lessons and limitations. *Journal of Mental Health*, 6: 367–380.

Safran, J.D., Crocker, P., McMain, S. and Murray, P. (1990) Therapeutic alliance rupture as a therapy event for empirical investigation. *Psychotherapy*, 27: 154–165.

Schulberg, H.C., Katon, W., Simon, G.E. and Rush, A.J. (1998) Treating major depression in primary care practice: an update of the Agency for Health Care Policy and Research Practice Guidelines. *Archives of General Psychiatry*, 55: 1121–1127.

Schwartz, D. and Lellouch, J. (1967) Explanatory and pragmatic attitudes in therapeutic trials. *Journal of Chronic Disease*, 20: 637–648.

Seligman, M.E.P. (1995) The effectiveness of psychotherapy: the Consumer Reports study. *American Psychologist*, 50: 965–974.

Shapiro, D.A. (1996) 'Validated' treatments and evidence-based psychological services. *Clinical Psychology: Science and Practice*, 3: 256–259.

Shaw, B.F. and Dobson, K.S. (1988) Competency judgements in the training and evaluation of psychotherapists. *Journal of Consulting and Clinical Psychology*, 56: 666–672.

Shoham, V. and Rohrbaugh, M. (1995) Aptitude x treatment interaction (ATI) research: sharpening the focus, widening the lens, in M. Aveline and D.A. Shapiro (eds) *Research Foundations for Psychotherapy Practice*. Chichester: Wiley, 73–96.

Smith, M.L. and Glass, G.V. (1977) Meta-analysis of psychotherapy outcome studies. *American Psychologist*, 32: 752–760.

Stiles, W.B., Elliott, R., Llewelyn, S.P., Firth-Cozens, J.A., Margison, F.R., Shapiro, D.A. and Hardy, G. (1990) Assimilation of problematic experiences by clients in psychotherapy. *Psychotherapy*, 27:411–420.

Stiles, W.B. and Shapiro, D.A. (1994) Disabuse of the drug metaphor – psychotherapy process outcome correlations. *Journal of Consulting and Clinical Psychology*, 62: 942–948.

Strupp, H.H., Butler, S.F. and Rosser, C. (1988) Training in psychodynamic therapy. *Journal of Consulting and Clinical Psychology*, 56: 689–695.

Taylor, D. (1998) Critical review of the review of psychotherapy services in England. *Psychoanalytic Psychotherapy*, 12: 111–118.

Part 2

Generating the evidence

Chapter 6

Randomised controlled trials and the evaluation of psychological therapy

Peter Bower and Michael King

One of the key tenets of evidence-based health care (EBHC) is that objective evaluation of the outcome of health service interventions is a requirement for their provision in clinical practice (Sackett *et al.*, 1996). Psychological therapies[1] are no exception. Concerns about the effectiveness of such therapies have a long history, dating back to Eysenck's seminal article challenging the view that the effectiveness of psychological therapy had been established (Eysenck, 1952).

Although there are a number of methods of evaluating such interventions, it is widely agreed that such evaluations should use the most rigorous methods possible in order to ensure that only safe, effective and economic treatments are delivered to patients. This chapter will consider one particular form of evaluation which has been accorded significant status in EBHC because of its rigour: the randomised controlled trial (RCT).

The first part of the chapter (the 'logic of experiment') will consider the reasons why RCTs are so important in the evaluation of treatments. The second part will consider a wider range of issues specific to the use of RCTs in the evaluation of psychological therapy.

THE LOGIC OF EXPERIMENT

If the challenge of evidence-based practice is to be met, mental health practitioners need to be able to answer two distinct but related questions about the treatments they provide. The first is 'Does it work?'; that is, can psychological therapy be said to *cause* beneficial effects in those who receive it (Basham, 1986). The second key question is 'Which works best? (Basham, 1986). If psychological therapies are responsible for beneficial effects, comparisons are important to determine which of the large number of alternative approaches achieves the best outcomes.

Observational studies

One method of evaluating the effects of interventions is to measure the relationships between treatment and outcome as they occur in routine clinical situations. For example, distress may be measured in patients[2] before and after they receive psychological therapy, or patients who have received therapy may be compared with those who have not. Such studies, which do not involve any changes imposed by researchers, are described as observational, naturalistic or non-experimental (Black, 1996). The relationships observed in such research (for example, that patients' distress is lower after therapy than before) are described as associations between variables.

Although such studies can be highly informative and useful in generating hypotheses, they do not provide conclusive evidence to answer either the causal or comparative questions described above. The mental health of patients is potentially related to a large number of factors, and the provision of treatment is only one factor together with other influences such as the patient's pre-existing personality or changes in their social environment. The existence of an association between treatment and outcome does not necessarily imply a cause, because the changes observed in a patient's mental health may be due to other, unobserved factors which happen to be related to the provision of treatment (such as differences between patients who are and are not referred for therapy, or simply the passage of time). Variables that operate so as to confuse real cause and effect relationships are known as confounding variables (Davey Smith and Philips, 1992). For example, patients with problems of recent onset usually do better in psychological therapy than those with long-term symptoms. However, patients with severe, long-term problems may be more likely to be referred for psychological treatment, and those with less severe problems may generally receive no specialist help. A straightforward comparison of outcome in these groups might paradoxically show that those who receive treatment have worse outcomes than those who do not. This is not because the treatment is making patients worse, but because receiving treatment is confounded with the severity of the problem.

Experimental studies

In contrast to observational studies, experimental studies involve active manipulation of some parameters (called independent variables) followed by examination of the effects of these manipulations on other parameters (called dependent variables). Experimental procedures are designed to exclude the possibility that other variables are responsible for the observed findings. The confidence with which a researcher can conclude that an experiment has demonstrated either a causal relationship between a treatment and outcome (i.e. that the treatment 'works') or provided an unbiased demonstration of the comparative effectiveness of treatments (i.e. that one treatment is superior to another) is described as the internal validity of the experiment. Confounding variables and biases are described as threats to internal validity. Randomised controlled trials are research designs that provide safeguards against key threats to internal validity through three interrelated mechanisms (Spector, 1981; Mahoney, 1978): control, comparison and randomisation.[3] The different procedures used to implement each of these three mechanisms will determine the type of trial that is undertaken and how the results should be interpreted.

Internal validity is contrasted with external validity, which relates to the confidence with which a researcher can expect relationships found in the context of one particular experiment to generalise to other contexts. For example, will the relationships hold true in different settings, with different therapists, patients, and at different times (Cook and Campbell, 1979)? External validity issues will be dealt with later in the chapter.

Control

Control is the basis of experiment, and involves holding variables constant or varying them systematically so that their effect can be examined. For example, if a researcher wishes to compare two treatments, one of which is routinely provided over six sessions and one over twelve, then any differences in outcome may simply relate to differences in the amount of treatment provided rather than the superiority of one treatment over another. By comparing the two treatments over nine sessions (i.e. 'controlling the length of treatment'), the researcher ensures that differences in outcome cannot be due to differences in the length of treatment. Similarly, a study might be conducted only on a specific diagnostic group (e.g. patients with 'major depression') to ensure that differences in the natural history of the disorders cannot be responsible for differences in outcome.

It is important to distinguish between the meaning of 'control' used here, in the sense of power over the operation of important variables in the experiment, and control in the sense of 'control group', which is dealt with in the 'comparison' section below.

The degree of control that a researcher can maintain will depend in part on the setting of the study. For example, it may be easier to ensure that patients in a study do not receive treatments other than those under test if the evaluation is in an in-patient setting rather than out-patients or primary care, because patients in the latter environments are much more able to act in a manner that is not within the overall plan of the study (what is called the study protocol).

Comparison

Experimental comparison involves three steps:

a   setting the independent variable at different levels (e.g. giving some patients psychological therapy and some no therapy, or giving them different amounts of psychological therapy);
b   allocating patients to these different levels (called groups or trial arms);
c   examining the differences in outcome between the group receiving the different levels of the independent variable.

Groups receiving psychological therapy are called the active, intervention, or treatment groups. When some patients do not receive psychological therapy at all, this group is called the control group; when they receive an alternative type or administration of therapy, they are called a comparison group.[4]

What is the function of such groups? One key validity threat is history i.e. changes over time outside the research context that account for patient outcome (Campbell and Stanley, 1966). It is well known that a significant proportion of psychological and psychiatric disorders will improve over time without any professional intervention (spontaneous remission). Exactly how such remission occurs is not clear, but such changes are particularly likely to be confused with the effects of treatment. Control and comparison groups provide protection against such a threat by ensuring that it effects both groups. If, after treatment, outcome in the experimental and control groups is very similar, all other things being equal we can conclude that the effects of treatment plus the effects of spontaneous remission in the intervention group are no greater than the effects of spontaneous remission alone in the control group. Therefore, it is unlikely that the treatment is having a significant effect on outcome. Control groups also allow examination of negative effects of psychological therapy. If patients who receive a treatment have worse outcomes than those who do not, it might suggest that treatment is doing more harm than good. Without a control group, it would be difficult to tell whether such negative effects existed because they could not be disentangled from the natural history of the disorder.

In order to answer the causal question, 'Does psychological therapy work?', it is necessary to ensure that the treatment group differs from the control group in only one way: the treatment under test. A particular problem for such studies is caused by the operation of placebo effects or expectancy artefacts (Basham, 1986). It is generally accepted that almost all treatments, including psychological therapy, may work in part because of the expectation of recovery brought about in the patient or clinician by the offer of treatment. For example, if patients are allocated to treatment or no treatment conditions (such as a waiting list for treatment), patients in both groups will develop specific expectancies about the possible outcome of their disorder based on their assignment. Thus, patients allocated to a 'new' treatment may have more confidence in a good outcome, while those on a waiting list may expect no change or even deterioration. Therefore, the patients will differ both in terms of whether they receive treatment at all *and* whether they are expecting a positive outcome (i.e. expectancy is confounded with treatment).

In trials of medication, it is possible to overcome this problem by blinding patients and their clinicians to the treatment group to which they have been allocated. This involves the use of identical pills and administration procedures to ensure that it is unclear during the study who received an 'active' medication and who received an inert placebo pill. Assuming the blinds are not broken (Greenberg and Fisher, 1994; Moncrieff *et al.*, 1998), this procedure ensures that the expectancies in both groups will be similar and thus will not bias the results. However, it is impossible to conduct psychological therapy trials in genuinely 'blind' conditions: clinicians will always be aware whether the treatment is active or not, and patients may well develop hypotheses concerning which treatment group they are in (Orne, 1962). Therefore, these expectancy artefacts cannot normally be differentiated from the effect of the treatment. The basic question, 'Does psychological therapy work?', is therefore very difficult to answer in a formal experimental sense.

A related difficulty concerns the question of how psychological therapies achieve their effects. Most psychological therapies are based on a theory of human function and dysfunction, and the theories underlying psychological therapies are often highly dissimilar. However, despite these differences, some authors have suggested that these different therapies tend to be of similar effectiveness. This is known as the 'Dodo bird verdict' (Luborsky and Singer, 1975) after the result of the Caucus race in *Alice in Wonderland*: 'everyone has won, and all must have prizes'. It has been suggested that psychological change may be related to the contact and support from a caring professional (non-specific treatment effects or common factors) rather than any specific psychological mechanisms suggested by the underlying theory (Kazdin and Wilcoxon, 1976; Shapiro, 1980). Thus a psychoanalyst and behavioural therapist may achieve outcomes because of the similarities in the way they relate to their patients, not the different methods they use.

Attention-placebo control groups are designed to determine whether a particular psychotherapeutic procedure provides additional advantages over and above non-specific effects by providing patients with time and support without offering any active therapeutic procedures (Kazdin and Wilcoxon, 1976) – for example, through non-specific discussion groups and bogus treatments. However, convincing placebos have proved difficult to develop for a number of methodological and ethical reasons (O'Leary and Borkovec, 1978). A particular problem is that it is necessary that both the active treatment and attention-placebo conditions are viewed by patients as equally credible (Parloff, 1986). However, checks on credibility are rarely done (Shapiro and Shapiro, 1983), and without them expectancy artefacts may once again be confounded with treatment.

Comparative studies

In contrast to causal studies, comparative studies assume some benefit from psychological therapy, but seek to determine which treatments are associated with the best outcome. Assuming the treatments are broadly similar in format and credibility (Borkovec and Castonguay, 1998), a comparison of two treatments lessens the threats from expectancy artefacts because the treatments are more similar than the treatment/no-treatment design, and thus expectancies would be more alike. Since non-specific effects are expected to occur in all therapies, they will also be equivalent and that threat to validity will be controlled as well (Basham, 1986). However, if two therapies differ significantly in format and administration (e.g. the number of sessions, content of the treatment), the number of uncontrolled factors between the therapies increases, and it becomes less clear which particular aspects of therapy were responsible for therapeutic change.

Finally, it is possible to answer questions about 'what works in psychological therapy?' through a form of comparative design, where the comparison involves a complete form of treatment and another form which is identical in all features (e.g. number of sessions, types of therapists, key therapeutic techniques) except for the one key issue under test (Borkovec and Castonguay, 1998). For example, one study (Jacobson *et al*., 1996) compared outcome from three forms of cognitive-behaviour therapy: behavioural activation (BA); behavioural activation plus cognitive work on automatic thoughts (AT); and full cognitive therapy (CT). In this study, the CT condition contained elements of the BA and AT, while the AT condition contained elements of the BA condition. As no significant differences in patient outcome were found between the treatments, the causal efficacy of the additional cognitive elements of the treatment (over and above BA) were thrown into doubt. Such studies are called dismantling studies or component analyses and can assist in the identification of cause and effect relationships between specific therapeutic procedures and patient outcomes.

The nature of the control or comparison group determines the types of questions that can be answered by a trial. Control group designs (and dismantling studies) seek to answer *scientific* questions, in the sense that they attempt to uncover causal processes that underpin a treatment. Such studies enable researchers to specify with increasing accuracy just what was responsible for the changes that were observed (Borkovec and Castonguay, 1998). In contrast, comparative designs are examples of *evaluative* research. Such work uses rigorous methodology, but is focused on determining the basic worth or value of a procedure in terms of its effects on the recipients, rather than uncovering the processes by which such effects occur (Smith *et al*., 1980). For example, treatment trials in primary care are increasingly using 'usual general practitioner care' as a control condition, because patients in both groups will always have access to such care and it thus represents a sensible baseline for outcome. 'Usual GP care' is varied in nature and may involve some psychotherapeutic processes, and the lack of control means that identification of exact causal processes is impossible. Rather, the design seeks to determine if the addition of psychological therapy adds anything of value to the outcome that patients would ordinarily achieve under the care of their GP.

Randomisation

Control groups provide protection against bias with one all-important proviso: 'all other things being equal' (Latin: *ceteris paribus*). If the patients making up the intervention and control groups in the study differ significantly in characteristics relating to the outcome of their disorder (for example, the severity of their problems), then any conclusions made about them will be vulnerable because these differences could very well account for the observed differences in outcome rather than the treatment provided. This validity threat is called selection bias (Campbell and Stanley, 1966; Kleijnen *et al.*, 1997), and it is countered by allocation of patients to treatment and control groups through a process of randomisation.

In one sense, randomisation is the opposite of experimental control, as it involves letting parameters vary freely. However, the fact that allocation is random ensures that the groups will both contain roughly equal levels of each patient variable, because every idiosyncratic value assigned to the first group will tend to be balanced later in the random process by assigning a similar variable to the other group or an opposite variable to the same group. With sufficient numbers of patients, randomisation should ensure that there are no systematic differences in the average 'score' on any variable between the groups. Thus any differences in outcome cannot reasonably be attributed to any pre-existing differences between the groups, and any comparison between the groups will be unbiased. Although it is theoretically possible to match patients in each group on key variables (such as age, sex, and initial degree of psychological distress), randomisation has the advantage that it will ensure that there are no systematic differences in relation to both measured variables *and* those which are not measured but may potentially influence outcome (Cook and Campbell, 1979).

Non-randomised studies which use control or comparison groups are described as quasi-experiments or controlled before-and-after (CBA) designs. Empirical comparisons between randomised and CBA designs suggest the latter are prone to overestimate the effects of interventions, although underestimates also occur (Kunz and Oxman, 1998). Although quasi-experiments are more vulnerable to bias and therefore more difficult to interpret, they have significant uses when randomisation is not possible because of ethical or other barriers (Cook and Campbell, 1979).

RESEARCH DESIGN ISSUES

Despite the importance of randomisation, comparison and control, they are only aspects of the overall research design among a host of others (Cook and Campbell, 1979), some of general importance and others which are specific to the evaluation of the psychological therapies. A number of these issues will now be considered.

Explanatory and pragmatic designs

The preceding section has focused on threats to the internal validity of study design. One of the main issues in the interpretation of studies relates to their external validity. Population validity is the degree to which the results will generalise to other patients, while ecological validity refers to other variables in the study such as the clinicians, the treatments and the specific setting of the study (Bracht and Glass, 1968).

Although studies high on internal and external validity are the ideal, in practice there is often conflict between the two types of validity, such that there is a trade-off between the scientific rigour of a study and its external validity. This is because the conditions that optimise the former (i.e. randomisation, comparison and control) are so rarely features of real world settings to which the results are to be generalised (Cook and Campbell, 1979; Shadish *et al.*, 1997; Weisz *et al.*, 1992). For example, use of a highly homogeneous group of patients in a trial leads to greater precision in the results, but may be a poor representation of clinical practice where the types of presenting problems may be variable. Equally, the types of therapy practised in clinical settings may be very varied, so that controlling for issues such as length of therapy may sacrifice some external validity. A number of factors have been described (Clarke, 1995) that might potentially limit the external validity of RCT studies, including therapist training; the quality and format of treatments provided; the use of combination treatments; multiple roles for the therapist; homogeneity of patients entered into the trial; and the type of control group used (e.g. placebo control or usual care).

Depending on the way in which trials deal with such threats to external validity, they can be described as explanatory or pragmatic in nature (Schwartz and Lellouch, 1967). Explanatory trials are similar to the control group designs discussed earlier in that they require high levels of control over variables to provide rigorous demonstrations of the causal link between treatment and outcome. Double-blind, placebo controlled drug trials are paradigm examples of explanatory designs. Interventions are clearly specified, the effects of placebos are controlled, and the types of patient entering the trial are defined by a rigid protocol. Such trials prioritise internal validity to answer basic scientific questions. For example, the rigid definition of the treatment in an explanatory trial means that it is necessary that patients receive high-quality treatments in a format and dose defined by the study protocol.

In contrast, pragmatic trials seek to balance internal and external validity to provide results that are more generalisable to routine settings than the specialised conditions usually found in explanatory trials. Treatments are provided flexibly, in that the exact nature of the treatment is left to the judgement of the clinician, and there is variation in quality and process of care as would be found in routine settings. Placebo effects and expectancies are not controlled; if one treatment is viewed more favourably by patients, then such views are considered part of normal practice and a component of the treatment itself. Furthermore, it is not necessary that all patients attend for treatment, since failure to attend is a common aspect of clinical work. The lack of control and the increased number of confounding variables means that causal questions cannot be answered: it will not be clear whether outcome differences are due to the effects of the treatments, placebo or expectancy or other uncontrolled factors. However, to the degree that the conditions in such trials reflect usual practice, pragmatic trials do provide evidence that the treatment is in some way responsible for the changes observed in the treatment group over and above those found in the controls (Chambless and Hollon, 1998). Although pragmatic trials do not seek to control key variables, it is important that they report the values that those variables took (e.g. the training and experience of the therapists) so that the conditions of the trial (and their relationship to routine practice) can be clearly judged.

The potency of interventions evaluated under highly controlled conditions is known as the efficacy of the treatment. When potency is considered under routine conditions, it is described as effectiveness[5] or clinical utility. Explanatory and pragmatic trials use different techniques to answer different questions, and it is important to understand what sort of trial type is being considered before it is possible to interpret the methodology and results. Table 6.1 shows the main types of RCT, the threats to internal validity that they control for and the interpretation of the results.

Allocation

The fact that a study reports using random allocation is not enough to ensure the complete removal of selection bias; it is necessary that the decision about whether a patient is eligible to participate in the study is separate from knowledge of the patient's allocation. For example, if a clinician is entering a patient in a trial, it is important that the patient's eligibility is not altered because the clinician knows that the next treatment allocation is one that he or she views as unfavourable (e.g. a wait-list control). There are a number of methods of randomising patients, and studies have shown that bias is less likely in those where allocation is

Table 6.1 Types of randomised trial

Trial design	Trial type	Controls for patient expectancy?	Controls for non-specific effect of treatment?	Interpretation of results
Double-blind, placebo controlled trial	Explanatory only	Yes	Yes	Does psychological therapy cause change?
Placebo controlled trial	Explanatory only	Yes – to the degree that the placebo is viewed as of equal effectiveness by patients	Yes	Does psychological therapy cause change?
Comparative trial of active treatment and wait-list control	Explanatory or pragmatic	No	No	Does psychological therapy and associated expectancy and placebo cause change?
Dismantling study	Explanatory only	Yes	Yes	Does a specific aspect of psychological therapy cause change additional to the basic treatment?
Comparative trial of two active treatments	Explanatory or pragmatic	Yes – to the degree that each treatment is viewed as of equal effectiveness by patients	Yes	Which psychological therapy causes most change?
Comparative trial of active treatment and usual GP care	Pragmatic	No – unless usual care is viewed as of equal effectiveness to the active treatment	No – only to the degree that usual care involves significant therapeutic attention	Does psychological therapy plus usual care cause more change than usual care alone?

adequately concealed – for example, where randomisation is done centrally rather than by clinicians, or through the use of numbered, sealed and opaque envelopes which can be checked by a trial administrator (Chalmers *et al.*, 1983; Schulz *et al.*, 1995). Other methods (such as alternation of allocation based on case numbers) in which the allocation is transparent and decisions about eligibility can be made with fore-knowledge of the next allocation are more vulnerable to selection bias.

Randomisation in psychological therapy trials is complicated by ethical and logical difficulties. In some contexts, ethical committees are less willing to sanction trials where patients may be deprived of treatment (such as the use of wait-list controls). Clinical trials are meant to be undertaken when there is genuine uncertainty about the overall risks and benefits of different treatments (equipoise). However, equipoise in the minds of researchers and managers may not always be shared by clinicians and patients, who may use different evidence on which to base their decisions. Some trials have been abandoned because of problems in recruiting patients where they risk randomisation to a non-preferred treatment arm (Fairhurst and Dowrick, 1996).

Furthermore, where patient motivation is an important component of treatment, randomisation may interfere with treatment processes and threaten internal validity (Brewin and Bradley, 1989). Allocating patients to treatments that they do not want may lead to resentful demoralisation (Cook and Campbell, 1979; Seligman, 1995), which may worsen outcome in those participants if they are not sufficiently motivated to attend for treatment or otherwise react negatively to their treatment allocation.

Patient preference trials

One solution is to use a patient preference design (Brewin and Bradley, 1989), in which only patients without preferences are randomised; patients with strong preferences are allocated to their preferred treatment and followed up. The increased acceptability of the trial to patients and partici-pating clinicians may increase recruitment rates and the representativeness of the trial population, and the results from the randomised and preference cohorts can be used to investigate the influence of preference on outcome. However, such trials are potentially much larger than simple randomised trials (Brockelhurst, 1997). Analysing the data from the preference patients is also hampered by the fact that selection biases will operate to make the preference and randomised arms differ in variables other than their preferences. The relationship between preferences and motivation for treatment is also poorly understood at present. Studies that have compared randomised and preference cohorts in psychosocial treatments do not suggest any marked differences in outcome (Gossop et al., 1986; McKay et al., 1995). Other solutions to the problems include Zelen's design, where patients are randomised before their consent is sought, and only those patients in the new treatment are asked for informed consent – patients randomised to the 'usual care' arm of the trial are not asked for consent (Zelen, 1979; Torgerson and Sibbald, 1998). Such a procedure is limited by the fact that only patients in one arm are aware of the trial (which means that the two groups are not alike with respect to the information they have received), and also has ethical implications concerning informed consent. Alternatively, if preferences are not expected to influence recruitment, all patients may be randomised, but with patient preferences measured and used as a variable in later analyses (Torgerson et al., 1996).

Although randomisation is usually effective in producing baseline equivalence in patient characteristics, it is not a certainty (Scott and Freeman, 1992). The likelihood with which it will produce equivalence in groups depends on the sample size; small samples are more likely to lead to randomised groups differing by chance on confounding variables (Strube, 1991). Baseline imbalance may also suggest subversion of the allocation procedure (Roberts and Torgerson, 1999). To avoid such problems, stratification can be used to assist in maintaining equivalence when it is known that certain variables are highly likely to influence treatment outcome. Patients are split into different groups (or 'strata') defined by levels of these crucial variables (for example, problem severity), and random assignment is carried out within each stratum. Significant imbalances are thus less likely to occur because it is impossible for all the extreme values of the stratified variable to be randomised by chance to one group rather than the other. An alternative method is called minimisation. This involves allocation of the next patient in a trial to a group based on the degree to which the allocation will minimise the differences between the groups that have been formed by patients already recruited to the trial (Treasure and MacRae, 1998). Alternatively, techniques such as analysis of covariance can be used to adjust for baseline differences, although such adjustments should be specified in advance rather than after any imbalance is detected (Roberts and Torgerson, 1999).

Treatment allocation (through randomisation) refers to the initial decision about which group the patient has been assigned to. However, it is also necessary that a significant proportion of patients are followed-up in order to measure treatment outcome. Loss of patients to follow-up is known as attrition. High levels of attrition may jeopardise the results of a study in terms of their external validity. Differential attrition (the loss of significantly more patients from one of the groups) can undermine the benefits associated with randomisation and lead to selection bias, especially if attrition is related to aspects of the allocation procedure (e.g. high attrition amongst those allocated to a no-treatment group).

Finally, allocation may be compromised by contamination when patients in one group receive the intervention meant for the other group. For example, patients in a wait-list control group may receive the intervention through other channels (e.g. private treatment). In explanatory designs, such contamination is critical, because it means that the control group is no longer differentiated from the intervention group in terms of whether each has received psychological therapy. In pragmatic trials, such contamination is less problematic if it represents normal practice. However, with both trial types the effect of the therapy may be diluted (because control patients may receive active treatments) and the results of the study may be more difficult to interpret.

The intervention

There are many theoretical models of psychological therapy (Kazdin, 1986). Six main approaches have been delineated (Roth and Fonagy, 1996): psychodynamic psychotherapy, behavioural and cognitive-behavioural psychotherapy, interpersonal psychotherapy, strategic or systemic psychotherapies, supportive or experiential psychotherapies, and group therapies. However, even these broad groupings can conceal considerable overlap between therapeutic techniques, especially as they are applied in routine practice settings, when formal technique may be moulded to the specific characteristics of both therapist, patient and the context of treatment. Dismantling studies can be used to determine which particular aspects of a treatment are responsible for the observed effects, although some therapies (e.g. behavioural therapies) are far more suited to such research than others (e.g. psychodynamic therapy).

There are a number of different dimensions that can be used to describe therapies. The format concerns the number, length and spacing of therapy sessions. Ideally, such factors should be held constant in order to avoid confounding (Kazdin, 1986), but this can be difficult when different therapeutic orientations are compared (e.g. psychodynamic and behavioural therapies, traditionally long- and short-term therapies respectively). Adherence concerns the degree to which the patient received the treatment as planned (e.g. a minimum number of sessions, compliance with therapeutic procedures such as homework). Integrity concerns the degree to which patients in a particular treatment arm receive that form of treatment and not another form, while differentiation concerns differences between treatments in how they are carried out (i.e. the degree to which the therapies share common techniques and processes). The suggestion that therapeutic effects may operate through common factors has encouraged psychological therapy researchers to test therapies that have been 'manualised'; that is, by producing a written specification of the content and process of the therapy according to its theoretical description. In this way, integrity and differentiation can be maximised. Taping of sessions and rating the adherence of the therapists to their particular treatment is an additional check. Such checks are particularly important in comparative studies: if the treatments provided are not of equal quality, then the comparison between them will be biased towards the treatment of higher quality (Borkovec and Castonguay, 1998; Jacobson and Hollon, 1996). One additional complication concerns the therapists who provide the treatments. If different therapists are used for each treatment type (i.e. therapists are nested within therapies), therapists are confounded with therapy and the results of the study may be highly dependent on the particular therapists used. A preferred strategy is to have all therapists provide each of the treatments under test (therapists crossed with therapy) to control for such confounding, but finding therapists skilled in a variety of different approaches may be difficult (Barkham and Shapiro, 1992).

The external validity of treatments provided in trials has been called into question. Participant therapists tend to have greater training and experience than that normally found in routine settings, and control may be exercised over the use of concurrent treatments such as medication and social interventions which are routinely used (Clarke, 1995). The use of manuals may be a poor representation of actual clinical work (Shapiro and Shapiro, 1983; Roth and Fonagy, 1996) and may limit normal clinical practice which is flexible, self-correcting and responsive to the patient's presentation (Seligman, 1995; Persons, 1991). However, the effectiveness of such clinical judgement processes has been queried, and it is possible to compare 'manualised' and 'naturalistic' versions of psychological therapy within the format of a clinical trial (Jacobson and Christensen, 1996).

The patient population

A significant amount of psychological therapy research has traditionally been conducted on accessible populations such as students or volunteers (so called analogue research) rather than 'real' patient populations, which has severely restricted the external validity of study findings. Similarly, explanatory trials use highly selected patient groups, recruited in specialist trial centres and subject to exclusion criteria such as the rejection of patients with significant co-morbidity – for example, a psychiatric diagnosis secondary to the main problem, such as depression with personality disorder (Kendall and Lipman, 1991). The use of such criteria provides greater control and precision in the measurement of outcome, because outcome will not vary widely through different diagnoses or problem types (Charlton, 1996). However, the patients may not be representative of usual practice and may be simpler cases to treat (Seligman, 1996), although this may not always be true (Jacobson and Christensen, 1996).

Furthermore, the choice of the system used to describe disorders or diagnoses can be controversial. Many studies use a psychiatric classification system such as DSM IV (American Psychiatric Association, 1994), but the validity of systems of this type has been called into question, both in general (Mirowsky and Ross, 1989) and in their particular application outside the hospital settings in which they were developed; for example, their relevance to primary care populations (Von Korff and Simon, 1994).

More pragmatic trials use broader inclusion criteria which better represent normal practice. However, they are handicapped by the greater variability in patients which makes the identification of causal relationships more difficult, reduces the precision of the results, and means that average outcomes may mask significant differences in outcome among patients with different characteristics (Charlton, 1996). For example, a treatment may work with one particular diagnostic group involved in a trial, but such an effect may not be detected by the study because the treatment is not effective with the broader mix of patients included in the treatment groups.

Outcome measurement

It is generally accepted that measurement of the effects of psychological therapy requires a broad approach, although this has led to a profusion of measures which complicates the comparison of studies and makes adequate testing difficult (King, 1997). First, outcome measures must meet the psychometric requirements of validity and reliability. Reliable measures are those that give the same result at different times and in different contexts, assuming there has been no change in the underlying attribute (Kline, 1992). A measure is described as valid when there is evidence that it is an accurate indicator of what it purports to measure.

Outcome measures need to represent the multiple perspectives of the patient (e.g. their sense of subjective well-being), the clinician (e.g. therapeutic change related to an underlying theory of personality) and the wider society (e.g. behaviour, especially its social and economic impact) (Strupp, 1996). Outcome measures are often completed by the patient (self-report scales), although clinician-rated scales may be used to provide an alternative perspective. In such cases it is important that the clinicians providing the ratings are not aware of which treatment group the patient is in so as to remove any potential bias. Such blinding is often difficult to maintain because patients may unwittingly give information away. Where different treatments are being compared, it is useful to include both generic measures of outcome relevant to each, as well as measures specific to the treatment under test (e.g. measures of depressive schema in cognitive therapy, and object relations in psychodynamic therapies) (Barkham and Shapiro, 1992). It has been suggested that certain instruments may be biased towards certain therapeutic orientations (Roth and Fonagy, 1996). Commonly used measures include the Hamilton Rating Scale for Depression (Hamilton, 1967), Beck Depression Inventory (Beck and Steer, 1987) and Brief Symptom Inventory (Derogatis, 1992).

A common criticism of RCT research in psychological therapy is that the subtle psychological changes that occur are not amenable to the relatively crude quantitative measurement methods available. While there is some truth in this charge, it may also be argued that treatment effects that are so subtle as to be invisible to measurement may not be a cost-effective use of health care resources.

Outcome measurements may be continuous in nature (e.g. the difference in scores on the Beck Depression Inventory before and after treatment). The advantages of such measurements is their precision, although the exact meaning of such changes in terms of functioning is often not clear. For example, the meaning of a drop in BDI score of 10 points has not been calibrated in relation to its equivalent in terms of functioning (e.g. number of days without significant depressive symptoms). Thus results can be difficult to interpret, especially to non-specialists such as managers or patients (Sechrest *et al.*, 1996). The use of categorical (i.e. qualitatively different) outcomes may ease interpretation. For example, treatment may be associated with a 50 per cent likelihood of moving from a symptomatic to asymptomatic state. A number of definitions of such categories as remission, recovery, relapse and recurrence are used in reporting outcomes (Roth and Fonagy, 1996). Unfortunately, the use of categorical variables is also associated with a potential drop in precision because information may be lost (Mirowsky and Ross, 1989).

Economic analysis is increasingly regarded as an important dimension in the evaluation of treatments; different methods of economic evaluation are discussed by Alan Maynard in this volume (see Chapter 4).

Outcome measurements can be made at a number of points. Post-treatment measurements are conducted at the end of the specified treatment period, while long-term follow-up measures the stability of treatment effects after a significant period of time (e.g. six to twelve months). The length of follow-up that is appropriate for trials depends on a number of issues. Disorders with a natural history of recovery and relapse benefit from long-term follow-ups, as do trials with a significant economic component. However, the interpretation of long-term follow-ups is complicated by two key issues. Attrition of patients tends to be higher, which can ruin the initial comparability of randomised groups and bias long-term outcome assessments. Second, control over experimental variables often cannot be maintained. Patients may receive a number of interventions during the follow-up, which will often depend on the outcome of their trial treatment. This makes it increasingly difficult to ascribe change to the initial intervention (Roth and Fonagy, 1996).

Analytic issues

The analysis of RCT data involves a number of key issues. Randomisation, comparison and control reduce systematic bias in the results. For example, if selection bias occurs, the results of studies will differ from the 'true' value, and the direction of the bias will be consistent and depend on the nature of the selection bias. Thus, if more severely ill patients tend to enter the treatment group, the results may systematically underestimate the true effect of treatment relative to the control. In contrast, the play of chance will also cause error in the results of the study, but the direction of that error will vary randomly, sometimes inflating the effectiveness of a treatment and sometimes reducing it. All other things being equal, increasing the numbers of patients in a trial (the sample size) reduces the effects of such random error and provides a more reliable and precise estimate of the effects of therapies (Collins *et al.*, 1997). The power of a study concerns the probability of detecting differential effectiveness between the treatment arms when a difference exists: studies with low power may conclude that there is no difference between treatments when one actually exists (a Type II error). Power is related to the variability in the outcome measures and the sample size (Cohen, 1969). Although ostensibly an analytic issue, power should be calculated as part of the study design, taking into account the size of the expected effects, likely loss to follow-up and potential problems in recruitment. Studies comparing active therapies rather than a therapy and control may require larger sample sizes to achieve adequate power because the expected differences in effect between treatments will be smaller.

Another key analytic issue concerns the difference between intention-to-treat and on-treatment analyses. Intention-to-treat studies analyse the outcome of patients in the group to which they were randomised, whether they received that treatment or not. On-treatment analyses only analyse data from patients who receive a certain 'dose' of therapy or comply fully with treatment. The key advantage of an intention-to-treat analysis is that it avoids bias in the analysis associated with differential compliance with treatments. For example, a confrontational or demanding treatment may be very effective, but only with a minority of patients who can engage with the therapy successfully. Intention-to-treat analyses underestimate the true efficacy of the treatment, but the estimate may be more reflective of routine clinical effectiveness where compliance may be low relative to that found in research settings – such analyses are thus a feature of pragmatic trials. On-treatment analyses provide an estimate of the actual effectiveness of a treatment and are thus relevant to explanatory trials, but restricting the analysis to patients who are fully compliant with treatment protocols may mean that the advantages associated with randomisation are lost because there may be differences between the patients in each treatment group who actually receive the treatment.

Treatment effects are often described in terms of the statistical significance of the differences between the groups. Such tests assume that there is no difference in outcome between the treatment groups (i.e. the null hypothesis is true), and calculate the probability of actually obtaining the observed data from the trial. If the probability is low, then the null hypothesis can be rejected (Dar *et al.*, 1994). Such tests are highly dependent on sample size and do not provide information about the importance of effects; a study with hundreds of patients may report a statistically significant effect which is very minor in clinical terms. Measures of the magnitude of effects are thus required to ease interpretation (Dar *et al.*, 1994). A number are available, such as confidence intervals (Gardner and Altman, 1989), proportion of explained variance (Dar *et al.* 1994) or effect size (Smith *et al.*, 1980). For example, a meta-analysis (Smith and Glass, 1977) found that the average patient in psychological treatment was better off than 75 per cent of their respective controls. Other measures (so-called clinical significance criteria) involve measures designed to be useful for the practising clinician. This might involve calculation of the number of patients who would require therapy to avoid a particular outcome such as hospitalisation, which is called number needed to treat (Sackett *et al.*, 1991). Alternatively, a study might compare the outcome scores of patients in the trial with normative samples of psychologically healthy individuals (Hansen and Lambert, 1996) or use relatively arbitrary definitions of 'recovery' based on specific criteria – for example, a BDI score less than 9 indicates a successfully treated case (Roth and Fonagy, 1996).

The main analysis of an RCT concerns the original randomised comparison. Many authors go on to present subgroup analyses. For example, the effects of a therapy may be analysed using specific groups of patients, such as those with particular diagnoses or personality characteristics. Much of the interest in such analyses derives from the suggestion that the overall effects of psychological therapy are relatively modest, but that far more significant effects will occur with particular matching of therapy, therapist and patient. For example, it was suggested that the key question for psychological therapy outcome research was 'What therapy, by whom, is most effective with this individual with that specific problem under which set of circumstances?' (Paul, 1967: 111). Such aptitude–treatment interactions have obvious theoretical importance and may have practical application, although this is not always the case. For example, even if research indicated that certain therapist characteristics produced better outcomes in relation to certain patients, matching might be difficult to achieve in routine practice (Smith and Sechrest, 1991).

Using subgroups loses the equality gained through randomisation, because the subgroups were not formed by a random process (unless randomisation was stratified on that variable). Furthermore, studies often lack power to detect such secondary effects. The validity of findings based on subgroup analyses are suspect because they tend to capitalise on chance findings, unless specified in advance and according to an underlying theory (Collins *et al.*, 1997). They should be considered suggestive and hypothesis-generating rather than conclusive.

It has often been suggested that individual differences between therapists are as important in determining treatment outcome as differences between treatments. The existence of such effects can be tested and failure to deal with such effects can lead to incorrect conclusions (Crits-Christoph and Mintz, 1991).

Because of the multiple constraints operating within a single study design and the play of random error, replications are essential to ensure reliable results. Replicating study results in different contexts and different populations allows judgements to be made about the external validity of findings. Finally, replications are important because of the operation of what are known as allegiance effects: when treatments are evaluated by research teams known to be supportive of the therapy under test (e.g. by the originators of the therapeutic approach), the outcomes of those treatments are often superior to evaluations from neutral settings. While the exact mechanism underlying this bias is unclear (quality in treatment provision seems a more likely reason than anything more sinister), it does underline the need for replications (Chambless and Hollon, 1998).

Reviews and meta-analyses

Broad areas of clinical work (e.g. the treatment of depression) require many studies to provide coverage of the many variables involved (i.e. different therapeutic techniques, different types of depression). The interpretation of a significant body of literature on a subject requires an integration of the available literature through a review; systematic reviews are dealt with by Gilbody and Sowden in Chapter 9.

RCT methodology and the development of psychological therapy

The broad principle underlying EBHC is that planning, commissioning and provision of health care should be based on the best available evidence about what is effective (Sackett *et al.*, 1996). This philosophy derives in part from the economic pressures on health care systems, at a time when developments in health technology are rapid, along with an increasing focus on consumer empowerment, accountability of services and the consequent demand for information on the effectiveness of treatments.

Although few would argue with the general principle that health services provision should be based on sound evidence about which treatments lead to the best health outcomes for patients, there has been less agreement as to what constitutes 'sound evidence'. Cochrane's *Effectiveness and Efficiency* (1972) was important in suggesting that the RCT was the optimum source of evidence for such decisions when compared to the alternative sources of information (such as clinical opinion and observational studies). The reasons for this advantage have been set out in detail earlier in this chapter.

As a profession, psychological therapists stand to gain from the use of RCT-based evidence in a number of ways. It provides the necessary methodological underpinning to the 'scientist–practitioner' model espoused by some segments of the psychological therapy community (Barlow *et al.*, 1984). The results of RCTs can provide a necessary corrective to dogmatic adherence to particular methods and an impetus to further development of both effective and ineffective treatments (if there is the belief that some effective processes are contained within the latter). RCTs are able to indicate when therapies are actually doing more harm than good (Roth and Fonagy, 1996; Wessely *et al.*, 1998), and to provide protection for professionals in terms of legal challenges to the validity of their chosen clinical approach (Persons and Silberschatz, 1998). Finally, in the current economic climate, RCTs can provide support for the continued provision of cost-effective therapies that might otherwise be under threat (either in general, or from alternatives such as pharmacological treatments).

Further developments in managed care, clinical governance and clinical guidelines are dealt with elsewhere in this book; all provide the potential for an increase in the impact of RCT-based evidence on clinical practice. Nevertheless, despite the increasing acceptance of Cochrane's thesis, the impact of such evidence on service planning and clinical practice is still variable. Although institutional and professional inertia may be contributing factors, there are still a number of legitimate challenges to the 'gold-standard' position of RCTs as the basis for health services provision. These will be discussed briefly below.

Even among those who accept the primacy of RCTs as a method of scientific evaluation, there are a number of criticisms of their applicability to routine service provision. External validity is probably the key perceived weakness; if the treatments, patients and therapists evaluated in trials bear little or no resemblance to those encountered in practice, the implications of the trials may be highly ambiguous (Seligman, 1995, 1996; Parloff, 1982). Since RCTs are expensive, some therapies may be unevaluated if there is insufficient economic or professional impetus to fund such studies: no evidence of effectiveness is too often construed as evidence of no effectiveness (Persons and Silberschatz, 1998). Furthermore, differences between academic and practitioner views can cause difficulties. For example, RCTs which use strictly manualised treatments can lead to inappropriate assumptions about the effectiveness of a particular 'brand-name' therapy; a therapist ostensibly using the same 'evidence-based' model may be ineffective if he or she does not attend to other issues of relevance to efficacy, such as the quality of the therapist–patient relationship or therapeutic alliance (Roth and Fonagy, 1996). Equally, the biomedical paradigm underlying much RCT evidence (reflected in the wide use of DSM-based diagnoses) may fail to consider other variables of interest to clinicians outside the dominant academic paradigm (such as the importance of personality and interpersonal dynamics) (Goldfried and Wolfe, 1996). There is also a perception that

EBHC (in general) and RCTs (in particular) have less to do with the scientific basis of health services and function more as methods of curbing the behaviour of health professionals to the will of managers and policy-makers (Roth and Fonagy, 1996; Graham-Smith, 1995).

A second key challenge emanates from those who suggest that an excessive reliance on RCTs inappropriately denigrates other research paradigms such as observational studies or qualitative research. For example, there are a number of situations in which RCTs may be an inappropriate methodology (Black, 1996; Jadad, 1998). These include those situations where treatment has a profound effect, where significant outcome events are very rare, or where treatments are strongly influenced by patient preferences (as described earlier in the present chapter). A recent review cast doubt on the accepted wisdom that non-randomised studies always *overestimate* the effectiveness of interventions (Britton *et al.*, 1998). Some authors suggest that observational studies with appropriate statistical controls can provide information of similar utility to RCTs (Heckman, 1997; McClellan *et al.*, 1994). Equally, some complex issues in psychological therapy provision (such as issues in service structure and configuration), although amenable to trials in principle, are diffi-cult to conduct in practice because of the difficulties associated with randomisation when the experimental units are practices, units or districts (Roberts and Sibbald, 1998). Others point out that RCTs may not always be the most appropriate methodologies for understanding the processes by which psychological therapies achieve change; this may require in-depth quantitative or qualitative analysis of individual cases of therapy (so-called process research) (Persons and Silberschatz, 1998; Rice and Greenberg, 1984). Studies that show a therapy can work in the trial context must be complemented by other methodologies (such as audit and bench-marking) that can assure that their delivery in routine settings is still producing positive outcomes (Roth and Fonagy, 1996; Seligman, 1996). For example, the 'hourglass' model of treatment development has been described (Salkovskis, 1995), in which highly controlled studies are relevant for only one portion of the development cycle, while less controlled methods (such as case studies and effectiveness studies) have crucial roles early and late in the development of the therapy respectively. The relationship between RCT-based evidence and systematic data collection from routine settings (e.g. audit, benchmarking, quality evaluation) are developed further in Chapter 8, while the role of qualitative research is considered in Chapter 7.

The third major challenge to the role of RCTs comes from those who feel that an excessive reliance on the results of academic research downplays the role of clinical judgement processes (Tanenbaum, 1993) and leads to a 'cook-book' approach to therapy, where the complexity of patient presentation and professional response is reduced to a few broad guidelines written into a manual. Although some proponents of EBHC suggest that clinical judgement is a necessary complement to RCT-based evidence (Sackett *et al.*, 1996), the processes by which the two are to be integrated are far less clear (Dowie, 1996). Whereas trials provide information about the average responses of groups of patients, clinicians are faced with individual patients: the application of RCT-based evidence to individual patients is complex (Fahey, 1998; Charlton, 1996), especially when therapists must apply their treatments so as to be sensitive to the evidence as well as to the patient's psychological and social context (Greenhalgh and Worrall, 1997). RCTs often do not address the issues of greatest interest to clinicians, such as engaging with difficult patients, overcoming therapeutic impasse or dealing with multiple problems (Persons and Silberschatz, 1998).

In part, the academic view of clinical judgement processes reflects the legacy of a large number of research studies that have demonstrated the flaws associated with human judgement, which suggests that the supposed sensitivity of many such judgements is overrated (Meehl, 1954; Tversky and Kahneman, 1974; Dawes, 1988). Nevertheless, clinical judgement is likely to remain important, in so far as the complexity of psychological therapy cannot be captured in full by any research paradigm; such judgements also represent the prerogative of psychological therapists as a *profession*. However, clinical judgements should not be an obstacle to assimilation of evidence from RCTs. It has been suggested that in the case of clinical guidelines, the recommendations inherent in the guideline should represent a default position; clinical judgement may suggest an alternative course, but the reasons for deviating from the default position should at least be explicit (Roth and Fonagy, 1996).

Extreme positions concerning the role of RCTs are hard to justify. RCTs should not be considered the only legitimate source of evidence for health services. Not all aspects of health services are amenable to the methodology, and there are other issues beyond efficacy and effectiveness that impact on decision-making (such as patient preferences, availability of providers, equality and access) that call for a broader view of the decision-making process (Dowie, 1996; Haines and Donald, 1998). Overvaluing RCTs may lead to a number of unhelpful effects. These might include an excessive focus by therapists and managers on narrow technical concerns and 'pure' interventions as practised in RCTs, as well as inaccurate client expectations that their problems will follow the same clinical course as trial participants (Goldfried and Wolfe, 1996). It is also doubtful that any health service could *afford* to conduct enough trials and replications for every relevant treatment and patient group to meet the requirements of EBHC.

Nevertheless, for all their weaknesses, total rejection of the relevance of RCTs for psychological therapy provision is difficult to defend. When seeking evidence of causal relationships, or unbiased comparisons of treatments, the RCT methodology is likely to be the method of choice in most circumstances. Although there are obvious differences between pharmacological and psychological treatments, the broad requirement that treatments are proven to be safe, acceptable and effective is broadly applicable to both. Although external validity remains a key weakness of trials, it is an issue that can be examined empirically (Shadish *et al.*, 1997) and does not justify total rejection of the results: attempting to adapt the results of the RCT to the current patient's circumstances is still likely to be superior to basing decisions on preferred practice and clinical judgement (Persons and Silberschatz, 1998). One of the key impacts of RCTs and EBHC is not in the detail of randomisation, power and effect sizes; rather, it is in the broad aim of encouraging an openness to scientific evaluation, audit, feedback and external critique in the continued development of all treatment provision in health care.

CONCLUSIONS

The relative simplicity of the logic underlying RCTs belies the complexity involved in their planning and conduct, and the analysis and interpretation of the data. However, the history of psychological therapies suggests that the gulf between the claims of therapeutic effectiveness and the empirical results can be relatively wide and RCTs function as a necessary corrective to such claims (Shapiro, 1980). The development of a secure base of evidence about what is effective is increasingly demanded by those who fund and manage health care systems and the patients who seek help, and is necessary if psychological therapies are to maintain their credibility and continue to develop in the years ahead.

NOTES

1 The term 'psychological therapies' will be used as an umbrella term to refer to the broad range of psychological treatments, from formal psychotherapies

through counselling, cognitive-behavioural treatments and problem-solving approaches.
2 The use of the term 'patient' rather than 'client' reflects the medical setting which predominates in much of the research described in this chapter, and has been retained for convenience.
3 RCTs are experiments using groups of patients, but many of the experimental mechanisms can also apply with modification to the analysis of experiments using single cases. Such experiments are beyond the scope of the present chapter (see Chambless and Hollon, 1998; Kazdin, 1982).
4 Even when there is no formal control group, trials are often described as RCTs, even though 'randomised trials' might be a more accurate term.
5 Some authors also use the term 'effectiveness' to refer to observational studies of the effects of treatments, as compared to experimental studies (e.g. Seligman, 1995).

REFERENCES

American Psychiatric Association (1994) *Diagnostic and Statistical Manual of Mental Disorders* (4th edn). Washington, DC: American Psychiatric Association.
Barkham, M. and Shapiro, D. (1992) Response, in W. Dryden and C. Feltham (eds) *Psychotherapy and its Discontents*. Bristol: Open University Press, 86–96.
Barlow, D., Hayes, S. and Nelson, R. (1984) *The Scientist-Practitioner: Research and Accountability in Clinical and Educational Settings*. New York: Pergamon Press.
Basham, R. (1986) Scientific and practical advantages of comparative design in psychotherapy outcome research. *Journal of Consulting and Clinical Psychology*, 54: 88–94.
Beck, A. and Steer, R. (1987) *Beck Depression Inventory: manual*. San Antonio: Psychological Corporation.
Black, N. (1996) Why we need observational studies to evaluate the effectiveness of health care. *British Medical Journal*, 312: 1215–1218.
Borkovec, T. and Castonguay, L. (1998) What is the scientific meaning of empirically supported therapy? *Journal of Consulting and Clinical Psychology*, 66: 136–142.
Bracht, G. and Glass, G. (1968) The external validity of experiments. *American Educational Research Journal*, 5: 437–474.
Brewin, C. and Bradley, C. (1989) Patient preferences and randomised clinical trials. *British Medical Journal*, 299: 313–315.
Britton, A., McKee, M., Black, N., McPherson, K., Sanderson, C. and Bain, C. (1998) Choosing between randomised and non-randomised studies: a systematic review. *Health Technology Assessment* 2 (13).
Brockelhurst, P. (1997) Partially randomised patient preference trials. *British Journal of Obstetrics and Gynaecology*, 104: 1332–1335.

Campbell, D. and Stanley, J. (1966) *Experimental and Quasi-Experimental Designs for Research*. Chicago: Rand McNally.

Chalmers, T., Celano, P., Sacks, H. and Smith, H. (1983) Bias in treatment assignment in controlled clinical trials. *New England Journal of Medicine*, 309: 1358–1361.

Chambless, D. and Hollon, S. (1998) Defining empirically supported therapies. *Journal of Consulting and Clinical Psychology*, 66: 7–18.

Charlton, B. (1996) The future of clinical research: from megatrials towards methodological rigour and representative sampling. *Journal of Evaluation in Clinical Practice*, 2: 159–169.

Clarke, G. (1995) Improving the transition from basic efficacy research to effectiveness studies: methodological issues and procedures. *Journal of Consulting and Clinical Psychology*, 63: 718–725.

Cochrane, A. (1972) *Effectiveness and Efficiency: Random Reflections on Health Services*. London: The Nuffield Provincial Hospitals Trust.

Cohen, J. (1969) *Statistical Power Analysis for the Behavioural Sciences*. San Diego: Academic Press.

Collins, R., Peto, R., Gray, R. and Parish, S. (1997) Large scale randomised evidence: trials and overviews, in A. Maynard and I. Chalmers (eds) *Non-random Reflections on Health Services Research*. London: BMJ Publishing Group, 197–230.

Cook, T. and Campbell, D. (1979) *Quasi-Experimentation – Design and Analysis Issues for Field Settings*. Chicago: Rand McNally.

Crits-Christoph, P. and Mintz, J. (1991) Implications of therapist effects for the design and analysis of comparative studies of psychotherapies. *Journal of Consulting and Clinical Psychology*, 59: 20–26.

Dar, R., Serlin, R. and Omer, H. (1994) Misuse of statistical tests in three decades of psychotherapy research. *Journal of Consulting and Clinical Psychology*, 62: 75–82.

Davey Smith, G. and Philips, A. (1992) Confounding in epidemiological studies: why 'independent' effects may not be all they seem. *British Medical Journal*, 305: 757–759.

Dawes, R. (1988) You can't systematize human judgement: dyslexia, in J. Dowie and A. Elstein (eds) *Professional Judgement: A Reader in Clinical Decision Making*. New York: Cambridge University Press, 150–162.

Derogatis, L. (1992) *The Brief Symptom Inventory (BSI): Administration, Scoring and Procedures Manual*. Baltimore: Clinical Psychometric Research Inc.

Dowie, J. (1996) The research–practice gap and the role of decision analysis in closing it. *Health Care Analysis*, 4: 5–18.

Elkin, I., Gibbons, R., Shea, T. and Shaw, B. (1996) Science is not a trial (but sometimes it can be a tribulation). *Journal of Consulting and Clinical Psychology*, 64: 92–103.

Eysenck, H. (1952) The effects of psychotherapy: an evaluation. *Journal of Consulting and Clinical Psychology*, 16: 319–324.

Fahey, T. (1998) Applying the results of clinical trials to patients in general practice: perceived problems, strengths, assumptions, and challenges for the future. *British Journal of General Practice*, 48: 1173–1178.

Fairhurst, K. and Dowrick, C. (1996) Problems with recruitment in a randomised controlled trial of counselling in general practice: causes and implications. *Journal of Health Services Research and Policy*, 1: 77–80.

Gardner, M. and Altman, D. (1989) *Statistics with Confidence*. London: British Medical Association.

Goldfried, M. and Wolfe, B. (1996) Psychotherapy practice and research. *American Psychologist*, 51: 1007–1016.

Gossop, M., Johns, A. and Green, L. (1986) Opiate withdrawal: inpatient versus outpatient programmes and preferred versus random assignment to treatment. *British Medical Journal*, 293: 103–104.

Graham-Smith, D. (1995) Evidence-based medicine: Socratic dissent. *British Medical Journal*, 310: 1126–1127.

Greenberg, R. and Fisher, S. (1994) Suspended judgement. Seeing through the double-masked design: a commentary. *Controlled Clinical Trials*, 15: 244–246.

Greenhalgh, T. and Worrall, J. (1997) From EBM to CSM: the evolution of context-sensitive medicine. *Journal of Evaluation in Clinical Practice*, 3: 105–108.

Haines, A. and Donald, A. (1998) *Getting Research Findings into Practice*. London: BMJ Books.

Hamilton, M. (1967) Development of a rating scale for primary depressive illness. *British Journal of Social and Clinical Psychology*, 6: 278–296.

Hansen, N. and Lambert, M. (1996) Clinical significance: an overview of methods. *Journal of Mental Health*, 5: 17–24.

Heckman, J. (1997) Instrumental variables: a study of implicit behavioural assumptions used in making program evaluations. *Journal of Human Resource*, XXXII: 441–461.

Jacobson, N. and Christensen, A. (1996) Studying the effectiveness of psychotherapy: how well can clinical trials do the job? *American Psychologist*, 51: 1031–1039.

Jacobson, N., Dobson, K., Truax, P., Addis, M., Koerner, K., Gollan, J., Gortner, E. and Prince, S. (1996) A component analysis of cognitive-behavioural treatment for depression. *Journal of Consulting and Clinical Psychology*, 2: 295–304.

Jacobson, N. and Hollon, S. (1996) Cognitive-behaviour therapy versus pharmacotherapy: now that the jury's returned its verdict, it's time to present the rest of the evidence. *Journal of Consulting and Clinical Psychology*, 64: 74–80.

Jadad, A. (1998) *Randomised Controlled Trials: A User's Guide*. London: BMJ Books.

Kazdin, A. (1982) *Single Case Research Designs: Methods For Clinical and Applied Settings*. New York: Oxford University Press.

Kazdin, A. (1986) Comparative outcome studies of psychotherapy: methodological issues and strategies. *Journal of Consulting and Clinical Psychology*, 54: 95–105.

Kazdin, A. and Wilcoxon, L. (1976) Systematic desensitization and nonspecific treatment effects: a methodological evaluation. *Psychological Bulletin*, 83: 729–758.

Kendall, P. and Lipman, A. (1991) Psychological and pharmacological therapy: methods and modes for comparative outcome research. *Journal of Consulting and Clinical Psychology*, 59: 78–87.

King, M. (1997) Brief psychotherapy in general practice: how do we measure outcome? *British Journal of General Practice*, 47: 136–137.

Kleijnen, J., Gøtzsche, P., Kunz, R., Oxman, A. and Chalmers, I. (1997) So what's so special about randomisation? in A. Maynard and I. Chalmers (eds) *Non-random Reflections on Health Services Research*. London: BMJ Publishing Group, 93–106.

Klein, D. (1996) Preventing hung juries about therapy studies. *Journal of Consulting and Clinical Psychology*, 64: 81–87.

Kline, P. (1992) Problems of methodology in studies of psychotherapy, in W. Dryden and C. Feltham (eds) *Psychotherapy and its Discontents*. Bristol: Open University Press, 64–99.

Kunz, R. and Oxman, A. (1998) The unpredictability paradox: review of empirical comparisons of randomised and non-randomised clinical trials. *British Medical Journal*, 317: 1185–1190.

Luborsky, L. and Singer, B. (1975) Comparative studies of psychotherapies: is it true that everyone has won and all must have prizes? *Archives of General Psychiatry*, 32: 995–1008.

McClellan, M., McNeil, B. and Newhouse, J. (1994) Does more intensive treatment of acute myocardial infarction in the elderly reduce mortality? *Journal of the American Medical Association*, 272: 859–866.

McKay, J., Alterman, A., McLellan, T., Snider, E. and O'Brien, C. (1995) Effect of random versus non-random assignment in a comparison of inpatient and day hospital rehabilitation for male alcoholics. *Journal of Consulting and Clinical Psychology*, 63: 70–78.

Mahoney, M. (1978) Experimental methods and outcome evaluation. *Journal of Consulting and Clinical Psychology*, 46: 660–672.

Meehl, P. (1954) *Clinical Versus Statistical Prediction: A Theoretical Analysis and Review of the Evidence*. Minneapolis: University of Minnesota Press.

Mirowsky, J. and Ross, C. (1989) Psychiatric diagnosis as reified measurement. *Journal of Health and Social Behaviour*, 30: 11–25.

Moncrieff, J., Wessely, S. and Hardy, R. (1998) Meta-analysis of trials comparing antidepressants with active placebos. *British Journal of Psychiatry*, 172: 227–231.

O'Leary, K. and Borkovec, T. (1978) Conceptual, methodological and ethical problems of placebo groups in psychotherapy research. *American Psychologist*, 33: 821–830.

Orne, M. (1962) On the social psychology of the psychological experiment: with particular reference to demand characteristics and their implications. *American Psychologist*, 17: 776–783.

Parloff, M. (1982) Psychotherapy research evidence and reimbursement decisions: Bambi meets Godzilla. *American Journal of Psychiatry*, 139: 718–727.

Parloff, M. (1986) Placebo controls in psychotherapy research: a sine qua non or a placebo for research problems? *Journal of Consulting and Clinical Psychology*, 54: 79–87.

Paul, G. (1967) Strategy of outcome research in psychotherapy. *Journal of Consulting Psychology*, 31: 109–118.

Persons, J. (1991) Psychotherapy outcome studies do not accurately represent current models of psychotherapy: a proposed remedy. *American Psychologist*, 46: 99–106.

Persons, J. and Silberschatz, G. (1998) Are results of randomised controlled trials useful to psychotherapists? *Journal of Consulting and Clinical Psychology*, 66: 126–135.

Rice, L. and Greenberg, L. (1984) *Patterns of Change*. New York: Guilford Press.

Roberts, C. and Sibbald, B. (1998) Randomising groups of patients. *British Medical Journal*, 316: 1898.

Roberts, C. and Torgerson, D. (1999) Baseline imbalance in randomised controlled trials. *British Medical Journal*, 319: 185.

Roth, A. and Fonagy, P. (1996) *What Works for Whom? A Critical Review of Psychotherapy Research*. London: Guilford.

Sackett, D., Haynes, R., Guyatt, G. and Tugwell, P. (1991) *Clinical Epidemiology: A Basic Science for Clinical Medicine* (2nd edn). Boston: Little, Brown & Company.

Sackett, D., Rosenberg, W., Gray, J., Haynes, R. and Richardson, W. (1996) Evidence-based medicine: what it is and what it is not. *British Medical Journal*, 312: 71–72.

Salkovskis, P. (1995) Demonstrating specific effects in cognitive and behavioural therapy, in M. Aveline and D. Shapiro (eds) *Research Foundations for Psychotherapy Practice*, Chichester: Wiley, 191–228.

Schulz, K., Chalmers, I., Hayes, R. and Altman, D. (1995) Empirical evidence of bias: dimensions of methodological quality associated with estimates of treatment effects in controlled trials. *Journal of the American Medical Association*, 273: 408–412.

Schwartz, D. and Lellouch, J. (1967) Explanatory and pragmatic attitudes in therapeutic trials. *Journal of Chronic Diseases*, 20: 637–648.

Scott, A. and Freeman, C. (1992) Edinburgh primary care depression study: treatment outcome, patient satisfaction, and cost after 16 weeks. *British Medical Journal*, 304: 883–887.

Sechrest, L., McKnight, P. and McKnight, K. (1996) Calibration of measures for psychotherapy outcome studies. *American Psychologist*, 51: 1065–1071.

Seligman, M. (1995) The effectiveness of psychotherapy: the consumer reports study. *American Psychologist*, 50: 965–974.

Seligman, M. (1996) Science as an ally of practice. *American Psychologist*, 51: 1072–1079.

Shadish, W., Navarro, A., Crits-Christoph, P., Jorm, A., Nietzel, M., Robinson, L., Svartberg, M., Matt, G., Siegle, G., Hazelrigg, M., Lyons, L., Prout, H., Smith, M. and Weiss, B. (1997) Evidence that therapy works in clinically representative populations. *Journal of Consulting and Clinical Psychology*, 65: 355–365.

Shapiro, D. (1980) Science and psychotherapy: The state of the art. *British Journal of Medical Psychology*, 53: 1–10.

Shapiro, D.A. and Shapiro, D. (1983) Meta-analysis of comparative therapy outcome studies: a replication and refinement. *Psychological Bulletin*, 92: 581–604.

Smith, B. and Sechrest, L. (1991) Treatment of aptitude x treatment interactions. *Journal of Consulting and Clinical Psychology*, 59: 233–244.

Smith, M. and Glass, G. (1977) Meta-analysis of psychotherapy outcome studies. *American Psychologist*, 32: 752–760.

Smith, M., Glass, G. and Miller, T. (1980) *The Benefits of Psychotherapy*. Baltimore: Johns Hopkins University Press.

Spector, E. (1981) *Research Designs*. London: Sage Publications.

Strube, M. (1991) Small sample failure of random assignment: a further examination. *Journal of Consulting and Clinical Psychology*, 59: 346–350.

Strupp, H. (1996) The tripartite model and the Consumer Reports study. *American Psychologist*, 51: 1017–1024.

Tanenbaum, S. (1993) What physicians know. *New England Journal of Medicine*, 329: 1268–1270.

Torgerson, D., Klaber-Moffett, J. and Russell, I. (1996) Patient preferences in randomised trials: threat or opportunity? *Journal of Health Services Research and Policy*, 1: 194–197.

Torgerson, D. and Sibbald, B. (1998) What is a patient preference trial? *British Medical Journal*, 316: 360.

Treasure, T. and MacRae, K. (1998) Minimisation: the platinum standard for trials? *British Medical Journal*, 317: 362–363.

Tversky, A. and Kahneman, D. (1974) Judgement under uncertainty: heuristics and biases. *Science*, 185: 1124–1131.

Von Korff, M. and Simon, G. (1994) Methodologic perspective: getting answers to the most important questions, in J. Miranda, A. Hohmann, C. Attkisson and D. Larson (eds) *Mental Disorders in Primary Care*. San Francisco: Jossey-Bass, 421–447.

Weisz, J., Weiss, B. and Donneberg, G. (1992) The lab versus the clinic: effects of child and adolescent psychotherapy. *American Psychologist*, 47: 1578–1585.

Wessely, S., Rose, S. and Bisson, J. (1998) A systematic review of brief psychological interventions (debriefing) for the treatment of immediate trauma and the prevention of PTSD (Cochrane Review), in *The Cochrane Library*, Issue 3. Oxford: Update Software.

Zelen, M. (1979) A new design for randomised clinical trials. *New England Journal of Medicine*, 300: 1242–1245.

Chapter 7

The contribution of qualitative research to evidence-based counselling and psychotherapy

John McLeod

One of the striking features of the psychotherapy research literature has been the number of outcome studies that have been published. The question of whether psychological therapy is effective has preoccupied the profession and its community of researchers. Reviews of this literature can be found in Bergin and Garfield (1994), Roth and Fonagy (1996) and many other places. Yet in these reviews there are no examples of qualitative research. It seems to have become generally accepted that the best or sometimes even the *only* way to evaluate the effectiveness of psychotherapy is to apply measures before and after treatment. The aim of this chapter is to present the case for using qualitative methods in evaluating the effectiveness of psychotherapy and other psychological interventions. It will be argued that the absence of qualitative studies has diminished the usefulness of the outcome findings that are currently available, and that their inclusion would make a significant contribution to evidence-based health care policies. Because faith in the validity of existing methods is so deeply ingrained, the chapter begins with a critique, which aims to show that there are some fundamental problems involved in applying existing quantitative techniques in therapy outcome research. This critique is followed by a discussion of some examples of qualitative outcome research in psychotherapy. The chapter ends by proposing increased methodological pluralism in outcome research.

CURRENT METHODS OF EVALUATING THE EFFECTIVENESS OF COUNSELLING AND PSYCHOTHERAPY: A CRITIQUE

The standard research design currently used within psychotherapy and counselling outcome research comprises a randomised controlled trial (RCT) using standardised psychometric questionnaire self-report measures. All the studies cited in the recent Roth and Fonagy (1996) review are controlled trials of this type. In a review of 116 psychotherapy outcome studies published in the *Journal of Consulting and Clinical Psychology* between 1986 and 1991, Lambert (1994) found that self-report was used in 90 per cent of studies.

The limitations of RCTs in psychotherapy outcome research

Methodological issues associated with the use of randomised controlled trials in psychotherapy outcome research are discussed more fully in Chapters 6 and 8, and so are only summarised here. Unlike much medical research, these studies cannot be 'blind', since at least the therapist must know the nature of the treatment being offered. Clients have preferences regarding the type of therapy they would choose, and as a result it is difficult to control for their reactions to randomisation, or even to achieve randomisation (see Fairhurst and Dowrick, 1996) although patient preference trials address this. It is no easy matter to create an appropriate or meaningful control condition in psychotherapy research. Many studies have used waiting list controls, but it can be argued that being allocated to a waiting list can instil hope in some applicants for therapy, and therefore functions as a minimal treatment condition. On the other hand, other applicants may perceive the waiting list as a rejection, with potential deleterious effects on their mental health and their willingness to engage with therapy once the waiting period is over. The effects of the waiting-list condition are therefore highly uncertain, but unlikely to be neutral. The external validity or generalisability of RCTs can also be questioned. The use of treatment manuals to ensure adherence to a specific therapeutic modality creates a clinical situation that is aberrant in terms of everyday practice. The homogeneous treatment groups required by the RCT design are rarely found in real life clinical work: many clients report with multiple problems. These are just some of the limitations of the RCT as a method of generating reliable knowledge of the effectiveness of therapy. RCTs are also expensive, and so an over-reliance on this approach has the result of limiting the number of therapies that can be accepted as empirically validated. Finally, as Henry (1998) has argued, the bulk of research into therapy outcome suggests that it is the therapeutic relationship or qualities of the therapist, rather than their model of therapy, that makes a difference.

The limitations of standardised psychometric questionnaire self-report measures

The limitations of standardised psychometric questionnaire self-report measures are discussed here in more detail, because readers may be less familiar with the evidence on this topic. There has been a great deal of research carried out over the last forty years on the psychological processes involved in completing self-report personality adjustment questionnaires such as the Beck Depression Inventory (BDI) and the Minnesota Multiphasic Personality Inventory (MMPI). With the exception of Meier (1994) and Lambert (1994), psychotherapy researchers do not appear to have paid much attention to this body of theory and research. Because the literature in this area is extensive, the account which follows will focus on identifying a number of key themes, before going on to offer an integrative overview.

Method factors

Following the pioneering work of Campbell and Fiske (1959), it has been generally accepted that the assessment of trait or adjustment variables will reflect the assessment method used. Lambert (1994) has reviewed studies which show a lack of consensus across outcome measures of the same variable. For example, there are only weak correlations between outcome ratings made by clients, therapists and external observers. Different self-report questionnaires (e.g. depression questionnaires) completed by clients yield different patterns of change. Campbell and Fiske (1959) used the term *method factor* to describe this phenomenon. The implication is that, in psychotherapy outcome research, the likelihood of being able to report positive change will depend on the instrument used (i.e. which depression or anxiety self-report scale is used in the study). Also, as Cartwright *et al.* (1963) found, the estimates of change found in self-report questionnaire data do not necessarily match those found in data derived from other viewpoints (i.e. therapists or significant others). Given the heavy reliance placed on self-report measures in the recent literature, this means that perhaps a quite different picture of which therapies have been supported by evidence would have emerged if different measures had been employed.

Item response processes

Several researchers have explored the processes through which a person formulates their response to a questionnaire item, and the factors which influence this process. It is clear that when a person is faced with a typical questionnaire item (for example a statement from the BDI such as 'I am not particularly pessimistic or discouraged about the future') then he or she does not engage in a simple process of self-observation based on tracking back through recent memories of occasions of pessimism. What happens instead, it is suggested, is that the question evokes a set of cognitive schema that function as what has been called an 'implicit personality theory' (Shweder, 1975; Kuncel and Kuncel, 1995). In other words, in answering a questionnaire item the person does not report directly on their behaviour but on their sense of self, as mediated through the cognitive schema that acts as a personal framework for making sense of how people behave.

Looking more closely at the particular type of conceptual schema that are activated by answering self-report questionnaires in therapy research, it seems clear that central to this process are evaluative schema. Measures of psychological dysfunction (e.g. depression, anxiety) load heavily on social desirability (SD) (Edwards, 1957; Kelly *et al.*, 1996; McCrae and Costa, 1983). When answering a questionnaire, the person implicitly compares himself or herself against a social ideal. Paulhaus (1986) has suggested that social desirability comprises two components: impression management and self-deception. Impression management can be defined as 'conscious dissimulation of test responses designed to create a favourable impression in some audience' (Paulhaus, 1986: 144). Self-deception refers to 'any positively biased response that the respondent actually believes to be true' (ibid.). These elements of social desirability differ in terms of the conscious intentions of the respondent. In impression management, there is at least some degree of strategic intention and awareness of presenting a particular image to the world. Depending on the situation, this image may be positive or negative. As Paulhaus (1986: 156) points out, some impression management may be motivated by self-promotion (the desire to appear competent) while in other instances the person may be adopting the role of supplicant, in seeking to appear helpless and thereby to elicit help.

The presence of impression management and self-deception as factors in self-report measures used in psychotherapy research creates a number of problems for researchers. The existence of significant correlations between social desirability and measures of anxiety, depression and other adjustment scales opens up the whole question of what is being measured in outcome research and what changes. It would seem reasonable to suppose that, as far as impression management is concerned, therapy clients would be more likely to present themselves as supplicants at intake (through reporting high depression and anxiety scores), and as competent at follow-up (reporting low depression and anxiety scores). Moreover, there is evidence reviewed by Paulhaus (1986) which shows that well-adjusted people have a positively biased (rather than accurate or realistic) view of themselves. The well-adjusted person tends to:

> ignore minor criticisms . . . discount failures . . . avoid negative thoughts, and . . . have a high expectancy of success in new endeavours. In contrast, the anxious or depressed individual accepts criticism and failures as being informative of his abilities and character.
>
> (Paulhaus, 1986: 150)

From this perspective, approaches to therapy which emphasise self-awareness and insight could be expected to be associated with poor outcomes as measured on self-report scales. Conversely, good outcomes on such measures could be construed as suggesting that clients have learned to practise a kind of benign self-deception.

When questionnaires are used in 'pure' personality research, respondents may feel little need to engage in impression management. When questionnaires are used in personnel selection, the level of impression management and self-deception can be taken as a background 'constant'. In therapy research, by contrast, the intervention process influences impression management and self-deception in complex ways. Unfortunately, the nature and extent of this influence is as yet poorly understood. There is a need for more research on item response factors in psychotherapy research situations.

Impression management and self-deception are factors associated with the *evaluative* aspects of the cognitive schema which a person uses in order to respond to a questionnaire item. There is, however, also a more general aspect of the schema which reflects the way the person conceptualises the domain of knowledge or experience being accessed. For instance, a person responding to the BDI statement 'I am not particularly pessimistic or discouraged about the future' might evoke a 'pessimism' schema, or an 'orientation to the future' schema. In psychotherapy outcome research, the interpretation of change in scores depends on whether there is reason to believe that the schema has changed. It is easy to see that the process of therapy might lead a person to develop a much more differentiated and reflective understanding of pessimism. If that person's response to that BDI item shifts, how can we know whether he or she has indeed become less pessimistic, or has merely re-defined pessimism?

There are studies from the training literature which can be used to shed some light on this issue. For example, Howard *et al*. (1979) carried out an evaluation of a series of training workshops designed to reduce social prejudice and racism in air force personnel. Although these workshops were well received, with positive qualitative feedback, the scores of participants on measures of prejudice showed them to be *more* prejudiced following the workshops. Howard *et al*. (1979) ran the study again, but this time at follow-up asked participants also to complete retrospective questionnaires on how prejudiced they remembered being, before the first workshop they had attended. Analysis of this data showed that the retrospective ratings were much higher in prejudice than the actual pre-workshop ratings. What seemed to have happened was that the workshops had enabled participants to see how prejudiced they were. In effect, the intervention had the effect of recalibrating participants' *concepts* of prejudice, as well as (in some cases) changing their prejudiced behaviour.

Unfortunately, Howard *et al*. (1979) was not actually evaluating the outcomes of psychotherapy. One might anticipate that the shifts in such cognitive schema brought about by participation in psychotherapy might depend on a variety of factors. Nevertheless, studies of training by Howard and others (Goedhart and Hoogstraten, 1992; Manthei, 1997) give some indication of the magnitude and pervasiveness of response shift effects which might well also be occurring to a significant extent in psychotherapy outcome investigations. Golombiewski *et al*. (1976) and Golombiewski (1989) have argued that response shifts occur in many different types of intervention, and are difficult to detect with existing statistical methods.

Summary: methodological issues in the use of self-report measures in psychotherapy outcome research

The aim of this brief review has been to show that there are some difficult methodological issues associated with the current ways in which psychometric self-report scales are employed in psychotherapy outcome research. No one reading a self-report questionnaire used in a therapy study could have any doubt that how a client or patient answers will bear *some* relationship to how anxious or depressed that person is, in terms of how he or she acts, feels and relates in everyday life. The face validity and common-sense appeal of self-report questionnaires cannot be disputed. But, from a more critical perspective, there are a number of unresolved methodological problems which make it difficult to interpret the results of psychotherapy outcome studies which utilise self-report measures. Some of these problems (e.g. impression management) could be interpreted to imply that the findings of such studies overestimate the effectiveness of therapy. Other issues (e.g. schema recalibration/response shifts) are difficult to interpret and may operate differentially for clients at different stages of therapy, or in different types of therapy.

QUALITATIVE EVALUATION METHODS IN COUNSELLING AND PSYCHOTHERAPY RESEARCH

Qualitative methods represent the main alternative to the quantitative paradigm described and critiqued in earlier sections of this chapter. In principle, it would be feasible to evaluate the effects of therapy by analysing qualitative data sets generated by such techniques as: individual or focus group interviews with clients, therapists and significant others; transcripts of therapy sessions; personal documents such as diaries and case notes; open-ended questionnaires or written accounts; narrative responses to projective techniques; ethnographic participant observation; biographies and novels. To the best of my knowledge, very few of these methods have been employed in published therapy outcome research. It is possible that unpublished qualitative studies exist in the form of internal reports for agencies and clinics, or student dissertations. The mindset that prevails within the counselling and psychotherapy world, of equating evaluation with the application of 'measures', may have impeded publication of such studies.

The discussion here will focus on three studies: Howe (1989), McKenna and Todd (1997) and Dale *et al.* (1998). None of these studies comprises a wholly satisfactory approach to the question of qualitative evaluation of psychotherapy. They represent tentative steps towards a qualitative evaluation methodology for psychotherapy, but are nevertheless valuable in terms of showing what is *possible* in terms of qualitative outcome research.

Howe (1989) comprises the most detailed example of qualitative evaluation of psychotherapy currently available. This investigation examined the effectiveness of the family therapy provided in a social work agency, as experienced by the members of thirty-four families who had been offered therapy over a twelve-month period. Twenty-three of the families (68 per cent) had entered therapy, with the remainder either declining or failing to turn up for the first session. Qualitative data was collected on thirty-two families, including twenty-two of those who had received therapy. Family members were interviewed (between two and three months after the end of therapy), and further information was obtained on the outcome and process of therapy from agency files and therapist notes. This material was analysed using an approach based on grounded theory (Glaser and Strauss, 1967). Further information on aspects of the analysis of the data have also been reported in Howe (1996).

What kind of evaluative picture does this qualitative study generate? Clearly, Howe (1989) does not offer estimations of improvement assessed through changes in scores on standardised measures. Nevertheless, the study as a whole does supply a readily understandable and practicable account of the effectiveness of this form of therapy with this group of clients. Only five of the families reported that they had gained from therapy. Another five were ambivalent about their experience of therapy. The other twelve families left before the end of therapy, usually after two or three sessions, and were critical or dismissive of the treatment they had received. It is important to recognise that the effectiveness of this therapy was being judged in terms of the criteria employed by the families. What Howe (1989) was interested in was whether they saw themselves as having benefited from therapy. Unlike most outcome studies, the rich descriptive detail provided by this qualitative research allows the reader to gain a detailed appreciation of *how* the therapy operated, and to understand *why* the therapy was effective or ineffective. The study generated a number of suggestions regarding what this team of therapists might do to improve their success rate.

From a qualitative research perspective, there are certainly a number of limitations to the Howe (1989) study. He focused entirely on one set of stakeholders (the families). There was an absence of 'informant checking', where findings are taken back and discussed with research participants. There was no use of an independent 'adversary' or 'auditor' (Hill *et al.*, 1997) to review the adequacy of his interpretation of the data.

Other researchers conducting qualitative evaluation studies of psychotherapy would undoubtedly be able to improve on Howe's work. But the key point is that the Howe (1989) study demonstrates that qualitative evaluation of psychotherapy is *possible*. The study shows that qualitative research could, in principle, deliver on the basic questions that therapy outcome research needs to consider: 'how much do users benefit from the intervention?', and 'how do success rates compare with other studies?' Compared to (most) quantitative outcome studies, a qualitative approach can be seen to have the advantage of *also* being able to address questions such as: 'what actually happens in this kind of therapy?', 'what aspects of practice enhance or reduce outcomes?', and 'what can be done to make this therapy more effective?'

The study by McKenna and Todd (1997) consisted of lengthy (90–120 minute) interviews with nine clients of a university psychotherapy clinic in the USA. The main aim of the study was to examine patterns of longitudinal utilisation of psychotherapy services over time. However, in responding to questions about their pattern of involvement with psychotherapy and other mental health agencies, most informants were able to articulate their personal assessments of the value of each treatment episode in relation to their needs at that point in their life. McKenna and Todd (1997) used the technique of the *time line* to assist informants in ordering their accounts of previous therapies. Interview material was transcribed and analysed with the help of a computer qualitative analysis software program. Findings were presented in the form of individual case vignettes and an analysis of general themes.

The results of the McKenna and Todd (1997) study illustrate one of the strengths of qualitative research – its sensitivity to categories employed by informants to make sense of their life-experience. In qualitative research, rather than the researcher imposing his or her analytic categories on experience (e.g. in the form of questionnaire items or rating codes), the aim is to be as open as possible to the ways in which informants themselves construe events. Here, it emerged that the clients interviewed by McKenna and Todd (1997) differentially evaluated the effectiveness of therapy episodes depending on what they were looking for at that stage in their life. Some therapy episodes were characterised as introductory and intended to do no more than allow the service user a preliminary *exposure* to therapy. One informant described such an experience as 'breaking the ice'. Other episodes, labelled *discrimination* therapy encounters, were seen as enabling the person to 'shop around' to find a good match between himself or herself and a therapist. There were also *formation* episodes, where the person felt that significant and lasting change had occurred; *consolidation* therapies, where the person was not seeking to change but merely to reinforce what had been gained in a previous formative experience; and finally *holding* therapies, in which the person did not feel that he or she was making much progress. These holding therapies could be perceived as useful ('kept things from getting worse') or frustrating ('wanting more but not knowing how to get it').

The McKenna and Todd (1997) study is based on a small number of clients who had used one therapy centre (although in the past they had all used other therapy services too). It would not be sensible to claim that the types of episode identified in this study could be generalised to all clinical settings or clients. All the same, their work opens up an understanding of how clients perceive the effectiveness of therapy. For one client, a brief 'exposure' to therapy may be just what they need at that point in their life. For another client, who has been exposed to different approaches and learned to discriminate between them, only a formative therapeutic experience would be regarded as effective. For some time after that experience, further transformative therapy would not be welcome, whereas opportunities to consolidate would be rated highly. Formative experiences are the only ones that would be able to provide *quantitative* evidence of their worth, but this would give a most misleading impression of effectiveness.

The research by Dale *et al.* (1998) reports on interviews carried out with forty people who had received counselling in relation to abuse they had experienced in childhood. These informants supplied information on 130 counselling experiences. As might be expected in a qualitative study, the interviews generated useful insights into the processes associated with effective and ineffective therapy. However, the researchers were also able to estimate the success rate of these counselling episodes. Although virtually all of these clients reported having had a positive overall experience of counselling, around one-quarter described counselling experiences that they felt had been harmful to them. In many of these cases they had been unable to tell their counsellors about their dissatisfaction, adopting instead the strategy of 'pretending to be better'.

All three studies described in this section demonstrate that qualitative interview data can be used to generate useful information about the effectiveness of therapy. Some of the methodological issues associated with this form of evaluation research are discussed in the following section.

The logic of qualitative research

Different evaluation 'logics' prevail within quantitative and qualitative research. In a randomised controlled trial, the causal link between intervention and outcome is established through statistical analysis of group data. For example, the anxiety scores on the group of clients who receive therapy are compared with the scores of those in a control condition. If randomisation has been successful, then it can reasonably be concluded that differential outcomes are due to the intervention. This is a powerful framework for attributing cause and effect relationships. In a qualitative study, on the other hand, the link between intervention and outcome is established through descriptive accounts given by therapy participants. Howe (1989) found that the families he interviewed were able to be explicit about whether or not their problems had improved over the course of treatment. Howe's report gives many examples of families reporting attitudes and behaviour that had changed or remained the same over the period of time before, during and following therapy. However, informants would sometimes attribute these changes to therapy, sometimes to their own efforts, and at other times to external or chance influences. As one mother said: 'everything's fine at home now . . . but what we did at home was ten times more use than what they did' (Howe, 1989: 77). In a qualitative interview, events are constructed into a *narrative* account. The use of the time-line technique by McKenna and Todd (1997) is an example of one of the ways in which informants can be helped to reconstruct the story of their therapy.

One way of understanding the methodological issues associated with the use of self-report measures in psychotherapy outcome research is that, here too, respondents attempt to 'narrativise' their experience but that the linguistic constraints of the questionnaire format impedes their capacity to do so. Their answers to questionnaire items are not straightforward behavioural reports, but reflect the story they tell themselves about their life and their therapy. At least in qualitative research the fact that the research is concerned with how clients (or indeed, other stakeholders) construe or 'narrativise' their experience is openly acknowledged.

One of the interesting aspects of the Howe (1989), McKenna and Todd (1997) and Dale *et al.* (1998) studies is that therapy clients appeared to be quite willing to be critical of their therapists in these interviews. In research that employs client satisfaction questionnaires at the end of therapy it is usual to observe a 'ceiling effect' in which the majority of clients give ratings at the extreme positive end of the scale (Attkisson and Greenfield, 1994). Why are clients more willing or able to give a balanced view of their therapy in the context of an in-depth interview, where they tend to give an exaggerated positive evaluation on rating scales? It may be that satisfied clients fill in satisfaction questionnaires while unsatisfied ones do not complete them, or that less satisfied clients are more willing to be interviewed. However, it may also be that the interview situation encourages a reflective stance which allows the person to give a more complete account of the meaning of an important experience in their life. The 'demand characteristics' of a brief end-of-therapy satisfaction questionnaire may contribute to answers dominated by a wish not to undermine the reputation of the therapist who has done his or her best to help. Schwartz (1996) has described some of the ways in which the language used in questionnaire items invites particular answers. By contrast, the 'demand characteristics' of an extended interview with a neutral researcher give permission for the person to express the ambiguities and complexities of their sense of whether, and how much, therapy has helped them. The logic of qualitative evaluation, therefore, must be seen as being grounded in a willingness to accept diversity, or even ambiguity, rather than being wedded to a 'horse race' mentality in which the therapy with the highest gain score is the winner. In terms of producing new knowledge that contributes to debates over evidence-based therapy, it would appear that qualitative evaluation is better able to explore the limits of therapeutic *ineffectiveness*. Participants in the Howe (1989) and Dale *et al.* (1998) studies reported somewhat *lower* success rates than in other published research. For example, in the Dale *et al.* (1998) research, some 10 per cent of counselling episodes were described by informants as being positively harmful.

Qualitative methods have traditionally been considered as most appropriate for research which seeks to uncover the *meanings* embedded within a slice of social life or piece of action. Qualitative research is seen as contributing to the growth of *understanding*, rather than to the collection of factual knowledge and construction of causal explanation. In research into the outcomes of psychotherapy, attention to the meaning of treatment and the development of an understanding of therapeutic gain are important goals. But outcome research also needs to feed in to policy debates where there is a demand for more precise statements about *who* benefits from *which* therapy and *how much*. In recent years, researchers employing quantitative methods and clinical trials have begun to estimate the comparative benefits of different types of therapy by constructing estimates of reliable clinically significant (or socially significant) change. The estimates are derived by working out for each individual client whether that person has or has not achieved enough in therapy to be considered as a 'success' case. In principle, there is no reason why this kind of statement about individual cases cannot just as easily be generated from qualitative data. There exist techniques within qualitative methodology, such as the use of triangulation and external auditing (Hill *et al.*, 1997), that would allow the reliability of statements about clinically significant change to be built on inter-observer consensus. So, although there are important differences between the 'logic' or 'rhetoric' of qualitative and quantitative approaches, it is also possible to see how these approaches can converge around, for example, a requirement to make specific recommendations to external audiences. It is also possible to envisage ways in which qualitative and quantitative approaches might be combined within outcome studies (Dennis *et al.*, 1994). Mixed-method strategies include: using the findings of qualitative analysis to interpret quantitative results; drawing on qualitative material when sample sizes are too small to allow statistical analyses of sufficient power to be carried out; employing qualitative methods as a heuristic device to develop hypotheses that can be tested using quantitative methods; using change scores to identify subgroups of clients to be studied more intensively using qualitative techniques. In future, a fundamental use of mixed methods might be to establish a greater understanding of the parameters of clinical effectiveness for different treatments. For example, it seems clear that client satisfaction question-naires tend to produce the most optimistic estimates of effectiveness, while open-ended in-depth interviews yield the most conservative picture, with randomised trials reporting effectiveness rates that are somewhere between. Qualitative interviews appear to be, at present, the most sensitive method for evaluating the harmful effects of therapy and also for recording its greatest individual successes. The standardised self-report methods used in randomised trials appear both to inhibit criticism of therapists and reporting of deterioration, and also give little scope for clients to describe the hugely positive transformational experiences that can sometimes take place in counselling. For example, informants in the Dale *et al.* (1998) study used phrases such as 'changed my life' and 'its made such an incredible difference'.

CONCLUSIONS

This chapter has attempted to establish two propositions. First, that psychotherapy outcome studies based on self-report measures of adjust-ment may not be as methodologically sound as they are assumed to be. Second, that qualitative evaluation methods may have something to offer. Qualitative studies of the effectiveness of interventions have been used for some time in fields such as education (see Greene, 1998, for a recent review of this work). Within the counselling and psychotherapy research community, Howard (1983) has made a powerful plea for increased methodological pluralism. However, while pluralism (in the form of qualitative methods or mixed methods) has become acceptable in psychotherapy process research it has had little impact on outcome methodology. Although the qualitative outcome studies reviewed in this chapter must be seen as pilot studies, as limited and tentative, they do provide a basis for moving forward. There are many other qualitative research techniques which can be applied in psychotherapy outcome research, either in isolation or in conjunction with quantitative measures. When there are 480 qualitative outcome studies (the number of controlled trials reviewed in the Smith *et al.* meta-analysis published in 1980) we will be in a better position to judge the contribution of this approach.

REFERENCES

Attkisson, C.C. and Greenfield, T.K. (1994) Client Satisfaction Questionnaire-8 and Service Satisfaction Scale-30, in M.E. Maruish (ed.) *The Use of Psychological Testing for Treatment Planning and Outcome Assessment.* Hillsdale, N.J.: Lawrence Erlbaum.

Bergin, A. and Garfield, S. (eds) (1994) *Handbook of Psychotherapy and Behavior Change* (4th edn). New York: Wiley.

Campbell, D.T. and Fiske, D.W. (1959) Convergent and discriminant validation by the multitrait-multimethod matrix. *Psychological Bulletin,* 56: 81–105.

Cartwright, D.S., Kirtner, W.L. and Fiske, D.W. (1963) Method factors in changes associated with psychotherapy. *Journal of Abnormal and Social Psychology,* 66: 164–175.

Dale, P., Allen, J. and Measor, L. (1998) Counselling adults who were abused as children: clients' perceptions of efficacy, client–counsellor communication, and dissatisfaction. *British Journal of Guidance and Counselling,* 26: 141–158.

Dennis, M., Fetterman, D.M. and Sechrest, L. (1994) Integrating qualitative and quantitative evaluation methods in substance abuse research. *Evaluation and Program Planning,* 17: 419–427.

Edwards, A.L. (1957) *The Social Desirability Variable in Personality Assessment and Research.* New York: Dryden.

Fairhurst, K. and Dowrick, C. (1996) Problems with recruitment in a randomized controlled trial of counselling in general practice: causes and implications. *Journal of Health Services Research and Policy,* 1: 77–80.

Glaser, B. and Strauss, A. (1967) *The Discovery of Grounded Theory.* Chicago: Aldine.

Goedhart, H. and Hoogstraten, J. (1992) The retrospective pre-test and the role of pre-test information in evaluative studies. *Psychological Reports,* 70: 699–704.

Golombiewski, R.T. (1989) The alpha, beta, gamma change typology. *Group and Organization Studies,* 14: 150–154.

Golombiewski, R.T., Billingsley, K. and Yeager, S. (1976) Measuring change and persistence in human affairs: types of change generated by OD designs. *Journal of Applied Behavioral Science,* 12: 133–157.

Greene, J.C. (1998) Qualitative, interpretive evaluation, in A.J. Reynolds and

H.J. Walberg (eds) *Advances in Educational Productivity. Vol. 7. Evaluation Research for Educational Productivity*. Greenwich, Conn.: JAI Press.

Henry, W.P. (1998) Science, politics and the politics of science: the use and misuse of empirically validated treatment research. *Psychotherapy Research*, 8: 126–140.

Hill, C.E., Thompson, B.J. and Nutt-Williams, E. (1997) A guide to conducting consensual qualitative research. *Counseling Psychologist*, 25: 517–572.

Howard, G.S. (1983) Toward methodological pluralism. *Journal of Counseling Psychology*, 30: 19–21.

Howard, G.S., Ralph, K.M., Gulanick, N.A., Maxwell, S.E., Nance, D.W. and Gerber, S.K. (1979) Internal validity in pretest–posttest self-report evaluations and a re-evaluation of retrospective pretests. *Applied Psychological Measurement*, 3: 1–23.

Howe, D. (1989) *The Consumer's View of Family Therapy*. Aldershot: Gower.

Howe, D. (1996) Client experiences of counselling and treatment interventions: a qualitative study of family views of family therapy. *British Journal of Guidance and Counselling*, 24: 367–376.

Kelly, A.E., Kahn, J.H. and Coulter, R.G. (1996) Client self-presentations at intake. *Journal of Counseling Psychology*, 43: 300–309.

Kuncel, R.B. and Kuncel, N.R. (1995) Response-process models: toward an integration of cognitive-processing models, psychometric models, latent-trait theory, and self-schemas, in P.E. Shrout and S.T. Fiske (eds) *Personality Research, Methods and Theory. A Festschrift Honoring Donald. W. Fiske*. Hillsdale, N.J.: Lawrence Erlbaum.

Lambert, M.J. (1994) Use of psychological tests for outcome assessment, in M.E. Maruish (ed.) *The Use of Psychological Testing for Treatment Planning and Outcome Assessment*. Hillsdale, N.J.: Lawrence Erlbaum.

McCrae, R.R. and Costa, P.T. (1983) Social desirability scales: more substance than style. *Journal of Consulting and Clinical Psychology*, 51: 882–888.

McKenna, P.A. and Todd, D.M. (1997) Longtitudinal utilization of mental health services: a time-line method, nine retrospective accounts, and a preliminary conceptualization. *Psychotherapy Research*, 7: 383–396.

Manthei, R.J. (1997) The response-shift bias in a counsellor education programme. *British Journal of Guidance and Counselling*, 25: 229–238.

Meier, S.T. (1994) *The Chronic Crisis in Psychological Measurement*. New York: Academic Press.

Paulhaus, D.L. (1986) Self-deception and impression management in test responses, in A. Angleitner and J.S. Wiggins (eds) *Personality Assessment via Questionnaires: Current Issues in Theory and Measurement*. Berlin: Springer-Verlag.

Roth, A. and Fonagy, P. (1996) *What Works for Whom? A Critical Review of Psychotherapy Research*. New York: Guilford Press.

Schwartz, N. (1996) *Cognition and Communication: Judgemental Biases, Research Methods, and the Logic of Conversation*. Mahwah, N.J.: Lawrence Erlbaum.

Shweder, R. (1975) How relevant is an individual difference theory of personality? *Journal of Personality*, 43: 455–484.

Smith, M., Glass, G. and Miller, T. (1980) *The Benefits of Psychotherapy.* Baltimore, Md.: Johns Hopkins University Press.

Chapter 8

Rigour and relevance

The role of practice-based evidence in the psychological therapies

Michael Barkham and John Mellor-Clark

INTRODUCTION

Evidence-based health care has moved through successive phases, each with a different focus: from efficacy, through quality improvement, and towards increased effectiveness. We argue that researchers and clinicians can collaborate to take forward the broad agenda of evidence-based psychological health and health care through the complementary agenda of *practice-based evidence*. Such an initiative is consistent with other calls identifying the need to close the gap between research and practice (e.g. Geddes and Harrison, 1997). Our views have been informed by work in three key areas central to current concerns. First, a recognition of the complexities and vulnerabilities inherent in designing and implementing efficacy studies of psychological treatments (Shapiro *et al.*, 1994). Second, a recognition of the need to extend experimental designs into field settings and implement naturalistic studies (e.g., Barkham *et al.*, 1996; Shapiro and Barkham, 1993). Third, the need to set a scientific and strategic agenda for the role of measurement and its related issues as they apply to the evaluation of the psychological therapies.

These three areas have led us to incorporate the concept of *practice-based evidence* within our research agenda and to espouse the central role of *quality evaluation* to act as both focus and method (Mellor-Clark and Barkham, in press). Accordingly, in this chapter we view the concept of evidence as a continuum emphasising the role of practice-based evidence as the natural complement to evidence-based practice. We present our material in two parts. In the first, we consider the efficacy–effectiveness continuum and associated models driven by (top-down) funded research traditions. In the second part, we consider some of the practical components of practice-based evidence driven by (bottom-up) research/ practitioner initiatives.

THE EFFICACY–EFFECTIVENESS CONTINUUM

A key assumption underlying the drive towards evidence-based health care is the central role played by randomised controlled trials (RCTs) or *efficacy* studies – that is, studies carried out with scientific rigour under optimum conditions. These are primary studies that also subsequently provide the data for meta-analyses and Cochrane reviews that are seen as the gold standard for information underpinning evidence-based practice. The hallmarks of efficacy studies, as well as some of their shortcomings, have been detailed elsewhere (see Bower and King, in Chapter 6). However, it needs to be recognised that designing an RCT is as much of an art as it is a science. Thus, Shapiro *et al.* (1995) provide an extensive account of the series of trade-off decisions that were made relating to the design, implementation and analysis in carrying out a large RCT of contrasting treatments of depression. For example, setting exclusion criteria to ensure a homogeneous sample also acts to make the sample less representative of patients in the population from which they were drawn.

In terms of the positive impact of RCTs to health care generally, three of the seven increased years of life expectancy over the past fifty years have been attributed to results arising specifically from randomised trials (Bunker *et al.*, 1994). Similarly, the RCT tradition has delivered an average of five additional years of partial or complete relief from poor quality of life associated with chronic disease (Bunker *et al.*, 1994). Such an attribution is in stark contrast to alternative views of RCTs suggesting 'a massive amount of research effort, the goodwill of hundreds of thousands of patients, and millions of pounds have been wasted' (Chalmers, 1998: 1167).

In the current context, the call is for 'unbiased, relevant, and reliable assessments of health care' (Chalmers, 1998). Considering each of these components does not, however, necessarily mean designing and implementing more stringent RCTs. Thus, the issue of *bias* is endemic in research and it is unlikely that any research within the area of psychological health will not, in some way, be biased. For example, there is growing evidence that differential outcome effects between psychological therapies can be attributable to researcher allegiance (Gaffan *et al.*, 1995; Robinson *et al.*, 1990). The implication is that such allegiance leads researchers, unwittingly, to introduce bias into their design and methodology. A more realistic expectation might be for researchers to understand what potential biases are present and what impact they might have on results. The concept of *relevance* is also a major issue for all research studies. For example, many practitioners want to be informed about ways of tackling therapeutic difficulties within sessions. RCTs are not necessarily the best way to address this issue, either scientifically or economically. And finally, the notion of *reliable assessments* need not place a premium on psychometric properties in which the fidelity (i.e. purity) of a measure or procedure is paramount. Within a broader perspective, there is a sense in which the notion of 'good enough' is sufficient when set against other criteria such as user-friendliness and clinical or therapeutic utility.

Replication and representativeness

Since Eysenck's (1952) critique of the outcomes of psychotherapy, efficacy research has progressed through a number of research generations (Russell and Orlinsky, 1996). Each phase reflects an increased sophistication in the areas of design, methodology, and analysis. However, for many researchers and practitioners, studies of both outcomes and processes within the psychological therapies – and more importantly the paradigms upon which they are based – have produced a low yield to practitioners relative to their financial cost. A central axiom of the scientific method has been *replication*. Relatively few attempts have been made to replicate efficacy trials in service settings. Those replication studies that have been carried out indicate that different findings from those reported in efficacy trials can occur. For example, a small but highly controlled field replication of the Second Sheffield Psychotherapy Project suggested that clients in NHS service settings benefited more from sixteen sessions than from eight sessions, irrespective of their presenting severity level (Barkham *et al.*, 1996). This finding contrasted with those obtained in the original trial in which only those clients presenting with severe depression showed an advantage in the sixteen-session condition (Shapiro *et al.*, 1994). The smaller sample size of the replication study was not a plausible explanation for this different finding. Such disparity in findings, which could have considerable bearing on the design of psychological services, needs to be considered.

Whilst replication is seen as the axiom of traditional efficacy research, prediction is perhaps more appropriate to effectiveness research. Here the requirement is for services to be able to predict the course of response (recovery or deterioration) in the context of a range of factors. Hence, change in response to interventions can be predicted on the basis of accumulated knowledge. Huge samples are required to model differential responses as a function of, for example, diagnosis, theoretical orientation, gender, severity, co-morbidity, etc. This is a very different approach to RCTs, but may provide a highly representative basis for informing practice and policy.

There have been efforts to extrapolate results obtained from efficacy studies to field settings (Shadish *et al.*, 1997; Weisz *et al.*, 1995). Findings from such studies are usually reported using an *effect size* (ES) which gives an indication of the magnitude of any effect rather than whether or not there was an effect.[1] In the area of child psychotherapy, efficacy studies have suggested a large effect (ES = 0.77) favouring active interventions when carried out in research settings. However, most important for the present debate has been the finding that when the evidence from clinical settings was evaluated, there was no effect (ES = 0.01; Weisz *et al.*, 1995).

Table 8.1   Three stages and their criteria of defining clinical representativeness

	Stage 1 criteria	Stage 2 criteria	Stage 3 criteria
	1 Carried out in non-university settings	1 Did not use treatment manual	1 Clients heterogeneous in personal characteristics
	2 Usual referral routes for clients	2 Did not monitor treatment implementation	2 Clients heterogeneous in presenting problems
	3 Experienced therapists with regular caseloads		3 Therapists not trained specifically for study
			4 Therapists free to select treatment methods
Number and % of 1,082 studies meeting criteria:	56 studies (5.2%)	15 studies (1.4%)	1 study (0.1%)
Average effect size:	0.68	0.58	0.51
Pooled effect size:	0.56	0.52	0.51

A similar study carried out by Shadish *et al.* (1997) utilising studies investigating adult populations arrived at different findings. These authors identified 1,082 studies of psychotherapy outcomes that showed an effect size between medium and large (ES = 0.59). The studies were categorised into three stages based on criteria that reflected the extent to which studies were clinically representative (i.e. on a continuum from efficacy to effectiveness). The hallmarks of each stage are set out in Table 8.1. The overall effect size for all studies was 0.59. Shadish and colleagues carried out increasingly stringent analyses to determine the effect sizes across the three stages as shown in Table 8.1. Regardless of the exact analysis, the effect size was medium.

These results have several implications. First, unlike the findings from child psychotherapy studies, psychotherapy for adults still appears effective beyond the confines of efficacy studies. For example, an effect size of 0.51 reported in Table 8.1 indicates that the average treated person scores better after treatment than 70 per cent of the control group. Set against this is the point that there is a trend towards the effect size decreasing as studies move from an efficacy towards an effectiveness base. In addition, there is an obvious weakness in that the results for Stage 3 – the stage that best approximates procedures and practices in the field – are based on a single study. What is clear is that there is a need for research efforts to place greater emphasis on the interface between efficacy and effectiveness studies. Accordingly, we briefly consider various models of how this interface might be achieved.

Models of the efficacy–effectiveness interface

In considering the approaches to evidence-based psychological health, there needs to be an overarching coherence between the methodologies employed. One way forward would be to place studies or research programmes within an overall strategy. Here, we outline two approaches to how models of efficacy and effectiveness studies might be co-ordinated. The first reflects the adoption of a linear approach and the second that of a dimensional approach.

Linear approach

One approach is to view studies as needing to progress through successive stages. This approach prioritises internal over external validity. Table 8.2 sets out three models: Salkovskis's (1995) 'hour-glass' model, Linehan's

Table 8.2 Three linear models of the efficacy–effectiveness continuum

'Hour-glass' model (Salkovskis, 1995)	Stage-wise treatment development model (Linehan, 1997)	Technology transfer model (Office of Technology, 1982)
1 Clinical problem of concern to large number of practitioners; possible answers based on theoretical framework and clinical hunch; small-scale exploratory testing; flexible designs used	1 Treatment development: a treatment generation b treatment standardisation c efficacy pilot testing	1 Pilots carried out for feasibility, acceptability, and risk 2 Evaluated in controlled clinical trials that comprise the full range of methods
2 More rarified research with narrower focus requiring control groups, stringent measurement, and statistical techniques	2 Treatment validation: a testing efficacy b testing mechanisms of action c testing utility	3 Defined population studies outside the research setting on sizeable samples 4 Demonstration and implementation studies on public health
3 Broadening out results of research to less selected sample, using settings closer to standard clinical practice	3 Treatment dissemination: a services development b programme evaluation c testing effectiveness	5 Evaluated as used in clinical practice (i.e., effectiveness studies)

Note: Similarly numbered stages do not necessarily infer similar content across the three models

(1997) treatment development model, and the Office of Technology's (1982) technology transfer model. While the three models differ in the extent to which they divide up the continuum, all three reflect the same progression from early/theoretical work, through a more concentrated phase of scientific testing, and then progressing to issues of generalising to larger and more homogeneous populations. However, as we all know, an hour-glass works by being continually inverted: the ending of one phase providing the beginning for another. Such iterative and dynamic processes are somehow lost in these linear representations.

Irrespective of the specific model, there is a disproportionate emphasis placed on the validation stage as the primary domain of scientific pursuit. This focuses on two areas. The first has been the outcome study comparing active treatment to either no-treatment conditions or comparative outcome trials in which two or more active treatments are compared. The second has been the process study which focuses on establishing the pathways or mechanisms of change (i.e. process – outcome links). The aim of these two forms of study has been to establish the most efficacious treatments for specific presenting problems. Whilst such studies deliver information on efficacy agenda, a further important stage involving more heterogeneous populations is required.

The aim of the dissemination stage is to take the efficacy-based findings and apply them in practical and clinical settings. The most relevant question here is 'Are psychosocial interventions effective in practical or applied settings?' Clinical guidelines, however, are based on the best available evidence and this is primarily drawn from efficacy studies. Clearly this linear model assumes that treatment efficacy should be replicated in service settings, rather than testing efficacy findings in practice – thereby closing the loop. This is a view which accords with the model of evidence-based practice set out in the NHSE Review of Psychotherapy Services in England (Department of Health, 1996) which proposes no *direct* feedback on the effectiveness of efficacy-based clinical practice guidelines (measured by service audit and outcome benchmarking) into local service utilisation.

Dimensional approach

Hoagwood *et al.* (1995) identified three dimensions (or axes) along which research studies can be placed: (1) intervention, (2) validity, and (3) outcome. These are described as continuous dimensions with poles that represent aspects of scope, range and generalisability. In such a model, the various types of validity, of interventions, and of outcomes enable any study to occupy a place in this three-dimensional space. The *intervention* axis refers to the extent to which any treatment or psychological intervention is structured. This invariably is manifest in the extent to which the intervention is manualised. In addition, it includes considering how pure the intervention is in terms of being derived from single or multiple modalities. It also considers the pragmatic issue of treatment length. The *validity* axis makes reference to the extent to which internal or external validity is the focus of the study. Hoagwood *et al.* (1995) argued that internal validity must be established before external validity. Also included is the definition of the population being investigated and the setting. Finally, the *outcome* axis aims to cover the broad range of dependent variables from individuals' symptoms to satisfaction with service delivery systems and costs.

Whichever approach is used, it is important that a clear relationship is established as to how the yields of efficacy and effectiveness research inform each other in service of the needs of practitioners. A 'benchmarking' research strategy offers an opportunity; point-by-point comparisons of the outcome data obtained in service settings are set against that derived from efficacy studies (see Wade *et al.*, 1998). In this approach, efficacy studies yield the extent of client change under optimum conditions which is used as a benchmark against which to judge whether the same intervention delivered in a field setting has a similar effect. To achieve this, data collected and analysed in field settings must be of the highest quality. Consequently, we argue for an approach to evidence that places an equal premium on data gathered from the practice setting – hence our focus on practice-based evidence.

PRACTICE-BASED EVIDENCE

We suggest that practice-based evidence is the natural complement to the current focus on evidence-based practice. Our aim in this part of the chapter is to present a view of practice-based evidence by looking at its structure, process and outcome. First, we introduce the concept of *practice research networks* as integral to the *structure* (or rather infrastructure) required to deliver practice-based evidence. Second, we present our position on quality evaluation as central to the *process* and detail some current national initiatives. Third, we conclude with the advantages of utilising clinically significant change to complement other ways of using data on *outcomes*.

Structure: practice research networks

In a similar way in which a complex infrastructure has developed to support the implementation and delivery of efficacy research, so too there is the need for a viable infrastructure to support effectiveness research. One component within such a structure is the practice research network (PRN). In the US literature, a PRN has been defined as typically consisting of 'a large number of clinicians who agree to collaborate to collect and report data' (Zarin *et al.*, 1996: 147). The PRN model is well equipped to help practising clinicians meet the dual agenda of evidence-based practice and practice-based evidence. First, the PRNs take a naturalistic approach in that they utilise data gathered in routine clinical practice settings rather than from any clinical research trials. Second, all practitioners use the same clinical measures and data collection tools, which enables the generation of large data sets and permits comparability between client populations, treatments, clinicians and services. Finally, the PRN structure enables the shared and consensual setting of standards and subsequent benchmarking of outcomes to enhance the delivery and development of services.

Adopting such a naturalistic and standardised approach has a number of advantages to offer traditional research, evaluation and audit designs:

- The PRN organisation is typically supported by an academic research centre. In addition, individual service administration, analysis and reporting costs can be optimised through centralisation.
- PRN membership allows both practitioners and researchers to collaborate in dissemination of data generated by the network as a whole. This may be relevant in the post-Culyer climate in which there is greater accountability over research activities within the NHS.
- The PRN model can help bridge the gap between practice and research by generating relevant and meaningful data reflecting the priorities of clinicians, facilitating the implementation of research findings in practice.
- PRN support is appropriate for helping practitioners to overcome resistance to effectiveness evaluation and reluctance to incorporating it into their routine practice (Mellor-Clark and Barkham, 1997).
- The PRN offers the opportunity to use standardised brief practitioner-completed instrumentation to help overcome problems with data attrition that can arise when the data collection procedure relies solely on patients.
- Finally, the PRN approach relates well to the current policy drive towards standards setting, monitoring effectiveness and improving the quality of psychological treatment provision (Department of Health, 1996), and clinical governance (Department of Health, 1997).

The PRN model has the potential to produce large bodies of data which allows comparisons to be made between patients, problems, practitioners and services and enables the setting of standards and the benchmarking of practice against those standards (Barkham *et al.*, 1998). In sum, PRNs in any health care domain give clinicians the opportunity to become involved in research that not only serves to expand the knowledge base in treatment effectiveness and efficiency but also offers important implications for policy and planning.

Process: quality evaluation

We believe that the *raison d'être* of evaluation should be to enhance the quality of service provision. This requires methods and measures capable of providing information on the quality of service provision, including inadequacies, thereby giving information to assist the development of service delivery. *Quality evaluation* should be the cornerstone of accountable service delivery and continuing professional development. The aims of quality evaluation should be:

- to demonstrate the *appropriateness* of service structures;
- to enhance the *accessibility* to service provision;
- to monitor the *acceptability* of service procedures;
- to ensure *equity* to all potential service recipients;
- to demonstrate the *effectiveness* of service practices;
- to improve the *efficiency* of service delivery.

Effectiveness (i.e., outcome) data is too often collected devoid of necessary contextual information addressing areas such as appropriateness, acceptability, and efficiency as some of the key determinants of the ultimate effectiveness. Hence, data on outcomes alone is open to misuse as it fails to take account of multiple factors that impinge on such outcomes. We see these interrelations as the hallmark of formal therapy research and would see their inclusion in evaluation methods and practice as a major advance.

In contrast to other forms of enquiry, evaluation research has been far less concerned with enhancing theory and adding to the established knowledge base. Instead, evaluations, whilst aspiring to scientific standards, have all too often used a ragbag of measuring tools to aid decision-making and solve operational problems, ultimately disseminated for purely local consumption (Parry, 1996). As a consequence, evaluation to date exists as a limited public information source relative to formal therapy research. We believe there is a critical requirement to enhance the credibility and utility of evaluation methods and measures to help inform national service development and guide others interested in evaluating their practice.

Outcomes auditing

Measures and measurement issues are important in that they invariably act as the currency by which service and treatment outcomes are evaluated. As indicated earlier, in such an outcomes-oriented climate, it is questionable whether there has been sufficient investment in these areas. For example, in the area of outcomes benchmarking prescribed by the Strategic Review of the Psychotherapies (Department of Health, 1996), there is a requirement that outcomes across studies can be compared. Individual and diverse measures can be converted to a common metric using such statistics as z-scores or effect sizes (as described on p. 136). In such an approach, diverse measures are standardised at a statistical level. An alternative approach would be to standardise measurement at the point of contact with the client through the adoption of a standard measure. One initiative set up to meet the Department of Health's agenda has been the development of the Health of the Nation Outcome Scales (HoNOS) (Wing *et al.*, 1994). The resulting scale, which is completed by the practitioner, comprises twelve items with psychometrics that tap four domains: behaviour, impairment, symptoms, and social aspects (Wing *et al.*, 1998). One key test for HoNOS, which is acknowledged by Wing and colleagues, is that 'clinicians should want to use it for their own purposes' (ibid.: 11). In that respect, the jury is still out.

The CORE outcome measure

In a parallel development, we have argued for the development of a systematic approach to ordering outcomes measurement (Barkham *et al.*, 1998). We have developed, validated and implemented a *core* (i.e. generic) outcome measure that can be used across services and populations to provide a common metric. The Clinical Outcomes in Routine Evaluation (CORE) measure (CORE System Group, 1998) is a brief two-sided, 34-item, client-completed questionnaire which addresses the clinical domains of *subjective well-being* (four items), *symptoms* (twelve items, which include anxiety, depression, trauma and physical symptoms), and *functioning* (twelve items, which include close relations, social relations, and life functioning). In addition, the measure contains six items which address components of *risk or harm* which can indicate whether clients are at risk to themselves or to others. The client completes the questionnaire at both the beginning and end of their contact with the service, although a shorter version can be used after each session. Consistent with our aim of placing outcomes in context, we have incorporated the outcome measure within a quality evaluation *system*.

The CORE (Information Management) System

The CORE System has been informed by extensive collaboration with practitioners, alongside a national survey of current measurement practice and preference (Mellor-Clark *et al.*, 1999). In essence, the CORE System takes a *hub and spoke* approach. The *hub* comprises fixed components that have generic applicability across all applications. By contrast, the *spoke* comprises components that are targeted specifically for the needs of particular user groups. The system allow both practitioners and clients to provide evaluation data. This paired data collection strategy facilitates the collection of a comprehensive set of context and outcome data.

FACE Assessment and Outcome System

No single evaluation system is likely to meet all the needs of providers without being overly cumbersome. While the CORE System was not developed for use with clients presenting with severe and enduring mental illness, the FACE Recording and Measurement System was designed for such use (Clifford, 1998, 1999). FACE (Functional Analysis of Care Environments) comprises three integrated functions: *systematic assessment* of needs, risk, and problems; *reliable measurement* of severity, dependency, outcome, and resource use; and *efficient communication* within and between professionals and associated agencies. A hallmark of the system is the FACE Framework that aims to provide a standardised conceptual structure having strong links to the Care Programme Approach. This was developed in order to bring clinical and research perspectives into a multi-axial framework that could be used for both assessment and measurement purposes. In effect, the framework represents a multidimensional model of human functioning comprising the following domains: psychological, physical well-being, activities of daily living, interpersonal relationships, social circumstances, and response to care. This Framework provides a comprehensive assessment and outcome system comprising interlinked clinical and social assessment packages.

The interface between the CORE and FACE Systems

It can be seen that there are differences between these two systems. The CORE System is clinically pragmatic and prescriptive, requiring a minimum standardised data set to be recorded ensuring maximum comparability between (inter- and intra-service) data sources. The FACE System is more flexible and has the potential for coding most clinical information. Where FACE is prescriptive is in the collection of data that relates to the Care Programme Approach through its utilisation of the Health of the Nation Outcome Scales (HoNOS) (Wing *et al.*, 1998).

However, the CORE and FACE Systems share many common features that have a significant bearing on their adoption and utilisation. The two systems target potentially different populations. The CORE System is directed towards NHS (out-patient) counselling, clinical psychology and psychotherapy services, alongside educational and employment settings. In contrast, the FACE System is targeted towards serious and enduring mental illness where practitioners predominantly adhere to the Care Programme Approach. However, the fact that the two systems share a similar philosophy (although targeting differing populations) can enable a high level of integration at both a technical and strategic level. This provides the realistic opportunity for tracking patient care from out-patient psychological therapy services (utilising the CORE System) through to in-patient care (utilising the FACE System). Indeed, the developers of both systems have collaborated to achieve practical and technological compatability between the CORE and FACE systems. Hence, these two systems and their level of integration provide a way forward for practitioners, service managers and policy and planning professionals to obtain comprehensive information on patient care at all levels of NHS provision. Moreover, the availability of such technologies provides a platform for the development of a comprehensive initiative to redress the balance whereby the evidence for practice is derived almost exclusively from efficacy studies. The national utilisation of the CORE and FACE systems provides an enormously rich database for practice-based evidence. However, data collection is one thing but making sense of it quite another, and it is to one aspect of the reporting of data that we now turn.

Outcomes: clinically significant change

In the preceding sections we have stated the importance of both infrastructure and process by emphasising the need for networking between practitioners and researchers, and the implementation of quality evaluation. However, much of the logic of evidence-based psychological health rests on outcomes and their associated processes and technologies (e.g. issues of measurement, outcome measures, etc.). In this respect, we need to ensure that outcomes reporting is both rigorous (i.e. reliable and based on a sound methodology) and relevant (i.e. meaningful and reflecting clinical reality).

Currently, the central paradigm within efficacy research has been to compare group means for treatments using statistical methods to determine whether change might be due to such factors as chance or sampling bias. In contrast, clinicians are more concerned with changes in particular individuals and often dichotomise outcome as 'success' or 'failure'. Hence, in the same way that elements of the existing infrastructure and process need to be adapted for the effectiveness agenda, so the same is true for the outcomes agenda.

One important procedure to be utilised in an effectiveness framework employs the concepts and methods of *reliable and clinically significant change* (RCSC) (Evans *et al.*, 1998; Jacobson and Truax, 1991). Jacobson and Truax summarised a model of the measurement of change that reflected the complementary concepts of statistical *reliability* of a change and its *clinical significance*. As such, the method is responsive to the need for change to be both meaningful and rigorous. In contrast, one of the major shortcomings of traditional ways of reporting client change has been that a criterion of statistically significant change can be met without any accompanying significant impact on health. For example, all obese people in a treatment trial might lose weight such that the weight loss is statistically significant. But this does not address the question as to whether the loss is sufficient to reduce significantly the probability of their being at high risk of having a heart attack. The criterion becomes one of making sufficient change that is deemed to be *reliable* such that the patient reaches a point at which their improvement in health status can be judged to be *clinically significant*. This is usually indicated by their being identified as having membership of a different (i.e. 'general' or 'non-distressed' rather than 'dysfunctional') population.

Differing criteria for determining clinical significance can be set according to particular objectives. For example, the criterion of 'success' might differ between professionals (e.g. a service manager compared with an individual clinician) and also within an individual (e.g. differing criteria might be appropriate during the course of training to reflect increasing experience). To facilitate adoption of such procedures and in order to be able to place individuals in context, there are now reasonably good cut-off points to define when a person moves from one population to another for a number of measures, including the Hamilton Rating Scale, Symptom Check List-90-R, Beck Depression Inventory and CORE Outcome Measure. These methods are a natural complement to traditional analytic methods that address the needs of practitioners in the management of their services.

These methods have been espoused within *Evidence-Based Mental Health* (Evans *et al.*, 1998), and we see them as the natural complement to traditional statistical methods – perhaps with the emphasis dictated by either audience or stakeholder.

CONCLUSIONS

In this chapter we have argued that the current focus on evidence-based practice needs to be complemented by an equal prioritisation of *practice-based evidence* and we have outlined several components to take this agenda forward. Although these can be achieved at a local and regional level, we believe that what is urgently required is a national effectiveness initiative with the purpose of delivering a national effectiveness database. This would complement the efficacy databases utilised for Cochrane reviews. Such effectiveness databases could be built through the development of multiple practice research networks, implementing quality evaluation via standardised systems, ultimately utilising meaningful outcome criteria to provide benchmarked outcomes auditing. Such an initiative not only directly enhances good working practice but can also provide a rich evidence base to test the generalisability of efficacy-based research. Ultimately, the combination of efficacy and effectiveness-based approaches will deliver rigorous and relevant evidence that will yield substantial benefits for the policy, planning and practice of the psychological therapies.

NOTE

1 An ES of 0.00 indicates no change; 0.2 is commonly taken to suggest a small improvement; 0.5 a medium-sized one; and 0.8 a large positive change. They can be negative, indicating a detrimental effect or may even exceed 1.0.

REFERENCES

Barkham, M., Evans, C., Margison, F., McGrath., G., Mellor-Clark, J., Milne, D., and Connell, J. (1998) The rationale for developing and implementing core outcome batteries for routine use in service settings and psychotherapy outcome research. *Journal of Mental Health*, 7: 35–47.
Barkham, M., Rees, A., Shapiro, D.A., Stiles, W.B., Agnew, R.M., Halstead, J., Culverwell, A. and Harrington, V.M.G. (1996) Outcomes of time-limited

psychotherapy in applied settings: replicating the Second Sheffield Psychotherapy Project. *Journal of Consulting and Clinical Psychology*, 64: 1079–1085.

Bunker, J.P., Frazier, H.S. and Mosteller, F. (1994) Improving health: measuring effects of medical care. *Millbank Quarterly*, 72: 225–258.

Chalmers, I. (1998). Unbiased, relevant, and reliable assessments in health care. *British Medical Journal*, 317: 1167–1168.

Clifford, P. (1998). M is for outcome: the CORE outcomes initiative. *Journal of Mental Health*, 7: 19–24.

Clifford, P. (1999) The FACE recording and measurement system: a scientific approach to person-based information. *Bulletin of the Menninger Clinic: A Journal for the Mental Health Professions*, 63: 305–331.

CORE System Group (1998) *CORE System (Information Management) Handbook*. Leeds: Core System Group.

Department of Health (1996) *NHS Psychotherapy Services in England: Review of Strategic Policy*. London: HMSO.

Department of Health (1997) *The New NHS: Modern, Dependable* London: HMSO.

Evans, C., Margison, F. and Barkham, M. (1998) The contribution of reliable and clinically significant change methods to evidence-based mental health. *Evidence-Based Mental Health*, 1: 70–72.

Eysenck, H. (1952) The effects of psychotherapy. *Journal of Consulting and Clinical Psychology*, 16: 319–324.

Gaffan, E.A., Tsaousis, I. and Kemp Wheeler, S.M. (1995) Researcher allegiance and meta-analysis: the case of cognitive therapy for depression. *Journal of Consulting and Clinical Psychology*, 63: 966–980.

Geddes, J.R. and Harrison, P. (1997) Closing the gap between research and practice. *British Journal of Psychiatry*, 171: 220–225.

Hoagwood, K., Hibbs, E., Brent, D. and Jensen, P. (1995) Introduction to special section: efficacy and effectiveness studies of child and adolescent psychotherapy. *Journal of Consulting and Clinical Psychology*, 63: 683–687.

Jacobson, N.S. and Truax, P. (1991) Clinical significance: a statistical approach to defining meaningful change in psychotherapy. *Journal of Consulting and Clinical Psychology*, 59: 12–19.

Linehan, M.M. (1997) Development, evaluation and dissemination of effective psychosocial treatments: stages of disorder, levels of care, and stages of treatment research. Paper presented at the Annual Meeting of the UK Chapter of the Society for Psychotherapy Research, Ravenscar.

Mellor-Clark, J. and Barkham, M. (1997) Evaluating effectiveness: needs, problems and potential benefits, in I. Horton and V. Varma (eds) *The Needs of Counsellors & Psychotherapists*. London: Sage, 166–182.

Mellor-Clark, J. and Barkham, M. (in press) Quality evaluation: methods, measures and meaning, in C. Feltham and I. Horton (eds.) *The Handbook of Counselling & Psychotherapy*. London: Sage.

Mellor-Clark, J., Barkham, M., Connell, J., Evans, C. (1999) Practice-based evidence and the need for a standardised evaluation system: Informing the design of the CORE System. *European Journal of Psychotherapy, Counselling and Health*, 3: 357–374.

Muir Gray, J.A. (1997) *Evidence-based Healthcare: How to Make Health Policy and Management Decisions*. Edinburgh: Churchill Livingston.

Office of Technology Assessment (1982) *Technology transfer at the National Institutes of Health. A Technical Memorandum* (Library of Congress Catalog Card Number 82–600529). Washington, DC: US Government Printing Office.

Parry, G. (1992) Improving psychotherapy services: applications of research, audit and evaluation. *British Journal of Clinical Psychology*, 31: 3–19.

Parry, G. (1996). Service evaluation and audit methods, in G. Parry and F.N. Watts (eds), *Behavioural and Mental Health Research: A Handbook of Skills and Methods*. Hove: Lawrence Erlbaum.

Robinson, L.A., Berman, J.S. and Neimeyer, R.A. (1990) Psychotherapy for the treatment of depression: a comprehensive review of controlled outcome research. *Psychological Bulletin*, 108: 30–49.

Russell, R.L. and Orlinsky, D.E. (1996) Psychotherapy research in historical perspective. *Archives of General Psychiatry*, 53: 708–715.

Salkovskis, P.M. (1995) Demonstrating specific effects in cognitive and behavioural therapy, in M. Aveline and D.A. Shapiro (eds) *Research Foundations for Psychotherapy Research*. Chichester: Wiley & Sons, 191–228.

Shadish, W.R., Matt, G.E., Navarro, A.M., Siegle, G., Crits-Christoph, P., Hazelrigg, M.D., Jorm. A.F., Lyons, L.C., Nietzel, M.T., Prout, H.T., Robinson, L., Smith, M.L., Svartberg, M. and Weiss, B. (1997) Evidence that therapy works in clinically representative conditions. *Journal of Consulting and Clinical Psychology*, 65: 355–365.

Shapiro, D.A. and Barkham, M. (1993) Relate – Information Needs Research. Final Report to the Department of Social Security. Rugby: Relate.

Shapiro, D.A., Barkham, M., Rees, A., Hardy, G.E., Reynolds, S. and Startup, M. (1994) Effects of treatment duration and severity of depression on the effectiveness of cognitive-behavioral and psychodynamic-interpersonal psychotherapy. *Journal of Consulting and Clinical Psychology*, 62: 522–534.

Shapiro, D.A., Barkham, M., Rees, A., Hardy, G.E., Reynolds, S. and Startup, M. (1995) Decisions, decisions, decisions: effects of treatment method and duration on the outcome of psychotherapy for depression, in M. Aveline and D.A. Shapiro (eds) *Research Foundations for Psychotherapy Practice*. Chichester: Wiley & Sons, 151–174.

Wade, W.A., Treat, T.A. and Stuart, G.L. (1998) Transporting an empirically supported treatment for panic disorder to a service setting: a benchmarking strategy. *Journal of Consulting and Clinicial Psychology*, 66: 231–239.

Weisz, J.R., Donenberg, G.R., Han, S.S. and Weiss, B. (1995) Bridging the gap between laboratory and clinic in child and adolescent psychotherapy. *Journal of Consulting and Clinical Psychology*, 63: 688–701.

Wing, J.K., Curtis, R. and Beevor, A. (1994) Health of the nation: measuring mental health outcomes. *Psychiatric Bulletin*, 18: 690–691.

Wing, J.K., Beevor, A.S., Curtis, R.H., Park, S.B.G., Hadden, S. and Burns, A. (1998) Health of the Nation Outcome Scales (HoNOS). *British Journal of Psychiatry*, 172: 11–18.

Zarin, D.A, West, J.C., Pincus, H.A. and McIntyre, J.S. (1996) The American Psychiatric Association Practice Research Network, in L.I. Sedderer and B. Dickey (eds) *Outcomes Asessment in Clinical Practice*. Baltimore: Williams & Wilkins.

Part 3

Synthesising the evidence

Chapter 9

Systematic reviews in mental health

Simon Gilbody and Amanda Sowden

INTRODUCTION

There has recently been a major shift in the way in which research evidence relating to the effectiveness of health care interventions is summarised. This chapter is intended to provide an introduction to systematic reviews, with special reference to their ability to inform rational decision-making in mental health. The history and rationale of systematic reviews will be discussed and two important sources of systematic reviews, those produced by the international Cochrane Collaboration and those summarised on the Database of Abstracts of Reviews of Effectiveness (DARE), will be used to illustrate the diversity of interventions which have been subjected to systematic review. A recent review, relating to the promotion of mental well-being, will be used to illustrate the process involved in conducting a systematic review. Lastly, there will be a discussion of the strengths and limitations of systematic reviews and how health care professionals, policy-makers, patients and carers might use them.

WHY DO WE NEED SYSTEMATIC REVIEWS?

Much research which is carried out to assess the effectiveness of an intervention, therapy, or policy initiative is likely to be replicated by several researchers, and (when published) is likely to be dispersed throughout the health care literature. Some research is likely to be more rigorous and valid than others and its results will be more reliable. In order to make sense of this disparate and often contradictory primary research literature, practitioners, policy-makers and consumers of health care have had to rely on the traditional 'review' article. Such articles are generally prepared by 'content experts' in a field and are intended to provide a digestible summary of research. Unfortunately, in many cases, such traditional research articles have been shown to be prone to a number of biases and their conclusions can be just as contradictory as the primary research which they are intended to summarise (Mulrow, 1987). Content experts come to a particular field with their own pre-formed opinions about the truth or effectiveness of a particular intervention. When experts produce review articles there is a danger that the research will be plundered selectively in order to confirm the authors' pre-formed opinion. It is often not clear how individual pieces of research evidence have been selected for inclusion and how a particular conclusion has been reached. In the face of growing dissatisfaction with the lack of transparency of methodology and lack of trust in the conclusions of traditional review articles, the systematic review article has emerged. The rationale and methodology behind systematic reviews is neatly summed up by Mulrow:

> Through critical exploration, evaluation and synthesis, the systematic review separates the insignificant, unsound or redundant deadwood from the salient and critical studies that are worthy of reflection.
> (Mulrow, 1994: 598)

Systematic reviews are explicit in their methodology and the reader is at all times aware of how a particular conclusion is reached. Systematic reviews take steps to seek out all the evidence on a particular topic using extensive (usually electronic) literature searches. From this evidence, only that of the highest quality is selected – ideally in the form of evidence from randomised controlled trials (RCTs). This evidence is synthesised in order to produce a clear message or conclusion regarding effectiveness and to highlight particular areas of uncertainty. In some cases, it is appropriate to produce a pooled summary statistic of the effectiveness of an intervention from several different studies. Here the systematic review employs a specific mathematical technique – meta-analysis (NHS Centre for Reviews and Dissemination, 1996).

Much health care research uses small sample sizes and consequently lacks the statistical power to detect small but important treatment effects (Altman, 1994). One of the major advantages of the systematic review is the ability to produce precise and powerful estimates from under-powered research. In the field of mental health, this shortcoming of the primary research literature has long been realised. Glass (1976) pioneered the use of meta-analysis in order to produce some overall estimate of the effectiveness of psychological therapies from the disparate, contradictory and under-powered studies that had been undertaken in this field. The techniques of systematic review and meta-analysis have evolved and become more refined in recent years, and have been employed to evaluate the effectiveness of a number of interventions in the area of mental health.

Sources of systematic reviews

Many journals now publish systematic reviews in preference to traditional narrative reviews. Unfortunately the increased acknowledgement of the validity and rigour of systematic reviews has meant that the term has come to be abused. Many authors claim that their reviews are 'systematic', whilst their content and methodology shows them to be far from so. The reader should remain critical of the quality of any review claiming to be systematic, as they should with all research (Oxman, *et al.*, 1994).

Two important sources of high-quality systematic reviews are those produced by the international Cochrane Collaboration and those summarised in the Database of Abstracts of Reviews of Effectiveness (DARE), maintained by the NHS Centre for Reviews and Dissemination at the University of York (Sheldon and Chalmers, 1994).

The Cochrane Collaboration

The international Cochrane Collaboration has set itself the task of 'preparing, maintaining and promoting the accessibility of systematic reviews of the effects of health care intervention' (Bero and Rennie, 1995). Since being set up in 1993, a diverse range of common interest 'review groups' have formed (see Chapter 2, this volume). The Collaboration is multidisciplinary and has produced reviews on a range of subjects including psychosocial interventions, pharmacological treatments, and evaluations of different models of care and service delivery. Reviews are published on the Cochrane Library of reviews, which is updated quarterly – both with new reviews as they are completed, and with new versions of reviews as they are updated in line with new evidence (Chalmers *et al.*, 1993). Some examples of reviews relevant to the field of mental health are given in Table 9.1 and an abstract of a review of the effectiveness of family intervention for schizophrenia (Mari and Streiner 1996) is given in Box 9.1 to illustrate the format of Cochrane Reviews.

Table 9.1 Examples of systematic reviews (or protocols for
systematic reviews) from the Cochrane Library

Cochrane Depression Anxiety and Neurosis Group
  Brief psychological interventions following trauma and in the
  prevention of PTSD
  Deliberate self-harm: the efficacy of psychosocial and pharmacolog-
  ical treatments
  Cognitive behaviour therapy for Chronic Fatigue Syndrome
  Anti-depressants for bulimia nervosa

Cochrane Dementia and Cognitive Impairment Group
  Reminiscence therapy for dementia
  Reality orientation for dementia
  Support for carers of people with Alzheimer's-type dementia
  Donepezil in the treatment of Alzheimer's disease

Cochrane Schizophrenia Group
  Assertive community treatment (ACT) for severe mental disorders
  Case management for severe mental disorders
  Community mental health teams for severe mental illness and
  disordered personality
  Family intervention for schizophrenia
  Clozapine vs 'typical' neuroleptic medication for schizophrenia

Database of Abstracts of Reviews of Effectiveness (DARE)

The Database of Abstracts of Reviews of Effectiveness (DARE) provides
a source of high quality systematic reviews that have been identified from
the medical, nursing, and psychological literature. Periodic literature
searches of the following electronic databases are made: Current Contents,
Medline, Cinahl, PsycLIT, Amed and BIOsis, along with hand searches
of a wide range of journals. DARE is one of the most up-to-date and
comprehensive sources of systematic reviews of effectiveness.

Reviews identified for potential inclusion in DARE must first meet a
basic minimum 'quality' standard, and those judged to be of sufficient
quality receive a critical commentary prepared independently by one CRD
reviewer and checked by a second. This commentary helps guide those
who might use the review and discusses critically aspects of methodological quality and the usefulness of the results of the review in informing
health care decision-making. The database contains some 700 individual
records, but this figure changes monthly as new records are added to the
database. Reviews of interventions likely to be of relevance to mental

Box 9.1 Family intervention for schizophrenia

Mari JJ, Streiner D

Date of most recent substantive amendment: 23 February 1996

Objectives: To estimate the effects of family psycho-social interventions in community settings for the care of those with schizophrenia or schizophrenia-like conditions. Search strategy: Electronic searches of Cochrane Schizophrenia Group's Register, EMBASE, MEDLINE, PsycLIT, and hand-searching the references of all identified studies.

Selection criteria: The inclusion criteria for all randomised studies were that they should focus on families of people with schizophrenia or schizoaffective disorders receiving any psycho-social intervention that required more than five sessions and was not restricted to an in-patient context/ environment. Twelve studies, stated to be randomised, were included.

Data collection and analysis: The reviewers extracted the data independently and Odds Ratios, weighted mean difference and number needed to treat were estimated. The reviewers assume that people who died or dropped out had no improvement and tested the sensitivity of the final results to this assumption.

Main results: Family intervention decreases the frequency of relapse (OR one year 0.42 95% CI 0.26–0.67) and hospitalisation (OR one year 0.45 95% CI 0.2–0.99). It encourages compliance with medication and may help people stay in employment. Family intervention does not obviously effect the tendency of individuals/families to drop out of care nor the levels of expressed emotion and family burden. This review provides no data to suggest that family intervention either prevents, or promotes suicide.

Conclusions: The results of this review are generalisable to other health service traditions. Families receiving this intervention may expect the member with schizophrenia to relapse less, be in hospital less, but that the family burden, and levels of emotion expressed, to remain the same. The number needed to treat (for example, for relapse at one year = 6.5 95% CI 4.3–14.0) may be more acceptable to clinicians and families than to purchasers and providers of care.

Note: Cochrane reviews are regularly updated and it is likely that this review may have been updated in line with emerging evidence. Please check the Cochrane library for the latest update of this review.

health professionals make up approximately 10 per cent of DARE records. Examples include reviews relating to the effectiveness of community mental health nursing, consultation–liaison psychiatry and cognitive-behavioural therapy in the treatment of panic disorder. An example of an abstract of a review taken from DARE is presented in Box 9.2. DARE can be accessed for free via the internet (http://www. york.ac.uk/inst/crd).

THE SYSTEMATIC REVIEW PROCESS

The systematic review process aims to ensure a rigorous and objective approach to evaluating and summarising available research findings. There are a number of stages in the review process, which are outlined below. For more detailed information about each stage see the guidelines developed by CRD for undertaking systematic reviews (NHS Centre for Reviews and Dissemination, 1996). Each stage of the review process is illustrated with examples taken from a recent systematic review on mental health promotion in high-risk groups, which was reported in the Effective Health Care Bulletin series produced by CRD (NHS CRD, 1997: see Box 9.3).

Stages involved in the systematic review process

The first step in the systematic review process is the identification of a need for the review. It is important to ensure that a good-quality review does not already exist and various sources can be checked for existing and ongoing reviews. Examples include the Cochrane Database of Systematic Reviews, DARE and the NHS National Research Register (a database of commissioned research, including systematic reviews).

If no review exists then a preliminary assessment of the volume and type of available primary research in the area is necessary to determine the scope of the review. At this stage it is also useful to discuss with experts in the field and potential users of the review the specific questions that the review might address. This preliminary information can be used to develop the review protocol.

The review protocol

The review protocol specifies the question(s) that the review will address and the methods that will be followed to answer it. Its purpose is to reduce

Box 9.2 Example of a structured abstract taken from DARE: a meta-analysis of treatment outcome for panic disorder

Gould R A, Otto M W, Pollack M H. A meta-analysis of treatment outcome for panic disorder. *Clinical Psychology Review*, 15 (8), pp. 819–844.

This record is a structured abstract written by CRD reviewers. The original has met a set of quality criteria.

Author's objective
To compare the effectiveness of pharmacological, cognitive-behavioural and combined pharmacological and cognitive-behavioural treatments for panic disorder.

Type of intervention
Treatment.

Specific interventions included in the review
Pharmacological interventions, cognitive-behavioural therapy and combined pharmacological and cognitive-behavioural treatments.

Participants included in the review
Patients with panic disorder with or without agoraphobia.

Outcomes assessed in the review
Panic frequency.

Study designs of evaluations included in the review
Randomised controlled trials (RCTs). Both single treatments and multiple treatments of combination treatments were included as long as they included a control group (no-treatment, wait-list, drug or psychological placebo).

What sources were searched to identify primary studies?
PsycLIT and MEDLINE (1974 to January 1994) using the following keywords: panic, agoraphobia, treatment outcome, long term, short term. Reference sections of identified articles were examined, and articles in press identified from national conferences prior to January 1994.

Criteria on which the validity (or quality) of studies was assessed
Not stated.

How were the judgements of validity (or quality) made?
Not stated.

continued . . .

How were decisions on the relevance of primary studies made?
Not stated.

How was the data extracted from primary studies?
Not stated.

Number of studies included
Forty-three studies (4,133 patients).

How were the studies combined?
Two average standardised effect sizes were calculated, one across all outcome measures and the second using panic frequency alone. Long-term outcome effect size was calculated within each group using post-treatment and follow-up measures standardised by the post-treatment standard deviation. The minimum follow-up was six months.

How were differences between studies investigated?
Studies were classified by their treatment intervention as pharmacotherapy, cognitive-behavioural therapy, or a combination of the two. Pharmacological studies were broken down by drug type: anti-depressants, benzodiazepines and others. Cognitive-behavioural studies were classified as: cognitive, cognitive restructuring plus situational exposure, cognitive-restructuring plus interoceptive exposure, and other interventions. Studies that did or did not use independent evaluators were compared.

Results of the review
Pharmacotherapy Interventions: sixteen studies (2,708 patients) yielded an average overall effect size of 0.47 (p<0.0001). Nine separate study comparisons examined antidepressants vs control, the overall effect size was 0.55 (p<0.0001). Thirteen separate study comparisons examined benzodiazepines vs control, the overall effect size was 0.40 (p<0.0001). The difference in effect size between the two drug types was not significant (p=0.09). The proportion of drop-outs for subjects receiving pharmacological interventions alone was 19.8 per cent (25.4 per cent for antidepressants, 13.1 per cent for benzodiazepines), compared to 32.5 per cent for the drug placebo control groups. Cognitive-behavioural Interventions (based on comparisons of the previous two groups): nineteen studies (832 patients) yielded an average overall effect size of 0.63 (p<0.0001). The overall drop-out rate for these interventions was 5.6 per cent, and 7.2 per cent in the control groups. Pharmacotherapy vs Cognitive-behavioural Interventions: The overall effect size of cognitive-behavioural studies

(0.63) was significantly higher than that of medication treatments using placebo control groups (0.47), p=0.05. Mean attrition rates were higher among subjects receiving a medication intervention (20 per cent) than those receiving a cognitive-behavioural intervention (6 per cent). The control groups for cognitive-behavioural interventions (the majority of which were wait-lists) may perform worse than those for pharmacological interventions (the majority of which are pill placebos). Combined Pharmacological and Cognitive-behavioural Interventions: six of the eight studies which examined this, looked at imipramine and cognitive-behavioural interventions versus imipramine alone. There was no significant difference between the effect sizes for combined treatment (0.56), versus imipramine alone (0.55). Attrition rates were 22 per cent for both types of interventions. Long-term Outcome: The overall within-group effect size was −0.17. The values for pharmacotherapy (three studies, 363 patients), combined pharmacotherapy plus exposure (two studies, 199 patients), and cognitive-behavioural interventions (eight studies, 358 patients) were −0.46, −0.07 and +0.06 respectively. None of the differences were statistically significant.

Was any cost information reported?
Monthly costs for a typical course of treatment were estimated for both cognitive-behavioural and pharmacologic treatments. The lowest cost interventions were imipramine treatment and group cognitive-behaviour therapy, with a yearly total of approximately $600.

Author's conclusions
Both pharmacologic and cognitive-behavioural treatments offer significant advantages over control treatment. In general, cognitive-behavioural treatments yielded the largest effect sizes and the smallest attrition rates relative to pharmacotherapy and combined treatments and are cost-effective. For patients with a primary diagnosis with panic disorder, the currently available evidence confers a number of advantages for cognitive-behavioural treatment, and encourages increased clinical utilisation of these interventions.

CRD commentary
It is not clear from the search strategy whether the search was restricted to English language articles, no non-English language articles are included. Also, there is the possibility of publication bias, as there was no attempt to locate unpublished literature,

except for articles in press. No quality assessment of the included studies is reported. It would be useful to have more information about the primary studies, for example the outcome measures used, setting, follow-up. The authors have calculated an overall effect size for each study based on all of the outcome measures used in the study. However, details of what these outcomes measures are, are not given. The decision to pool a number of potentially disparate outcomes measures into one overall effect size estimate may be questionable. It would be informative to have confidence intervals around the estimated effect sizes. There are a few inconsistencies in the text and it is difficult to link the results given in the text with the tables.

Subject index terms
Subject indexing assigned by CRD: Antidepressive-Agents/ad [administration-and-dosage]; Benzodiazepines/tu [therapeutic-use]; Cognitive-therapy; Panic-Disorder/th [therapy]

Correspondence address
Dr. R. A. Gould, Behavior Therapy Unit, WACC 815, Massachusetts General Hospital, 15 Parkman Street, Boston, MA 02114, USA.

Copyright: University of York, 1998. Database no.: DARE-968034
Abstract taken from DARE and edited.

the likelihood of bias. It contains sections relating to the review question(s), inclusion/exclusion criteria, literature searching, assessing study validity, data extraction, data synthesis and plans for dissemination of the findings. As such it covers all stages in the review process.

Review question(s)

The main question(s) or hypotheses to be investigated in the review should be stated clearly in the protocol. Each specific question should include reference to the participants, the intervention and the outcomes of interest.

Literature searching

The aim of the literature search is to provide a comprehensive list of both published and unpublished studies of relevance to the review question(s).

Box 9.3 Stages in the systematic review process using the example of a review of 'mental health promotion in high risk groups' (NHS CRD, 1997)

Review question(s): to examine the effectiveness of interventions designed to promote mental well-being and prevent the deterioration of mental health in groups at high risk, using a range of outcomes such as self-esteem, anxiety and depression.

Literature search: search period 1980–1995, electronic databases: Medline, PsycLIT, Cinahl, Assia, Eric, Caredata, Crib, Dissertation Abstracts, Unicorn Database at the HEA and the National Database for Health Promotion in Primary Health Care. Specific search strategies were designed for each database. Hand searches of key journals, scanning of reference lists of papers retrieved and contact with experts in the field.

Inclusion criteria: participants – people at high risk of developing mental health problems such as children experiencing parental separation or divorce, children within families experiencing bereavement, adults undergoing divorce or separation, the unemployed, adults experiencing bereavement or who are long-term carers. Interventions – interventions designed to promote mental well-being and/or prevent the deterioration of mental health. Outcomes – mental health and well-being outcomes such as self-esteem, anxiety and depression. Study designs – randomised controlled trials.

Decisions about study inclusion: two reviewers.

Validity assessment: two reviewers.

Data extraction: two reviewers.

Data synthesis: qualitative narrative synthesis with study details presented in table format by target group. Children showing behavioural problems: school-based interventions and parent training programmes can improve conduct and well-being. Children of separating parents: mental health problems can be reduced by providing cognitive skills training and emotional support. Unemployed: social support and problem-solving or cognitive-behavioural training can improve mental health and employment outcomes. Long-term carers: mental health problems can be prevented by respite care and psychosocial support.

Dissemination: Effective Health Care bulletin, *Mental Health Promotion in High Risk Groups* (1997) 3 (3).

It is important to ensure that the process of identifying literature is as unbiased as possible, so as to minimise the possibility of the findings of the review being weakened through publication bias. Publication bias is the tendency for positive or interesting studies to be published more readily than studies with negative or uninteresting results. Reviews which fail to search for unpublished studies are therefore at risk of presenting a biased (overoptimistic) summary of the body of primary research (Egger and Davey Smith, 1995).

Electronic databases such as Medline, Embase and PsycLIT are available for searching using specially designed search strategies. Examples of search strategies for retrieving randomised controlled trials can be found in the Appendix of CRD Guidelines (NHS Centre for Reviews and Dissemination, 1996). In addition to electronic searching it is recommended that other forms of study identification are also carried out. This can involve scanning the reference lists of articles already located through database searches, handsearching of key journals in the field and contact with experts who may be aware of very recent studies or unpublished (grey literature) articles such as those from conference proceedings, university theses and commissioned reports. There are also several electronic databases which index grey literature, such as SIGLE (System for Information on Grey Literature) and DHSS-Data.

Inclusion/exclusion criteria

The inclusion criteria are used to select the primary studies for inclusion in the review. Predetermined selection criteria are specified so as to reduce the possibility of *post hoc* 'selection bias' which can occur if no predetermined criteria are stated (for example in the form of only including those studies which indicate positive results). Two basic criteria are usually specified: (a) relating to relevance to the review question(s) and (b) to study design. A third criterion (c) relating to the inclusion of foreign language articles should also be considered.

RELEVANCE

Selection criteria relating to relevance usually includes a definition of the intervention(s) of interest, the specific patient or client group and the outcome measures used to assess the effectiveness of the intervention.

STUDY DESIGN

Additional selection criteria specify the type of study design that will be included in the review, for example randomised controlled trials (RCTs), quasi-experimental studies or before and after studies.

FOREIGN LANGUAGE RESTRICTIONS

Decisions relating to the inclusion of non-English language studies should be stated in the protocol. Sometimes foreign language papers are excluded because of the resources available for translation. However, the exclusion of non-English language papers may introduce bias, and where feasible all relevant papers should be included, regardless of language. Empirical evidence suggests that language bias can influence the results of a systematic review. For example, studies with positive or interesting results are more likely to be published in English language journals – and the exclusion of foreign language studies can introduce a form of publication bias (Egger *et al.*, 1997).

Making decisions about study inclusion

Even with explicit inclusion criteria decisions concerning the inclusion or exclusion of specific studies remain subjective and susceptible to bias. The validity of the decision-making process can be increased if all studies are independently assessed for inclusion by more than one reviewer. Any disagreements should be discussed and resolved by consensus, referring back to the review protocol if necessary.

Validity assessment

Those studies selected for inclusion in the review are assessed for validity so as to rank them according to the reliability of their findings. Primary studies can be graded into a hierarchy according to their design (see Box 9.4). This hierarchy reflects the degree to which different study designs are susceptible to bias. Ideally a review should concentrate on studies which provide the strongest form of evidence.

In addition to ranking types of studies, each included study should be critically appraised to assess the strength of its design and analysis. A number of different checklists are available for assessing the quality of different study designs (for example see Moher *et al.*, 1995). Again, as with assessing studies for inclusion, validity assessment can be subject to bias.

Box 9.4   Example of a hierarchy of evidence

I   Well-designed randomised controlled trial
II–1a   Well-designed controlled trial with
          pseudo-randomisation
II–1b   Well-designed controlled trial with no
          randomisation
II–2a   Well-designed cohort (prospective study) with
          concurrent controls
II–2b   Well-designed cohort (prospective study) with
          historical controls
II–2c   Well-designed cohort (retrospective study) with
          concurrent controls
II–3   Well-designed case-control (retrospective) study
III   Comparisons between times and/or places with and
          without intervention (in some circumstances this
          may be equivalent to level I or II)
IV   Opinions of respected authorities based on clinical
          experience; descriptive studies and reports of
          expert committees

Source: From NHS CRD (1996).

Independent assessment by more than one reviewer can help to reduce such bias.

Data extraction

Data extraction forms are designed to ensure that all the necessary data from each study are extracted in a standard format. The data to be extracted usually includes bibliographic details, descriptions of the setting and study population, details of the exact form and delivery of the intervention, the outcome measures used and the results. In addition information about the number of participants in each group, the rate of drop-out, the study methodology and any other factors likely to affect the validity of the results should be noted. This information is used in the critical appraisal of each included study.

Data extraction can be prone to error, so where feasible data extraction should be performed independently by two people and the level of agreement assessed. Any disagreements should be discussed and resolved by consensus.

Data synthesis

There are two approaches that can be used in synthesising the results of the primary studies: a qualitative (narrative) overview or a formal statistical pooling (meta-analysis). A qualitative approach considers all study results, taking into account their methodological rigour. Other key elements and how such elements might affect outcomes are also explored, for example characteristics of study participants, interventions and settings, and the robustness of the outcome measures themselves. A qualitative synthesis is unlikely to report an estimate of the average effect of the intervention, but in some circumstances it can reliably inform on the effectiveness of a particular intervention.

In contrast a formal meta-analysis pools or combines estimates of the intervention effect from each study and so does produce an average effect size. However, a statistical pooling should really only be carried out within the framework of a qualitative overview. A qualitative assessment can highlight differences between studies and guide decisions about whether statistical pooling is appropriate when studies are particularly heterogeneous. There are a number of sources available for further information about data synthesis (see Laird and Mosteller, 1990; Cooper and Hedges, 1994; Slavin, 1995). See also CRD Guidelines for further references (NHS Centre for Reviews and Dissemination, 1996).

Writing up the results and dissemination of the findings

It is important that the report of the review communicates the purpose, methods, findings and implications in a clear and concise way. Once the report has been finalised, including peer review by both topic experts and potential users, the results need to be effectively disseminated to the relevant audiences (see Oxman *et al.*, 1995). This can also include dissemination to relevant patient groups.

STRENGTHS AND LIMITATIONS OF SYSTEMATIC REVIEWS

The task of summarising the research literature

Despite the efforts of reviewers in recent years, the task of summarising the available research evidence in a systematic way is still far from complete. We still do not know what works, what helps or what harms in many areas of health care, including mental health. These gaps in the knowledge base in health care in general and mental health in particular are still apparent for a number of reasons. First, the preceding discussion illustrates the substantial effort required to undertake a systematic review – they require time, resources and skills. The task of summarising all the available RCTs in health care has, for better or for worse, been likened to the human genome project (Naylor, 1995). There are still many important areas of genuine clinical uncertainty where there is not as yet a systematic review to provide an answer. As the body of primary research is summarised it will become apparent what we know and what we don't in the field of mental health.

It would be naive to believe that systematic reviews are going to provide all the answers to what works and what does not. Often, systematic reviews are unable to provide a firm conclusion – either positive or negative. In many cases, the primary research evidence is of insufficient quality or includes insufficient numbers of participants to allow us to know what the truth is. When a systematic review fails to provide an answer, this should not be seen as a failing of systematic reviews *per se*, but rather a more honest reflection of the real state of the research knowledge base. This is preferable to the creation of spurious certainty, which is often found in traditional review articles. An important function of systematic reviews is therefore to determine the limits of our knowledge and to inform the research agenda. It is therefore timely that major research funding organisations such as the UK Medical Research Council (MRC) now require that a systematic review be undertaken before primary research is funded. In such cases, systematic reviews perform two functions: first, the replication of unnecessary research is prevented when a systematic review is able to provide a sufficient answer. Second, when further research is justified through conducting a systematic review, then investigators will be able to learn from previous mistakes in the research literature. Gaps in the knowledge base identified in this way will hopefully ensure that subsequent research is correctly designed to answer specific questions that are of relevance to practitioners, policy-makers and patients.

Abuses of systematic reviews

Just as there can be poor-quality primary research, there can be poor-quality systematic reviews. Fortunately, guides are available to allow the reader to distinguish 'good-quality' from 'poor quality' reviews. An example of simple questions which can be used to help guide the critical reading of a review and to allow the reader to decide whether the

Box 9.5   Questions to guide the critical appraisal of a systematic review

Are the results valid and believable?
- Is the research question stated and clearly focused?
- Are the inclusion criteria stated explicitly and are they appropriate?
- Is the search for relevant studies thorough?
- Is the validity of the individual studies assessed?
- Were the results similar from study to study?
- Were reasons for differences between studies explored?

What are the results?
- What are the overall results of the systematic review?
- How precise were the results?

Are the results useful to me?
- Can the results be applied to my patients or my clinical problem?
- Were all important outcomes assessed?
- Are the benefits worth the harms and costs?

Source: Adapted from Oxman et al. (1994).

conclusions of the review are believable and valid are given in Box 9.5 (Oxman *et al.*, 1994).

Poor-quality reviews are often ones where authors try to make more of the primary research evidence than is justified. For example, individual primary studies identified for inclusion can be different in terms of the interventions delivered and the patients that are included. Pooling such studies is generally not appropriate and represents an abuse of some of the statistical techniques that are available. A more appropriate and considered approach might be to acknowledge these fundamental differences and produce a narrative summary of the results of individual studies and compare them in a qualitative way, rather than to produce some (meaningless) summary statistic using meta-analytic techniques. Similarly, a systematic search of the research literature might only reveal primary research that is of poor quality and which is open to many biases. In these cases, the appropriate conclusion of a review would be that the research evidence is of insufficient quality to make any conclusion and that more (primary) research is justified. Authors have been known to apply meta-analytic techniques to such data, producing spurious certainty and more precise, but still biased, estimates of effect (Egger *et al.*, 1998).

An example of a review, which, in our view, over-ambitiously applies meta-analytic synthesis to poor-quality primary research, is one by Didden *et al.* (1997). The authors of the review attempt to evaluate the overall effectiveness of all treatments for 'problem behaviours' amongst individuals with 'mental retardation'. Broad inclusion criteria are adopted in that studies of any treatment, for any form of mental retardation, using any research design are selected for the review. The vast majority of 482 included empirical studies are case series reports or employ quasi-experimental methods which are open to numerous biases (see Box 9.4). Data from 1,451 individual interventions are pooled in the hope of establishing the true effect through increasing statistical power. Whilst the authors, in their discussion, do acknowledge that the methodological limitations of their primary data might have introduced bias, they clearly believe that pooling is the best approach. A more measured analysis of the data in this important area might have been to include only studies of similar methodological quality. Alternatively, the authors might state that the application of a systematic review methodology reveals the poor quality of the available research and that good-quality primary research is needed.

Gaps in the primary knowledge base

The examples of good-quality systematic reviews which we have presented, such as those included in DARE and those undertaken within the Cochrane Collaboration, are purposely chosen to highlight the diverse areas of mental health practice and policy which have been evaluated using this methodology. However, it might be the case that as researchers continue to look for high-quality research evidence to support or refute current practice, relative imbalances will emerge. In the area of mental health, for example, there may be more high-quality primary research which evaluates drug-based therapies than, say, psychodynamic psychotherapies. Systematic reviews cannot produce a conclusion when an area is under-researched or evaluated using biased research methodologies. An example of this relative imbalance and one such important gap in the knowledge base is given below.

Drug-based treatments have to be evaluated using rigorous methodologies as part of their product licensing process, whereas there is no such requirement for psychosocial interventions. Drug companies are able to fund this research by recouping development costs within the price of successful products. Unfortunately, no comparable source of income is available to evaluate psychosocial interventions. Indirect evidence for the predominance of (often commercially sponsored) primary research evidence into drug-based therapies comes from research by the US-based Agency for Health Care Policy and Research (AHCPR). This organisation has sought to produce evidence-based guidelines for a number of conditions, including depression and schizophrenia. In the case of schizophrenia, thirty specific recommendations were made where there was sufficient evidence to support a specific component of therapy and care (Lehman, 1998). Of these thirty, only six were psychosocial interventions, the rest relating to drug-based treatments (e.g. dosage, timing and choice of drug). This imbalance reflects a relative absence of high-quality research evidence that has been undertaken to investigate commonly used psycho-social interventions in the management of schizophrenia (Hargreaves, 1998). The extent to which many psychosocial interventions have been adequately evaluated using valid research methods will only become apparent as the research literature is subjected to the process of systematic review. Once again, systematic review will play an important part in defining the limits of our knowledge in mental health and in informing the research agenda.

A further source of ongoing debate surrounds what sort of evidence or methodology is appropriate or most valid in the evaluation of psychosocial or organisational interventions. The problems of applying RCT method-ologies in the evaluation of, for example, psychological therapies are discussed elsewhere in this text (see Chapters 6 and 8). Further, the role of qualitative methodologies is not yet well addressed within systematic reviews (see Chapter 7). A rigid adherence to the evidence hierarchy outlined in Box 9.4 is likely to mean that the primary research knowledge base for many interventions is shown to be 'poor'. Such hierarchies have helped produce a common agreement about what constitutes good and poor evidence, but they should not stifle debate about how they should be applied in other areas. By summarising the primary research literature in a transparent and explicit way, we can hope that systematic reviews will contribute to this debate.

Making sure the right questions are asked

Even when good-quality research has been carried out, it is unfortunate that in many cases studies have been designed to answer questions that have little direct relevance to routine clinical practice or policy. Further, studies often employ outcome measures that are of little direct relevance to routine care and are not those which patients, clinicians or policy-makers would choose to measure. For example, a recent systematic review of a new drug treatment for schizophrenia, risperidone, reveals that, despite large numbers of primary studies and participants, the research is not designed to answer questions which might be of interest to clinicians, policy-makers or those with schizophrenia. Studies that have been conducted (largely by the pharmaceutical industry), are short term and fail to measure outcomes or end-points which are of real clinical relevance, such as whether the drug helps people to remain well, out of hospital and with a reasonable quality of life (Kennedy *et al.*, 1998; see also Baker and Kleijnan, Chapter 2, this volume).

Systematic reviews can help to ensure that questions that are of more direct relevance to 'stakeholders' are asked from the outset. Representatives, including practitioners, policy-makers, patients and carers can be included on review advisory panels, and can comment on review protocols to ensure that important questions are asked of the primary research. When primary research in important areas of practice and policy fails to provide answers to questions which are of direct relevance to 'stakeholders' to answer these questions, then the limits of our knowledge are defined in an explicit way. This can be used to justify further primary research which is designed to answer important and relevant questions. Furthermore, primary research often fails to give prime emphasis to outcomes that are of more direct relevance, but which have none the less been measured. By extracting these data across studies, systematic reviews can provide information that is of more direct relevance to the various stakeholders.

Translating research into a usable form

Research is often overly technical and is difficult to translate into routine clinical practice and policy. As previously noted, interesting outcomes are often buried within the results sections of original papers and results are expressed in complex mathematical terms. Systematic reviews provide an opportunity to translate the (unnecessarily) complex and technical language of research into that which might be readily understood by patients, carers, practitioners and policy-makers alike. For example, the use of intuitive statistics such as 'numbers needed to treat' allows statistically significant results (usually expressed as 'p values') to be translated into clinically meaningful terms (Cook and Sackett, 1995). The example of the review of family interventions in schizophrenia (Mari and Streiner, 1996) given in Box 9.1 expresses benefit in terms of the numbers of families who would need to receive this intervention in order to prevent one relapse or episode of hospitalisation. Further, when reports are compiled, the main results can be expressed with a number of perspectives in mind. Reviews produced by the Cochrane Schizophrenia Group are prepared with a specific summary section aimed at people with schizophrenia and their carers, as well as sections aimed at practitioners and policy-makers. The systematic review of the new atypical anti-schizophrenia drug risperidone (Kennedy *et al.*, 1998) includes such a section, which communicates potential benefits (patients in studies experienced slightly fewer symptoms associated with schizophrenia), as well as potential adverse effects (patients were more likely to experience severe weight gain with this drug), in a language which patients and carers find understandable. Asking carers of people with schizophrenia to comment upon draft versions of reviews and encouraging reviewers to communicate information in this way ensures this process (Dr Clive Adams, personal communication).

Other initiatives have sought to explicitly translate complex systematic reviews into 'evidence-based' patient information leaflets. These initiatives include leaflets about pregnancy (such as foetal monitoring, routine ultrasound scans and the consumption of alcohol), cataract and glue ear (see NHS CRD for more information about the infomed choice initiative.) In addition, there are other initiatives, such as the Centre for Health Information Quality (CHIQ) which has been set up with the specific remit of supporting the development of evidence-based information for patients as part of the UK NHS Patient Partnership Strategy (www.centreforhiq. demon.co.uk).

As yet there have been few initiatives to produce evidence-based information for patients with mental health problems, but this is a potential future development which could be applied in the field of mental health.

Reaching the target audience

It is important that the findings from systematic reviews are disseminated to the relevant target audiences so that both practice and policy can be changed in line with the evidence. As such, dissemination is viewed as a crucial step in the process of achieving evidence-based practice. Dissemination can be seen to embrace a spectrum of activity with more traditional activities at one end, geared towards raising awareness of research evidence, to implementation activities at the other end, concerned with changing practice. Effective dissemination requires a systematic approach which addresses the needs of the target audience(s). For a (non-systematic) review about designing and disseminating effective materials aimed at changing health care providers' behaviour, see Kanouse *et al.* (1995). The NHS Centre for Reviews and Dissemination has also published a recent Effective Health Care bulletin *Getting Evidence into Practice* (NHS CRD, 1999), which focuses on dissemination and implementation strategies for changing professional practice.

CONCLUSIONS

Systematic reviews have moved us beyond the traditional narrative review. Important initiatives have come about in recent years, such as the Cochrane Collaboration and the Database of Systematic Reviews of Effectiveness – which have made the findings of systematic reviews more accessible to practitioners, policy-makers, patients and their carers. In many important areas of practice it is now clear what works, what doesn't and what causes actual harm. Furthermore, key areas of clinical uncertainty have been identified, which can only be rectified or addressed by good-quality primary research. Completion of the systematic review is a necessary, but not complete, step in ensuring that research knowledge is translated into clinical practice. The dissemination of research evidence to relevant target audiences is a crucial step in ensuring that practice changes in line with emerging evidence. Research-based patient information leaflets are as yet a relatively under-used developed source of dissemination in mental health, but might be an important area for future development directive.

ACKNOWLEDGEMENTS

We thank Paul Wilson for his comments on an earlier draft of this chapter and thank Professor Jair Mari for permission to include the abstract of his review of family therapy in schizophrenia.

REFERENCES

Altman, D.G. (1994) The scandal of poor medical research. *British Medical Journal*, 308: 283–284.

Bero, L. and D. Rennie (1995) The Cochrane Collaboration: preparing, maintaining and disseminating systematic reviews of the effects of health care. *Journal of the American Medical Association*, 274: 1935–1938.

Chalmers, I. *et al.* (1993) Preparing and updating systematic reviews of randomized controlled trials of health care. *Milbank Quarterly*, 71: 411–437.

Cook, D. and Sackett, D.L. (1995) The number needed to treat: a clinically useful measure of treatment effect. *British Medical Journal*, 310: 452–454.

Cooper, H. and Hedges, L.V. (eds) (1994) *The Handbook of Research Synthesis*. New York: Russell Sage Foundation.

Didden, R. *et al.* (1997) Meta-analytic study on treatment effectiveness for problem behaviors with individuals who have mental retardation. *America Journal of Mental Retardation*, 101: 387–399.

Egger, M. and Davey Smith, G.D. (1995) Misleading meta-analysis. *British Medical Journal*, 310: 752–754.

Egger, M., Zellweger-Zahner, T., Schneider, M., Junker, C., Lengeler, C. and Antes, G. (1997) Language bias in randomised controlled trials published in English and German. *Lancet*, 350: 326–329.

Egger, M. *et al.* (1998) Spurious precision? Meta-analysis of observational studies. *British Medical Journal*, 316: 140–144.

Glass, G.V. (1976) Primary, secondary, and meta-analysis of research. *Educational Research* 5: 3–8.

Hargreaves, W.A. (1998) Commentary on – The schizophrenia Patient Outcomes Research Team (PORT) treatment recommendations. *Schizophrenia Bulletin*, 24: 23–24.

Kanouse, D.E., Kallick, J.D., Kahan, J.P. (1995) Dissemination of effectiveness and outcomes research. *Health Policy*, 34: 167–192.

Kennedy, E. *et al.* (1998) Risperidone versus 'conventional' antipsychotic medication for schizophrenia (Cochrane Review). *The Cochrane Library*, Issue 3. Oxford: Update Software.

Laird, N.M. and Mosteller, F. (1990) Some statistical methods for combining experimental results. *International Journal of Technology Assessment in Health Care*, 6: 5–30.

Lehman, A.F. (1998) Translating research into practice: the schizophrenia Patient Outcomes Research Team (PORT) treatment recommendations. *Schizophrenia Bulletin*, 24: 1–10.

Mari, J.J. and Streiner, D. (1996) Family intervention for those with schizophrenia. Schizophrenia module of The Cochrane Database of Systematic Reviews. Updated 6 June 1996. Oxford: Update Software.

Moher, D. *et al.* (1995) Assessing the quality of randomised controlled trials: an annotated bibliography of scales and check lists. *Controlled Clinical Trials*, 16: 62–73.

Mulrow, C.D. (1987) The medical review article: state of the science. *Annals of Internal Medicine*, 106: 485–488.

Mulrow, C.D. (1994) Rationale for systematic reviews. *British Medical Journal*, 309: 597–599.

Naylor, C.D. (1995) Grey zones of clinical practice: some limits to evidence based medicine. *Lancet*, 345: 840–842.

NHS Centre for Reviews and Dissemination (1996) *Undertaking Systematic Reviews of Research on Effectiveness: CRD Guidelines for those Carrying Out or Commissioning Reviews*. CRD Report 4. York: University of York.

NHS CRD (1997) *Mental Health Promotion in High Risk Groups*. Effective Health Care Bulletin 3 (3): York: University of York.

NHS CRD (1999) *Getting Evidence into Practice*. Effective Health Care Bulletin 5(1). York: University of York.

Oxman, A.D. *et al.* (1994) Users' guide to the medical literature, VI. How to use an overview. Evidence-Based Medicine Working Group. *Journal of the American Medical Association*, 272: 1367–1371.

Oxman, A.D. *et al.* (1995) No magic bullets: a systematic review of 102 trials of interventions to improve professional practice. *Canadian Medical Association Journal*, 153: 1423–1431.

Sheldon, T. and Chalmers, I. (1994) The UK Cochrane Centre and the NHS Centre for Reviews and Dissemination: respective roles within the information systems strategy of the NHS R&D programme, co-ordination and principles underlying collaboration. *Health Economics*, 3: 201–203.

Slavin, R.E. (1995) Best evidence synthesis: an intelligent alternative to meta-analysis. *Journal of Clinical Epidemiology*, 48: 9–18.

Chapter 10

Clinical practice guidelines development in evidence-based psychotherapy

John Cape and Glenys Parry

INTRODUCTION

Psychotherapy encompasses a diverse range of activity. All psychotherapies have in common a systematic intervention, based on explicit
psychological principles, to improve health, well-being or self-efficacy
through the medium of a personal relationship. Beyond those commonalities, diversity reigns – in methods, theories, purposes, goals, client
groups – to the extent that practitioners have few agreed, overarching
principles. There is a plethora of training routes, and people practising
psychotherapy in the NHS often have diverse backgrounds in psychology,
medicine or nursing before training in psychotherapy. Practitioners tend
to hold strong allegiances to their own psychotherapeutic methods, and
many, if not most, remain ignorant of, or sceptical about, the large and
growing body of research findings.

Given this degree of pluralism, a common basis for psychotherapeutic
practice in evidence of what are effective, and shared, research-derived
understandings of process, seems, on the face of it, highly desirable.
Clinical practice guidelines hold enormous promise in fostering an
evidence-based approach to psychotherapy, but, given the state of the art
in relating research to psychotherapy practice, they have inevitable pitfalls.
Their development in this field is difficult and controversial, but, we shall
argue, immensely worthwhile.

Clinical practice guidelines have been promoted in the UK and USA
as a way of improving clinical effectiveness and reducing variation in
standards and outcomes of medical care. The UK Department of Health
has strongly endorsed their development and use, and has funded a
programme led in part through the medical Royal Colleges and other
professional bodies (Department of Health, 1996a). The establishment of
the National Institute for Clinical Excellence (NICE) in 1999 was intended

to carry forward programmes in evidence-based health care and to systematise initiatives. In the USA, the Agency for Health Care Policy and Research (AHCPR), funded by Federal Government, has organised a major national development and dissemination programme of clinical practice guidelines, including an electronic clearing house for evidence-based guidelines around the world (available on the World Wide Web at http://www.ahcpr.gov/clinic/ngcfact.htm).

Within this context, the development of guidelines in psychotherapeutic topics is relatively recent. In this chapter we explain what guidelines are, their purpose, methods of development and quality criteria. We also state the case *against* developing guidelines in this field, and attempt to address these objections. Finally, we give examples of guidelines of different types that have been developed, or are in the process of development, and sketch a possible future for guidelines development in this field.

WHAT ARE CLINICAL PRACTICE GUIDELINES?

Clinical practice guidelines, often in the UK shortened to 'clinical guidelines', are decision-making tools to assist in clinical decisions. The standard definition from the Institute of Medicine is that clinical practice guidelines are '*systematically developed statements to assist practitioner and patient decisions about appropriate health care for specific clinical circumstances*' (Field and Lohr, 1990, our emphasis). It is important to note that they are designed for use by practitioners and patients, and also that they are discretionary ('to assist decisions') and not mandatory. As any decision-making tool, they may be deemed useful by practitioners and adopted, or may not and be discarded. They are not management tools to define what clinicians should and should not do, nor commissioning tools to define what services should be purchased. However, some clinicians may decide to use a particular guideline and to audit their treatment against the guideline.

Any clinical circumstance can in principle be the subject of a guideline. Most common in medical and general mental health settings have been condition-based guidelines (e.g. assessment and management of depression in primary care: AHCPR, 1993a–d) and problem-based guidelines (e.g. management of violence in clinical settings: Royal College of Psychiatrists, 1997). The guideline sets out the specific clinical *process* that will lead to optimal *outcomes* for the specific circumstances and patients under consideration.

A guideline may vary in length from a sheet of A4 to a short book. Commonly both a brief practitioner desk-top version and a longer version with a summary of the evidence are produced. In general medical (family) practice, where there is a particular need for ready access to decision-making tools, computerised decision support versions of guidelines are being explored. Where relevant, it is recommended that patient versions of the guidelines are produced. The AHCPR depression in primary care guideline comprises a thirty-page A6 patient version, a twenty-page A5 practitioner version, and two 150-page full text versions.

Clinical practice guidelines differ from traditional literature reviews, chapters and textbooks in the manner of their construction. Their development is systematic and explicit, usually involving a representative guideline development group and a systematic approach to identifying, evaluating and incorporating evidence in the guideline.

Clinical guidelines may be developed either by local groups of clinicians or by national bodies and agencies. There is evidence that locally produced guidelines are more likely to be followed, although nationally produced guidelines are more likely to be valid (Grimshaw and Russell, 1993b). A common recommendation is that national and local efforts should be co-ordinated, with local clinicians adapting national guidelines to local circumstances.

Clinical practice guidelines are primarily advocated as a method to improve the effectiveness and appropriateness of health care. In medicine the performance of individual doctors is frequently found to be outdated and sub-standard compared to optimum care, when an agreed standard of optimum care is established (Ramsey et al., 1991; Sackett et al., 1997). The advice of clinical experts in textbooks and literature reviews is frequently inconsistent and in disagreement (Sackett et al., 1997) and is also at variance with systematic reviews of the evidence (Antman et al., 1992). Systematically developed evidence-based clinical practice guidelines are proposed as a more valid guide to clinicians, and the utilisation of such guidelines should result in better health outcomes for patients. Evidence that clinical practice guidelines can have this effect has been systematically reviewed by Grimshaw and Russell (1993a).

A secondary, less commonly noted purpose of clinical practice guidelines can be to promote equity in provision of treatment. Clinicians are often in the position of controlling access to valued treatments, and their decisions may be influenced by systematic biases (especially educational level and socio-economic status) rather than evidence-based criteria. Psychotherapy is such a valued treatment, and studies from the USA have noted the association of assessment of suitability for psychotherapy with the YAVIS factors (young, attractive, verbal, intelligent, single) and with ethnicity (Garfield, 1986; Weber *et al.*, 1985).

HOW ARE THEY DEVELOPED?

The emphasis of the national clinical practice guidelines programme in both the UK and the USA is on using systematic reviews of research evidence and, in particular, of randomised controlled trials as the basis of clinical guidelines, and then moderating and supplementing the research evidence against panels of expert clinicians and often also patients. Thus primacy is given to research evidence, but moderated in the light of consensual evidence and the preferences of service users.

Clinical practice guidelines, in order to be valid and helpful for practitioners and patients, need correctly to define the clinical practices that lead to optimal health outcomes. This raises questions of what are appropriate outcomes for psychotherapy and how best to evaluate evidence for the effectiveness of different clinical practices in psychotherapy. In medicine, symptom change, change in the underlying pathological disease process, and quality of life may all be relevant outcomes, depending on the particular circumstances.

In psychotherapy, brief cognitive behaviour and supportive therapies usually focus on symptom alleviation, while longer-term psychoanalytic psychotherapies more commonly target internal psychodynamic change, a measure of the underlying psychopathological process, and interpersonal change (Lambert and Hill, 1994; Malan, 1973; Mintz, 1981). In relation to clinical practice guidelines, it is consequently important to clarify the outcomes relevant for the specific clinical circumstances and interventions under consideration. The first step in a development process is therefore to agree the scope of the guideline, in terms of clinical circumstances, diagnoses or presenting problems, interventions and outcomes.

Summaries of research evidence can then be prepared, critically appraised and organised into the form of recommendations. The strength of research evidence for a given recommendation should be indicated.

Panels of clinicians can be established, using explicit selection criteria, to review the research evidence and address recommendations in areas where the research evidence is lacking or where clinical practice widely differs from a research-based recommendation. Such clinicians may be either well-respected skilled and experienced practitioners or the agreed experts in the field. A number of structured consensus methods are available to establish strength of agreement and to facilitate agreement

(Linstone and Turoff, 1975; Olson, 1995; Scott and Black, 1991; Woolf, 1992). Such structured consensus methods are important given the evidence about the inaccuracy of unstructured group decisions (Gigone and Hastie, 1997). This field of research is reviewed by Murphy *et al.* (1998) who make recommendations for the use of consensus methods in clinical guideline development.

Establishing consensus between psychotherapists about appropriate clinical practice is also not easy. The history of psychotherapy has been marked more by theoretical divisions and divergence than consensus, although some commentators perceive a recent trend towards convergence (Garfield and Bergin, 1994; Norcross and Goldfried, 1992). The tradition of autonomy of psychotherapy, with its strong individual private practice base and lack of dependence on third party or public reimbursement schemes, contains no particular incentive for agreeing common methods of practice. The valuable and special focus of psychotherapists on the uniqueness of the individual patient inevitably draws attention to differences between patients rather than to the commonalities of patients and treatment processes which are the necessary basis of agreement about practice. Together these factors contribute to a climate where consensus can be difficult to achieve.

Although a set of research-based and consensually agreed recommendations can be derived without input from patients, it is important to involve service users in the process of guideline development. Clinical guidelines, in order to be effective, need to be acceptable to and reflect the views of patients. A well-designed guideline will ensure that the health outcomes aimed for are those that are valued by patients (Duff *et al.*, 1996). At an individual level, choices available for a patient should be made explicit. For example, the Royal College of Psychiatrists monograph on clinical practice guidelines (Marriott and Lelliott, 1994) suggests that where the evidence indicates that a form of psychotherapy and antidepressant medication are equally effective, then a clinical guideline for depression should indicate that patient preference should guide choice of treatment.

What evidence is used on which to base the clinical practice recommendations will vary on the nature of the total evidence available. Of necessity in the psychotherapies, where there is often limited research evidence, there will be more dependence on consensual evidence than in some other areas. This is in part because of limited historic research funding and also because of intrinsic research design difficulties for some key questions. In the psychotherapies, there is a relative lack of large-scale primary empirical research compared to many areas of clinical medicine which benefit both from commercial research funding from drug companies and from funding from specialist research charities. The empirical research on psychotherapy that is conducted is heavily concentrated on brief and structured forms of psychotherapy (Bergin and Garfield, 1994; Roth and Fonagy, 1996). Thus there is both an overall lack of major empirical research in the psychotherapies and specific lacunae on empirical research on particular kinds of psychotherapies, especially longer ones. In addition, there is disagreement among psychotherapists as to appropriate research methodologies and even as to the validity of empirical research on psychotherapy at all. For example, the classical randomised controlled trial has major limitations in this field (Aveline *et al.*, 1995; see also Chapters 6, 7 and 8 in this volume) and, although there are a number of alternative methods of addressing effectiveness, the RCT is still seen as the gold standard in evidence-based health care. What is important is that the nature and strength of the evidence for each recommendation in the clinical guideline is made explicit. This allows those using the guideline to be clear on the evidence base and reasons for each recommendation.

ADDRESSING THE CASE AGAINST GUIDELINES DEVELOPMENT

There is considerable unease amongst psychotherapy practitioners about the wisdom of emphasising research and developing guidelines for practice. Ferguson and Russell point out that disproportionate emphasis on guidelines can result in a mechanistic approach (Chapter 3). Other major criticisms of guidelines can be summarised as follows:

- The research evidence is misleading, incomplete, and unfairly favours some approaches at the expense of others.
- Clinical judgements in psychotherapy cannot be reduced to algorithmic procedures. Guidelines unfairly favour those types of therapy which can most readily be so reduced.
- Guidelines can and will be used prescriptively by non-clinicians, for example as evidence in legal proceedings against practitioners, and as a basis for deciding which psychotherapeutic approaches to fund.

None of these objections is without some grain of truth, and each should be taken seriously, but they do not compel us to reject the development of practice guidelines and hence lose their benefits. We briefly sketch a response to these points.

- Although most research has been conducted in brief structured treatments (such as cognitive behavioural therapy), there is a respectable and growing body of work in other approaches, including longer-term therapy and psychoanalytic therapy. There is no reason in principle why good research should not be conducted in all forms of psychotherapy, and the publication of research-based guidelines will act as a spur to encourage such research. Where research is lacking, the inclusion of a process of clinical consensus should always include practitioners from all approaches.
- It is a profound misunderstanding to see a clinical guideline as an algorithmic replacement for complex clinical judgements. They are primarily an aide-memoire to help practitioners when making judgements. Clinicians retain both clinical freedom to do something different, and responsibility for their judgements. This point is strongly made by advocates of evidence-based medicine (Sackett et al., 1996) and is the policy of the Department of Health (1996a).
- There are reasonable and unreasonable uses of guidelines. The wrong use of them is not in itself an argument against them, any more than the wrong use of a car to ram-raid a shop window is an argument against the manufacture of cars. However, it is not unreasonable for those commissioning services to take account of all available sources of evidence in assessing need for services. Equally, guidelines can be used in medico-legal contexts in the same way as other evidence (e.g. expert witness evidence) relating to established standards of practice. In both cases, however, users should be aware of the degree of uncertainty that underlies recommendations, because of uncertainties in scientific evidence, biases in guideline development and patient heterogeneity (Woolf, 1998).

WHAT MAKES A GOOD GUIDELINE?

Desirable attributes of clinical practice guidelines have been suggested by the Institute of Medicine (Field and Lohr, 1992), the McMaster group (Hayward and Laupacis, 1993) and in the UK Effective Health Care Bulletin on Clinical Guidelines (Effective Health Care, 1994). The latter are usefully summarised in the Department of Health clinical guidelines document (Department of Health, 1996a). Key attributes of a good guideline are that the guideline:

- *Covers a significant topic*: topics for clinical guidelines, as topics for clinical audit, should address areas where clinical decisions are likely to have a significant impact on health care. This may be because they are common, resource intensive, have a significant impact on morbidity or where there is evidence of wide variation in practice (Department of Health, 1996a).
- *Includes a clear definition of the clinical circumstances covered by the guideline*: the patient populations and specific clinical circumstances covered by the guideline need to be unambiguously defined so that those using the guideline can be clear as to when and with what patients to use it.
- *Is based on a systematic and representative development process*: the guideline should be developed by a representative multi-professional group including patient representatives where appropriate, and be developed through a systematic structured development process. Ideally the methods of development should be described in the guideline document to allow others to understand how the recommendations in the guideline were derived.
- *Is soundly evidence based*: whether the recommendations are based on research evidence or on structured consensus, the specific evidence base and strength of evidence for each recommendation should be clearly specified.
- *Is user friendly*: clear, unambiguous language, understandable to practitioners and, where appropriate, patients, and easy to follow formats are used.

Several instruments incorporating desirable attributes into specific standards have been developed to evaluate clinical guidelines formally (Field and Lohr, 1992; Cluzeau *et al.*, 1997; Sutton, 1996).

MAKING GUIDELINES WORK

There is little purpose in developing guidelines if they are not used. Guidelines may not be used because the recommendations in the guidelines are not accepted by practitioners, because they are not sufficiently understood, or because there is some memory or other impediment to using the guideline when appropriate. Different strategies are needed in each of these circumstances.

Grimshaw and Russell (1994) have summarised evidence on strategies that facilitate the use of guidelines by clinicians. Ownership and hence use of guidelines may be facilitated by clinicians being involved themselves in the development of a guideline, or in adaptation of an existing guideline to local circumstances, or in derivation of local audit criteria for an existing guideline. Education about a guideline and its use appears to be helpful. Systems to remind clinicians when a guideline might be relevant (e.g. tagging patient files for whom the guideline might be appropriate) also appear to have some effect. There is also evidence that feedback to clinicians can be helpful from clinical audit or criteria related to a clinical guideline.

Clinical guidelines are not designed to be directly audited, but the recommendations of a guideline should be capable where possible of translation into explicit audit criteria (Department of Health, 1996a; Field and Lohr, 1992). The purpose of guidelines, to assist practitioners and patients in clinical decisions, is different to the audit function of providing feedback as to whether practice has met agreed standards, but there is evidently an overlap, with guidelines being prospective (guiding practice) and audit retrospective (providing feedback on practice).

The examples of existing psychotherapy guidelines we describe in the next section have generally not been translated into auditable criteria. In addition, for some, the guideline recommendations are not sufficiently precise to be capable of translation into explicit objective audit criteria. Although we are not aware of any published examples of audit criteria for the AHCPR depression guideline (AHCPR, 1993a, 1993b, 1993c, 1993d), these recommendations lend themselves easily to derivation of audit criteria. A UK audit proforma for treatment of depression in primary care focused on anti-depressant medication and cognitive therapy, based on the UK Effective Health Care Bulletin on treatment of depression in primary care (Effective Health Care, 1993) has been produced by the Eli Lilly National Clinical Audit Centre (1996).

Since it is unlikely that a clinical guideline will be able to specify all exceptions to its applicability, then 100 per cent conformance to audit criteria derived from a guideline is not desirable and should not be expected. Both overly slavish and overly lax conformance to audit criteria from guidelines should be cause for concern.

EXAMPLES OF PSYCHOTHERAPY PRACTICE GUIDELINES

This section gives examples of guidelines that have been developed for different groups of clinicians and specific clinical circumstances.

Guidelines for the psychotherapies can be classified into those that primarily relate to assessment and triage decisions and those that primarily relate to treatment decisions. By assessment and triage is meant the process of deciding whether psychotherapy and what form of psychotherapy might be most appropriate for a patient and making a referral accordingly, a decision that will be made both by GPs and other primary referrers for psychotherapy and also by assessing psychological therapists of different kinds. Guidelines about treatment decisions are those that relate to decisions made by psychological therapists (both generic and specialist) once they have decided to treat a patient.

In addition, guidelines for psychotherapy may be condition/disorder specific (e.g. focusing on borderline personality disorder) or general and of relevance to all patients.

We give two examples of clinical guidelines for GPs and primary care practitioners on matching patients to the most appropriate treatment including psychotherapy – the AHCPR guideline on treatment of major depression in primary care (AHCPR, 1993b) and a local UK clinical guideline on counselling and psychological therapies developed for GPs by a working group of the Camden and Islington Medical Audit Advisory Group (Cape *et al.*, 1996, 1998). A third example is work in progress – a Department of Health funded project developing a national clinical guideline for the psychological therapies targeted at GPs (Parry, 1998).

Other relevant clinical guidelines on appropriateness for psychotherapy, targeted primarily at general psychiatrists, have been developed by both the American Psychiatric Association (American Psychiatric Association, 1993a, 1993b) and the Royal Australian and New Zealand College of Psychiatrists (Quality Assurance Project, 1982a, 1982b, 1991a, 1991b). These focus on specific conditions/disorders and include guidance to assist in whether to treat with medication, psychotherapy or a combination of both.

A review by Persons *et al.* (1996) compared the evaluations and recommendations regarding psychotherapy in the American Psychiatric Association (APA) guideline for depression (APA, 1993b) and the AHCPR depression guideline (AHCPR, 1993a–d) and concluded that the APA guideline significantly understated the value of the psychotherapies compared to both the AHCPR guideline and the total evidence, and in addition the APA guideline made recommendations about choosing among psychotherapies that are not well supported by empirical evidence. The authors attributed this in part to the lack of use of a multidisciplinary, representative panel in the production of the APA guidelines.

AHCPR DEPRESSION IN PRIMARY CARE GUIDELINE

The AHCPR depression in primary care guideline (AHCPR, 1993a, 1993b) was developed by a multi-professional panel of experts, including a consumer representative, for use by primary care practitioners such as GPs, family physicians, internists, nurse practitioners, mental health nurses and other workers in primary care settings. It focuses on major depressive disorder and comes in two volumes, one on detection and diagnosis (AHCPR, 1993a) and the other on treatment (AHCPR, 1993b), as well as a quick reference guide for clinicians (AHCPR, 1993c) and a patient guide (AHCPR, 1993d).

The treatment guideline (AHCPR, 1993b) considers four main treatment options – medication, psychotherapy, combination of medication and psychotherapy, and ECT. The key recommendations on selection of the first three of these options for acute phase (first line) treatment are summarised in Table 10.1.

The AHCPR depression guideline treatment recommendations were favourably reviewed by Persons *et al.* (1996), with the exception that they considered the AHCPR guideline to understate the value of psychotherapy alone in the treatment of more severely depressed out-patients. Munoz *et al.* (1994) gave a less favourable review, although their criticisms were primarily targeted at the depression guideline Quick Reference Guideline for Clinicians (AHCPR 1993c). They concluded that the careful and balanced review in the main guideline was not reflected in the quick reference guide, which in consequence misrepresents the potential significance of psychotherapy as a first-line treatment. More recently, Schulberg *et al.* (1998) reviewed research published between 1992 and 1998 to update the guideline. They concluded that new evidence suggests both antidepressant pharmacotherapy and time-limited depression-targeted psychotherapies are efficacious in primary care settings, and that in most cases the choice between these two approaches should depend on patient preference.

THE CAMDEN AND ISLINGTON MAAG LOCAL GUIDELINE ON COUNSELLING AND PSYCHOLOGICAL THERAPIES

The Camden and Islington MAAG local guideline on counselling and psychological therapies (Cape *et al.*, 1996, 1998) was produced by a multi-

Table 10.1   AHCPR recommendations on selection of treatment for
acute phase (first line) treatment

Medication:
'Patients with moderate to severe major depressive disorder are
appropriately treated with medication, whether or not formal
psychotherapy is also used' (p. 39).

Psychotherapy alone:
'Patients with mild to moderate major depression who prefer
psychotherapy alone as the initial acute treatment choice may be
treated with this option. Psychotherapy alone is not recommended
for the acute treatment of patients with severe and/or psychotic
major depressive disorders' (p. 40).

Combined medication and psychotherapy:
'Combined treatment may have an advantage for patients with partial
responses to either treatment alone (if adequately administered) and
for those with a more chronic history or poor interepisode recovery.
However, combined treatment may provide no unique advantage for
patients with uncomplicated, non-chronic major depressive disorder'
(p. 41).

*Selection of a form of psychotherapy (i.e. psychodynamic,
cognitive-behavioural, interpersonal, etc.):*
'In most cases, therapies that target depressive symptoms (cognitive
or behavioural therapy) or specific interpersonal recurrent
psychosocial problems related to the depression (interpersonal
psychotherapy) are more similar than different in efficacy.
Long-term therapies are not currently indicated as first-line acute
phase treatments for patients with major depressive disorder'
(p. 84).

Source: AHCPR (1996b)

professional group comprising GP, practice counsellor, consultant
psychotherapist, clinical psychologist and lay representative (ex-director
of local mental health charity MIND). It was designed to assist GPs and
other local health practitioners in selecting adult patients for the most
appropriate of three psychological treatments – brief counselling,
cognitive behaviour therapy and psychodynamic psychotherapy. These
three psychological treatments were selected as they were the most
commonly provided psychological treatments locally, and for the most
part took place locally in different organisational settings – brief
counselling being provided primarily by practice counsellors in GP
premises, cognitive behaviour therapy in NHS psychology departments,
and psychodynamic psychotherapy in NHS psychotherapy departments.

Thus decisions by GPs locally about suitability for these three treatments were relevant in decisions as to referral pathways.

The guideline comprises a 22-page document with three separate easy reference guideline summaries. It defines pragmatically the three treatments, restricting counselling to brief (6–12 session) counselling, cognitive behaviour therapy to simple CBT (excluding complex approaches targeted at personality disorders) and psychodynamic psychotherapy to longer-term (over six months) psychodynamic psychotherapy. Its recommendations relate to the impact of four characteristics of patients' problems (nature of major problem/disorder, chronicity, severity, complexity) and three other characteristics of patients (treatment preference, interest in self-exploration, capacity to tolerate frustration and psychic pain) on decisions about suitability for the three treatments.

NATIONAL UK CLINICAL GUIDELINE FOR THE PSYCHOTHERAPIES

As part of the Department of Health funded clinical guidelines development programme in the UK, a project has been funded to develop a clinical guideline for the psychotherapies targeted at GPs and other primary referrers for psychotherapy to help them make good decisions on which form of psychological therapy is likely to be most effective for a given problem (Parry, 1998).

The project is a collaboration of the British Psychological Society Centre for Outcomes Research and Effectiveness, the Royal College of General Practitioners Clinical Practice Guidelines Programme, the Royal College of Psychiatrists Clinical Guidelines Programme, the Royal College of Psychiatrists Psychotherapy Section, the British Association for Counselling and the Eli Lilly National Clinical Audit Centre.

Development work began by defining the scope of the guideline, which is necessarily broad, potentially including cognitive and behavioural therapies, humanistic and client-centred therapies, systemic therapies, psychodynamic therapies, integrative therapies and eclectic or pragmatic therapies. It includes depression, anxiety, social anxiety and phobias, post-traumatic disorders, eating disorders, obsessive compulsive disorders, personality disorders, and will give guidance, where enough evidence exists, on those psychosomatic conditions which GPs rate as most important for considering psychological treatment: chronic pain, chronic fatigue, gastrointestinal disorders and gynaecological problems. It excludes disorders in childhood and adolescence, psychoses including schizophrenia, mania and bipolar disorder, alcohol and other drug addictions, sexual dysfunction and paraphilia and organic brain syndromes. It also excludes consideration of non-psychological treatments, such as drug treatment.

The development group commissioned a 'meta-review' of existing reviews of research in these fields (Mackay and Barkham, 1998), supplemented by review of primary studies which were too recent to have been included in published reviews. Eight quality criteria for reviews were used as recommended by Oxman and Guyatt (1988) (see Table 10.2), and only those which met all criteria were included in considering the effectiveness of psychotherapies for specific conditions. For evidence on other variables affecting outcome, a slightly lower-quality threshold of more than six of these criteria were included. Where good-quality review evidence was not available for a major topic within the guideline, leading researchers and educators within that field were approached for expert advice on key recommendations which could be authoritatively made on the existing state of knowledge, and these were subjected to consensual review.

Research findings were supplemented by expert consensus, to translate these into realistic recommendations for clinical practice. 'Experts' were nominated by the five national psychotherapy associations; namely, the British Psychological Society, Royal College of Psychiatrists, United Kingdom Council of Psychotherapy, British Confederation of Psychotherapy and British Association for Counselling, on the basis of being recognised by peers as having expertise in this field and a willingness to work with others to develop consensus. The Royal College of General Practitioners was also asked to nominate experienced GPs with knowledge

Table 10.2 Quality criteria for assessing research reviews

1 Were the questions and methods clearly stated?
2 Were comprehensive search methods used to locate relevant studies?
3 Were explicit methods used to determine which articles to include in the review?
4 Was the validity of the primary studies assessed?
5 Was the assessment of the primary studies reproducible and free from bias?
6 Was variation in the findings of the relevant studies analysed?
7 Were the findings of the primary studies combined appropriately?
8 Were the reviewers' conclusions supported by the data cited?

Source: Oxman and Guyatt (1988).

of mental health issues. Three workshops used structured consensus methods to outline best practice in areas where research is weak. This was the first time that expert therapists from a wide range of therapeutic approaches had been asked to develop a consensus on treatment choice decisions, and whether such a consensus was attainable was in itself an interesting empirical question. The guideline will be completed in 2000.

FUTURE DIRECTIONS: INTEGRATIVE TREATMENT GUIDELINES FOR SPECIFIC CONDITIONS

Many psychological therapy practitioners in both the USA (Jensen *et al.*, 1990) and the UK (Department of Health, 1996b) draw on more than one psychotherapeutic treatment orientation in their treatment of patients. In the UK this is the norm for clinical psychologists, is increasingly common for counsellors and counselling psychologists, and in addition there is an emerging trend for dedicated psychotherapy departments to offer a range of specialist psychotherapies rather than only psychodynamic psychotherapy. Integrative treatment guidelines would aim to inform such clinical practitioners in their treatment decisions.

At the time of writing, no such integrative treatment guidelines exist. Roth *et al.* (1996) give clinical examples of evidence-based practice in the psychotherapeutic treatment of post-traumatic stress disorder to demonstrate how appropriate treatment needs to vary according to a number of aspects of patients' presentation and history. These clinical examples and others could be used to construct an appropriate integrative clinical guideline for post-traumatic stress disorder.

Cape (1998) gives an example of panic disorder as an area where such a guideline could be developed.

- For patients whose panic symptoms involve catastrophic interpretation of bodily symptoms as indications of illness, madness or similar, use a cognitive approach (Clark, 1986; Clark *et al.*, 1994; Salkovskis and Clark, 1991).
- For patients with panic disorder accompanied by moderate or severe agoraphobia that has lasted longer than six months, use exposure therapy (Trull *et al.*, 1988).
- For patients whose panic disorder has been precipitated by and is associated with re-evocation of disturbing childhood memories (e.g. an early maternal death), use a psychodynamic approach.

- For patients whose panic disorder is part of a complex presentation of co-morbid problems, including personality disorder, consider alternative formulations of the patient's problems and their relationship with each other. Select a treatment approach based on these formulations that is most likely to optimise treatment goals that are considered important by both patient and therapist within the pragmatic (time) constraints of the specific therapeutic context of the treating psychological therapist and patient.

The above recommendations were speculative (as no review or research evidence or clinical consensus has been undertaken) and incomplete, but are an example of how such an integrative guideline could be developed.

In summary, the appropriate development and use of clinical practice guidelines in psychotherapy should be seen as important in a range of initiatives to improve mental health services by drawing on best evidence of good practice to inform both practitioners and service users. Guidelines development is in its infancy in this field. Over the next few years, we anticipate greater sophistication in both their development and use, greater awareness among psychotherapists of their value and an increase in appropriate and relevant research to inform them.

REFERENCES

Agency for Health Care Policy and Research (1993a) *Depression in Primary Care: Detection and Diagnosis.* Washington, DC: US Department of Health and Human Services.

Agency for Health Care Policy and Research (1993b) *Depression in Primary Care: Treatment of Major Depression.* Washington, DC: US Department of Health and Human Services.

Agency for Health Care Policy and Research (1993c) *Depression in Primary Care: Detection, Diagnosis, and Treatment. Quick Reference Guide for Clinicians.* Washington, DC: US Department of Health and Human Services.

Agency for Health Care Policy and Research (1993d) *Depression is a Treatable Illness: A Patient's Guide.* Washington, DC: US Department of Health and Human Services.

American Psychiatric Association (1993a) Practice guideline for eating disorders. *American Journal of Psychiatry*, 150: 207–228.

American Psychiatric Association (1993b) Practice guideline for major depressive disorder in adults. *American Journal of Psychiatry*, 150 (4): Supplement.

Antman, E.M., Lau, J., Kupelnick, B., Mosteller, F. and Chalmers, T.C. (1992) A comparison of results of meta-analyses of randomised control trials and recommendations of clinical experts. *Journal of the American Medical Association*, 268: 240–248.

Aveline, M., Shapiro, D.A., Parry, G. and Freeman, C.P.L. (1995) Building research foundations for psychotherapy practice, in M. Aveline and D.A. Shapiro (eds) *Research Foundations for Psychotherapy Practice*. Chichester: Wiley.

Bergin, A.E. and Garfield, S.L. (eds) (1994) *Handbook of Psychotherapy and Behavior Change* (4th edn). New York: Wiley.

Cape, J. (1998) Clinical practice guidelines for the psychotherapies, in R. Davenhill and P. Patrick (eds) *Rethinking Clinical Audit*. Routledge: London

Cape, J., Durrant, K., Graham, J., Patrick, M., Rouse, A. and Hartley, J. (1996) *Counselling and Psychological Therapies Guideline*. London: Camden and Islington MAAG.

Cape, J., Hartley, J., Durrant, K., Patrick, M. and Graham, J. (1998) Development of local clinical practice guideline to assist GPs, counsellors and psychological therapists in matching patients to the most appropriate psychological treatment. *Journal of Clinical Effectiveness*, 3: 97–140.

Clark, D.M. (1986) A cognitive approach to panic. *Behaviour Research and Therapy*, 24: 461–470.

Clark, D.M., Salkovskis, P.M., Hackmann, A., Middleton, H., Anastasiades, P. and Gelder, M. (1994) A comparison of cognitive therapy, applied relaxation and imipramine in the treatment of panic disorder. *British Journal of Psychiatry*, 164: 759–769.

Cluzeau, F., Littlejohns, P., Grimshaw, J. and Feder, G. (1997) Appraisal instrument for clinical guidelines. Version 1. St George's Hospital Medical School, London. May 1997. ISBN 1–8981–8311–2.

Department of Health (1996a) *Clinical Guidelines: Using Clinical Guidelines to Improve Patient Care within the NHS*. Leeds: NHS Executive.

Department of Health (1996b) *A Review of Strategic Policy on NHS Psychotherapy Services in England*. London: NHS Executive

Duff, L.A., Kelson, M., Marriott, S., McIntosh, A., Brown, S., Cape, J., Marcus, M. and Traynor, M. (1996) Clinical guidelines: involving patients and users of services. *Journal of Clinical Effectiveness*, 1: 104–112.

Effective Health Care (1993) *The Treatment of Depression in Primary Care*. Bulletin No. 5. Leeds: University of Leeds.

Effective Health Care (1994) *Implementing Clinical Practice Guidelines*. Bulletin No. 8. Leeds: University of Leeds.

Eli Lilly National Clinical Audit Centre (1996) *Management of Depression in General Practice*. Audit protocol CT11. Leicester: Eli Lilly Centre.

Field, M.J. and Lohr, K.N. (eds) (1990) *Clinical Practice Guidelines: Direction for a New Program*. Washington, DC: National Academy Press.

Field, M.J. and Lohr, K.N. (eds) (1992) *Guidelines for Clinical Practice: From Development to Use.* Washington, DC: National Academy Press.

Garfield, S.L. (1986) Research on client variables in psychotherapy, in A.E. Bergin and S.L. Garfield (eds) *Handbook of Psychotherapy and Behavior Change* (3rd edn). New York: Wiley.

Garfield, S.L. and Bergin, A.E. (1994) Introduction and historical overview, in A.E. Bergin and S.L. Garfield (eds) *Handbook of Psychotherapy and Behavior Change* (4th edn). New York: Wiley.

Gigone, D. and Hastie, R. (1997) Proper analysis of the accuracy of group judgements. *Psychological Bulletin*, 121: 149–167.

Grimshaw, J.M. and Russell, I.T. (1993a) Effects of clinical guidelines on medical practice: a systematic review of rigorous evaluations. *Lancet*, 342: 1317–1322.

Grimshaw, J.M. and Russell, I.T. (1993b) Achieving health gain through clinical guidelines I: developing scientifically valid guidelines. *Quality in Health Care*, 2: 243–248.

Grimshaw, J.M. and Russell. I.T. (1994) Achieving health gain through clinical guidelines II: ensuring guidelines change medical practice. *Quality in Health Care*, 3: 45–52.

Hayward, R.S.A. and Laupacis, A. (1993) Initiating, conducting and maintaining guidelines development programs. *Canadian Medical Association Journal*, 148: 507–512.

Jensen, J.B., Bergin, A.E. and Greaves, D.W. (1990) The meaning of eclecticism: new survey and analysis of components. *Professional Psychology: Research and Practice*, 21: 124–130.

Lambert, M.J. and Hill, C.E. (1994) Assessing psychotherapy outcomes and processes, in A.E. Bergin and S.L. Garfield (eds) *Handbook of Psychotherapy and Behavior Change* (4th edn). New York: Wiley.

Linstone, H.A. and Turoff, M. (1975) *The Delphi Method, Techniques and Applications.* Reading, Mass.: Addison-Wesley.

Mackay, H. and Barkham, M. (1998) *Report to the National Counselling and Psychological Therapies Clinical Guidelines Development Group: Evidence from Published Reviews and Meta-analyses, 1990–98.* University of Leeds: Psychological Therapies Research Centre.

Malan, D.H. (1973) The outcome problem in psychotherapy research: a historical review. *Archives of General Psychiatry*, 29: 719–729.

Marriott, S. and Lelliott, P. (1994) *Clinical Practice Guidelines.* College Report CR 34. London: Royal College of Psychiatrists.

Mintz, J. (1981) Measuring outcome in psychodynamic psychotherapy: psychodynamic vs symptomatic assessment. *Archives of General Psychiatry*, 38: 503–506.

Munoz, R.F., Hollon, S.D., McGrath, E., Rehm, L.P. and VandenBos, G.R. (1994) On the AHCPR depression in primary care guidelines: further considerations for practitioners. *American Psychologist*, 49: 42–61.

Murphy, M.K., Black, N., Lamping, D.L., McKee, C.M., Sanderson, C.F.B., Askham, J. *et al.* (1998) Consensus development methods, and their use in clinical guideline development. *Health Technology Assessment,* 2 (3).

Norcross, J.C. and Goldfried, M.R. (eds) (1992) *Handbook of Psychotherapy Integration.* New York: Basic Books.

Olson, C.M. (1995) Consensus statement: applying structure. *Journal of the American Medical Association,* 273: 72–73.

Oxman, A.D. and Guyatt, G.H. (1988) Guidelines for reading review articles. *Canadian Medical Association Journal,* 138: 697–703.

Parry, G. (1998) Guideline on treatment choice decisions for psychological therapies. *Audit Trends,* 6: 110.

Persons, J.B., Thase, M.E. and Crits-Christoph, P. (1996) The role of psychotherapy in the treatment of depression: review of two practice guidelines. *Archives of General Psychiatry,* 53: 283–290.

Quality Assurance Project (1982a) A treatment outline for agoraphobia. *Australian and New Zealand Journal of Psychiatry,* 16: 25–33.

Quality Assurance Project (1982b) A treatment outline for depressive disorders. *Australian and New Zealand Journal of Psychiatry,* 17: 129–148.

Quality Assurance Project (1991a) Treatment outlines for borderline, narcissistic and histrionic personality disorders. *Australian and New Zealand Journal of Psychiatry,* 25: 392–403.

Quality Assurance Project (1991b) Treatment outlines for antisocial personality disorders. *Australian and New Zealand Journal of Psychiatry,* 25: 541–547.

Ramsey, P.G., Carline, J.D., Inui, T.S., Larson, E.B., LoGerfo, J.P., Norcini, J.J. and Wenrich, M.D. (1991) Changes over time in the knowledge base of practising internists. *Journal of the American Medical Association,* 266: 103–107.

Roth, A. and Fonagy, P. (1996) *What Works for Whom? A Critical Review of Psychotherapy Research.* New York: Guilford Press.

Roth, A., Fonagy, P. and Parry, G. (1996) Psychotherapy research, funding, and evidence-based practice, in A. Roth and P. Fonagy, *What Works for Whom? A Critical Review of Psychotherapy Research.* New York: Guilford Press.

Royal College of Psychiatrists (1997) *Immediate Management of Violence in Clinical Settings: A Clinical Practice Guideline.* London: Royal College of Psychiatrists.

Sackett, D.L., Richardson, W.S., Rosenberg, W. and Haynes, R.B. (1997) *Evidence-based Medicine: How to Practice and Teach EBM.* New York: Churchill Livingstone.

Sackett, D.L., Rosenberg, W.M.C., Gray, J.A.M., Haynes, R.B. and Richardson, W.S. (1996) Evidence based medicine: what it is and what it isn't. *British Medical Journal,* 312: 71–72.

Salkovskis, P.M. and Clark, D. (1991) Cognitive therapy for panic attacks. *Journal of Cognitive Psychotherapy,* 5: 215–226.

Schulberg, H.C., Katon, W., Simon, G.E. and Rush, A.J. (1998) Treating major depression in primary care practice: an update of the Agency for Health Care Policy and Research Practice Guidelines. *Archives of General Psychiatry*, 55: 1121–1127.

Scott, E.A. and Black, N. (1991) When does consensus exist in expert panels? *Journal of Public Health Medicine*, 30: 35–39.

Sutton, P.A. (1996) *Clinical Guidelines Evaluation: Final Report of Department of Health Guidelines Evaluation Project*. Hull: University of Hull.

Trull, T.J., Nietzel, M.T. and Main, A. (1988) The use of meta-analysis to assess the clinical significance of behavior therapy for agoraphobia. *Behavior Therapy*, 19: 527–538.

Weber, J.J., Solomon, M. and Bachrach, H.M. (1985) Characteristics of psychoanalytic clinic patients: Report of the Columbia Psychoanalytic Centre Research Project (I). *International Review of Psychoanalysis*, 12: 13–26.

Woolf, S.H. (1992) Practice guidelines, a new reality in medicine II: methods of developing guidelines. *Archives of Internal Medicine*, 152: 946–952.

Woolf, S.H. (1998) Do clinical practice guidelines define good medical care? The need for good science and the disclosure of uncertainty when defining 'best practices'. *Chest*, 113 (3 Supplement):166S–171S.

Chapter 11

Getting evidence into practice

Stephen Goss and Nancy Rowland

In this final chapter we consider the challenge of getting evidence into practice and of producing evidence relevant to complex psychological therapies. Some of the barriers to change and strategies that may help practitioners integrate evidence into their work are considered. We outline a number of ways in which managers and practitioners can facilitate and extend evidence-based clinical practice. In considering the impact on psychological therapies of evidence-based commissioning and policy, a pluralist approach to generating evidence for psychological therapies is advocated. We conclude by noting the potential for shifting the balance of power created by EBHC in favour of its consumers because of the relative accessibility and immediate utility for *all* those with a stake in psychological therapy provision.

THE CHALLENGE FOR PRACTITIONERS AND MANAGERS

Evidence-based health care consists of three main stages – producing the evidence, making the evidence available and using the evidence (Muir-Gray, 1997). As Muir-Gray points out (1997), research evidence can be used to improve clinical practice and to improve health service management. Evidence-based clinical practice requires practitioners to use the best evidence available, in consultation with the patient, to decide which option suits that patient best. Managers, who are responsible for health services for groups of patients or populations, have to make wider decisions about policy, purchasing and management and the promotion of evidence-based clinical practice. The challenge to both practitioners and managers is unavoidable.

As the EBHC movement progresses, there will be few areas of psychological therapy practice or management that will not feel its impact, including non-NHS organisations. Other statutory agencies, non-statutory services, the voluntary sector and therapists in private practice will all be affected by the findings of systematic reviews which impact upon their work, and which may raise questions of effectiveness and cost-effectiveness. Clinical guidelines on specific conditions may make recommendations about optimum treatments which are generally applicable across service settings. Furthermore, while the activities of organisations such as the NHS Centre for Reviews and Dissemination, the National Institute of Clinical Excellence and the Commission for Health Improvement are concerned primarily with health matters, their findings will undoubtedly form the benchmark for good practice elsewhere. Finally, the ethical and legal ramifications of not implementing best practice may be considerable.

OVERCOMING THE BARRIERS TO IMPLEMENTATION: PRACTITIONER AND MANAGEMENT INVOLVEMENT IN EVIDENCE-BASED PRACTICE

The 'caucus race' conclusion regarding the relative effectiveness of alternative treatments (Beutler, 1991), that all the psychological therapies have won some evidence of effectiveness and 'all must have prizes', is not helpful in guiding purchasing decisions. It is both impossible and undesirable to fund everything: impossible because of finite budgets; undesirable because some treatments will help certain people more than others and we have an ethical duty to provide the best possible care within the resources available. It follows that purchasers must decide what to fund on the basis of guidance about what works best and how much it costs. Differentiation between the various forms of psychological therapy in terms of their clinical effectiveness and cost-effectiveness is not only desirable but essential.

Undoubtedly there are areas in which the various psychological therapies find themselves in competition. However, participants in the 'best care' debate will do well to avoid narrowing it into any form of turf war in which the winners are those that claim the biggest share of the territory. Cape and Parry (Chapter 10) note that, against a background of extraordinary diversity of models for psychological therapies, practitioners tend to hold strong allegiances to their chosen approach. While clinical judgement informed by training, experience and intuition is essential to best practice, practitioner allegiances provide an unreliable base for choice of treatment, and a developing knowledge base may either confirm or disconfirm theoretical models.

Challenging the culture of conservatism in the psychological therapies

Few practitioners would overtly disregard research evidence on the relative effectiveness or cost-effectiveness of their work. More common is a lack of awareness of the evidence base and a slowness in integrating findings into their clinical work. It is, perhaps, unsurprising that the possibility of having research demonstrate the superiority of a competing approach over one's own may be met with some resistance and scepticism. Clarkson describes one such emotional response to research as 'feeling threatened by anxiety about being scrutinised and the possibility of coming up with findings which do not support one's convictions' (1998: xvi). A serious challenge to any practitioner's theoretical orientation, especially if it is believed to be backed up by years of clinical experience, can be unnerving. The incentives to resist the rising tide of evidence for fear of what it may bring can be strong.

Wheeler and Hicks argue that many of the apparently logical arguments against changing clinical practice in the light of research findings are rooted in 'a deep-seated diffidence to undertake new activities' (1996: 532). Counsellors and psychotherapists, like other professionals, have been shown to have deeply conservative attitudes to many forms of innovation (e.g. Rosen and Weil, 1998; Goss and Baldry, 1999). Moreover, the integration of research and practice is hampered by a widespread lack of *active* commitment to, and sometimes understanding of, the principles, processes and products of EBHC. The tide is, perhaps, beginning to change, but, although Jenkinson (1997: 2) notes that 'increasingly attention is being paid to evidence derived from research', it is still often the case that 'in spite of a large and rather sophisticated research literature . . . there is widespread agreement that this research has done little to influence or improve clinical practice' (Richards and Longborn, 1996: 701).

If change is to come about, it will be necessary for practitioners to embrace the EBHC movement in practice as well as in principle. This needs to be supported by a deeper cultural shift: conservative attitudes to change will have to be addressed.

Evidence-based practitioner flexibility and lifelong learning: service integration and co-operation

The current emphasis on lifelong learning for health professionals should include information about recent developments in best practice and effectiveness data. Practitioners are already familiar with the notion of review: review of cases, of career development, of clinical skills, of performance. Such reviews should be a routine part of therapeutic work and should *systematically* incorporate evidence into practice.

Furthermore, as good evidence emerges that certain approaches are appropriate for certain clients with certain problems practitioners will need to change their approach. If a therapist is not trained to provide the best treatment indicated for certain clients or conditions, those clients will need to be referred elsewhere. Referral between services that offer different forms of therapy may be increasingly indicated and be a requirement of competent practice. Practitioners offering therapeutic interventions may find mutual benefits in working more closely and co-operatively together, despite the current inequalities in perceived status, contractual conditions, rates of pay and typical client groups – and the professional tensions that result. From a management perspective, the goals of effectiveness, efficiency and fairness (the key factors identified by Ferguson and Russell in Chapter 3) will necessitate high-quality assessment criteria, clearly defined interventions and clear referral guidelines. Such developments can only benefit practitioner, manager and patient.

Dryden (1994) has called for 'bespoke' psychological therapies in which a practitioner's response is tailored to the needs of each individual client. Some therapists may respond to the challenge of a developing evidence base by specialising in certain therapeutic work with certain patients; others may choose to continue training to acquire additional skills.

While the majority of psychological practitioners may require extensive further training to broaden their therapeutic approach, such flexibility, however, need not be limitless. As emphasis on the research base increases and guidance on what constitutes clinical excellence becomes clearer, so the influence (noted by Maynard in Chapter 4) of politically driven needs to respond to public or, worse, transient media concern must diminish. The increased flexibility involved in providing evidence-based therapies to varied client needs may be counteracted by increased stability in the interventions identified as being most beneficial and cost-effective for the population as a whole.

The need to develop practitioner research skills

One of the ways in which barriers to implementing evidence can be overcome is (as suggested by Parry in Chapter 5) in training mental health professionals in critical appraisal and in research skills. Such training, commonplace in some professional disciplines, would also serve to demystify research findings and provide an opportunity to address the cultural resistance both to research and to innovation in practice mentioned above.

Practitioners give a range of reasons for not involving themselves in research (Morrow-Bradley and Elliott, 1986; McLeod, 1994; Baker *et al.*, 1997; Clarkson, 1998); the first is that research is perceived to be irrelevant, with little to offer the practitioner concerned to maximise their efforts with clients. This is a challenge to research specialists and practitioners alike who *together* need to address questions that are directly relevant to daily practice.

Another theme is that participating in research may interfere with therapeutic work. Undoubtedly, any research will have an effect on the therapeutic work being examined – at the very least, patients in research trials tend to do better than those *not* in trials, whether in the treatment or control arm of the experiment. Moreover, given ethical requirements for informed consent, beneficent intent towards clients and appropriate levels of confidentiality and anonymity (Bond, 1993; McLeod, 1994), it is possible to design research that enhances rather than detracts from the therapeutic experience. This is not to suggest that it is easy to combine practice and research effectively. There are many complex issues relating to power-dynamics and boundaries within the relationship between practitioner-researcher and client (Etherington, 1996), as well as those surrounding methodology and giving meaning to data.

Finally, it emerges that practitioners are loath to do research due to a lack of skills, time, resources or support. Unless these obstacles are addressed at a managerial, contractual and cultural level a research ethos is unlikely to flourish. Managers would be well advised to give overt encouragement and practical support to therapists to prioritise research activities (such as those outlined in the next section), to enhance the ability of their services not only to incorporate current best evidence but to ensure that it is incorporated appropriately, effectively, efficiently and fairly.

None the less, whatever resistances there may be, all the different professional groups in the psychological therapies will have to participate actively and positively in all stages of EBHC – from conducting or supporting original research (including literature reviews), through debating the acceptability of different forms of evidence, to the implementation of practice guidelines. If they do not do so they will risk losing out to those groups which take on a more active or influential role. An example is the humanistic counselling models which risk becoming unfairly 'disenfranchised' (Bohart *et al.*, 1998) relative to those with a more easily quantifiable scientific base.

POSITIVE PRACTITIONER CONTRIBUTIONS TO THE EVIDENCE BASE

While large scale RCTs or other complex study designs are often inappropriate or impractical for practitioners to undertake themselves, there are a number of approaches that can help therapists develop evidence-based practice. Generating the evidence base does not comprise only large-scale, headline-making studies. While some of the methods noted below and in Box 11.1 may have little immediate impact on the development of evidence-based psychological therapies, they tend to influence the work of the individual practitioner and to contribute to the culture of evaluation.

1   Reflective practice is part of the everyday work of the competent practitioner. Although willingness to engage in a deliberate process of understanding one's work and using the evidence it generates to further develop professional skills can vary according to the

---

Box 11.1 Ways in which practitioners can enhance their involvement in EBHC

- Awareness of the findings of EBHC initiatives
- Reflective practice and supervision / case discussion
- Provision of case studies and case-series studies
- Undertaking small-scale, possibly qualitative, research
- Undertaking routine audit and evaluation of their work
- Training in research and critical appraisal skills
- Publishing research findings
- Site collaboration in large multi-centre randomised controlled trials

therapist's training, awareness, stress, motivation and personality (Dale, 1997), continuing professional development is recommended by the majority of professional bodies in the psychological therapies, as it is in the medical profession. Supervision entails establishing good standards of practice; developing the practitioner's knowledge and skills and working with his or her response to the process of conducting the therapy (Tolley and Rowland, 1995). Just as qualitative research can be sensitive to criticisms of therapy from clients (see McLeod, Chapter 7), consultative support or case supervision offers an opportunity for a 'warts and all' examination of a therapist's work. Although many psychological therapists who receive such supervisory support would not consider it a form of research, it is capable of routinely generating significant quantities of evidence of clinical relevance. Those professionals who are required to participate in regular consultative case supervision have, at the very least, a valuable means of quality control.

2   Reflective practice should demand that practitioners are informed of the findings of trials, systematic reviews and both the content and status of current practice guidelines. Practice must be influenced by evidence-based guidelines even where it is not driven by them. Where practitioners diverge from the recommended forms of care they should be able to explain why the alternative course of action is a better one. This is a teaching responsibility for supervisors and part of self-directed lifelong learning for practitioners.

3   Preparation of case studies or case-series studies (which consider a number of clients with clinically relevant characteristics in common) can be seen as part of ongoing professional development (Parker, 1995). Indeed, a great deal of the material presented in supervision could be considered an informal type of case study (Tolley and Rowland, 1995). It is a relatively straightforward step for verbal case discussion to be formalised and presented in a more systematic way – such as in detailed written form with explicit reference to the supporting literature and research. Such studies can then inform other practitioners and contribute to the culture of evaluation in the psychological therapies. As with other forms of qualitative research, what is lost in numerical precision is compensated for with accuracy of representation of the individuals concerned and the vivid, direct insights offered.

4   Qualitative investigation of specific points of recommended best practice is also a practicable way of contributing to the wider evidence base. Shafi (1998), for example, examined the view, widely accepted

in the published literature, that it is advantageous for clients to have a racially similar therapist. Shafi found that, among a purposively selected group of counselling clients, cultural awareness and sensitivity were far more important factors. Despite the limitations inherent in such small-scale work it is certainly capable of providing grounds for challenging accepted wisdom and of prompting further, larger-scale, research.

5   Making use of routine audit and evaluation as part of everyday work ensures that standards and benchmarks for effectiveness are rigorously applied and can also produce evidence of wider interest, especially if it can be collated with compatible forms of data from other agencies to form large data sets (such as contributing to a PRN). With the advent of standardised packages for audit and evaluation that can be applied in a range of settings, powerful indications of trends should be possible. Equality of access, different outcomes between different client groups or case types may be more readily identified and addressed than at present.

6   Many Masters-level and small-scale studies remain unpublished and read by a very small number of people. The contribution of practitioners could be far greater if this 'grey literature' was better placed in the public domain.

7   Finally, while practitioners are usually unable to access the skills and resources needed to organise controlled comparisons of therapeutic interventions, it is possible to co-operate with triallists as a site collaborator. Large multi-centre trials need large representative samples of patients, practitioners and practices. The benefits of collaboration for participants (whether patients or practitioners) in terms of treatments, understanding of the research process and in contributing to the evidence base can be significant.

The overall result is likely to be a large body of quantitative and qualitative evidence that could, at the very least, be used to target areas for future research and could also assist managers in evidence-based clinical decision-making, particularly where the knowledge base is lacking.

THE FUTURE OF EBHC IN THE PSYCHOLOGICAL THERAPIES

When guidance becomes tyranny: the limitations of evidence-based health care

Proponents of evidence-based health care will need to be aware of its limitations. There is potential for evidence-based guidance to be misused. Services can be commissioned on a poor or incomplete evidence base. Moreover, as Greenhalgh points out, the 'evidence based approach to clinical decision making is often incorrectly held to rest on the assumption that clinical observation is totally objective' (1999: 323) – a sort of naive empiricism. If this is indeed the case, the fears of practitioners, and their resistance to using the evidence, can be understood. Health professionals may feel frustrated when trying to apply evidence-based research findings to real-life cases, especially if they abandon the interpretive framework they use and attempt to get by on the evidence alone (Greenhalgh, 1999).

It is essential that guidelines are not used as rigid rule books, and that practitioners do not become over-reliant on guidance. Similarly, managers and policy-makers must not use guidelines as lists of acceptable methods, as in the empirically validated treatments movement in the USA. Such lists are inevitably based on generalised rules about which approaches *tend* to be most effective in *most* cases. Practitioners must always be free to use their best judgement on the basis of the specific details of each case and to have access to the treatments best suited to that individual – even if that means making an exception to the general rule.

Furthermore, as Ferguson and Russell note in Chapter 3, it is vital that the use of guidelines and statements of best clinical practice do not come to stifle innovation. The use of the evidence base to guide clinical and policy decision-making raises the possibility of practitioners and managers coming to rely increasingly on those practices for which there is greatest precedence. This may lead to defensive practice and a lack of innovation. Although there are certainly 'wrong' answers to particular clinical questions, it is often impossible to define a single right one that can be applied in every context (Greenhalgh, 1999). It has been stressed that the practice of EBHC is both a science and an art (e.g. Sackett *et al.*, 1996), and that we need to incorporate attributes of both if we are to respond most appropriately to the needs of individual patients and to managing psychological services.

Increasing the range, quantity and quality of EBHC

It is in the nature of EBHC that it should develop and evolve. While its fundamental principles remain constant, the evidence base which informs practice is subject to constant review and change. It is probable that sound evidence will become available on an ever-increasing range of areas and that guidance, informed by an increasing knowledge base, will be more reliable and more informative for clients, practitioners and policy-makers alike. It seems probable that the quality of the evidence base will also improve through the development of new tools and research methods, such as the introduction of standardised and widely applicable measures of clinical outcome.

Minimising bias

In addition to the undesirable consequences of therapeutic allegiance among *practitioners*, previously noted, it will also be essential to remove the influence of *researcher* allegiance to preferred models. The influence of researcher allegiance, for example on comparative studies of the relative effectiveness of psychological therapies, has been well documented. Luborsky *et al.* (1996) have even reported that while comparative outcome studies in psychological therapies often have conflicting results, researcher allegiance to one of the approaches under study was a more powerful predictor of which studies came to what conclusions than *any* other factor. Systematic reviews, of course, go a long way to minimising bias and, at the very least, take the important step forward of making their methods explicit and open to critique.

Overcoming such bias will be crucial at *all* stages involved in providing evidence-based health care. If this is to be achieved, we must start by ensuring that the paradigms on which research is based are capable of demonstrating the effects of widely differing approaches – from humanistic counselling to cognitive behavioural therapies. Researchers themselves must also take steps to address potential biases *and to make those steps explicit*. Those who review the research have an additional responsibility to ensure that their criteria and methods leave their work open to incorporating evidence produced by a range of methods, especially the method most appropriate for the therapy under review. Not all forms of therapy and counselling can be assessed equally well by a single research approach. We need further debate about how we constitute the evidence base for clinical practice and how it should evolve beyond its current state.

The need for pluralism

Calls for pluralist research that would do more than treat the different methods as separate contributions to be used in sequence or in parallel are neither uncommon nor new (Goss and Mearns, 1997). None the less, even when different research approaches are equally valued, their different types of evidence are frequently seen as being largely immiscible except to the extent that their separately derived findings merely corroborate or elaborate each other's findings or, when they disagree, generate new research questions (e.g. Miles and Huberman, 1984). That much work remains to be done is stressed by McLeod (1994) who notes:

> The field has been dominated by the positivist-paradigmatic monolith for so long that there is a long way to go before we will know what a truly pluralist methodology will look like, or even whether it is possible.
>
> (McLeod, 1994: 180)

Bergin and Garfield (1994: 828) endorse this view, noting that 'traditional experimental and multivariate methodologies have not consistently or adequately addressed the phenomenon of therapeutic change'.

At present, there are fundamental philosophical conflicts between the reductionism of RCTs and the phenomenology of qualitative and naturalistic studies. The breadth of perspectives represented by contributors to this book demonstrates the diversity of positions that can be taken.

If more than one approach is to contribute to the body of knowledge, we will have to ensure that these very different qualitative and quantitative paradigms can be combined. Even the most sophisticated attempts to achieve this (Howard, 1983; Rescher, 1977, 1993) have so far proved insufficient.

Kazdin (1994: 33) insists that 'the breadth of designs is vital to the field and contributes to its advances. The reason is that each particular design strategy alone has its weaknesses.' Furthermore, pragmatic methodological triangulation is well established (e.g. Jick, 1979; Duffy, 1987; Bryman, 1984; 1992) and the World Health Organization recommends that several investigative methods should be used to assess performance in health related professions, in the hope that each will offset the problems inherent in the others (WHO, 1981).

A *fully* pluralist approach to evidence-based health care would draw on quantitative and qualitative methods, and the reductionist and phenomenological paradigms that underpin them, at *all* stages of the research process. The formulation of research questions, study design, data collection and interpretation, presentation of the findings and collation of those findings into systematic reviews would *all* have to satisfy the requirements of *each* approach. This can lead to a surprisingly complex set of processes as the differing paradigms must then constantly interact with each other to ensure that their respective contributions are sustainable from each perspective. This has rarely been attempted but does raise the possibility of more fully meeting the needs of the various stakeholders in the output of evidence-based health care initiatives. In addition to having greater utility for this wide range of stakeholders, outcome data would be more robust: being supported by a range of methods at every stage, the findings are unlikely to be undermined by the criticisms that protagonists from each perspective typically level at alternative approaches. The evidence base as a whole, the clinical guidelines derived from it, and the clinical governance agenda driving EBHC would benefit from such pluralism and might more credibly meet the needs of practitioners and clients, policy-makers and service managers.

Shifting the balance of power

As patients and purchasers become better informed and better able to demand appropriate, effective interventions, it is possible that EBHC may lead to a significant shift in the provision of psychological therapies. In time, the general public and clients, as well as managers, purchasers, policy-makers and clinicians, will *all* have access to information on who should be doing what, for whom and how. This represents a fundamental shift in the balance of power from the expert educated few towards a more open, egalitarian body of knowledge. EBHC has the potential to dispel much, if not all, of the myth and mystique of the psychological therapies. How they work, who or what they are good for, what they cost and who should be providing them will be far more clearly discernible than has been the case so far.

CONCLUSION

The unfolding of evidence and the resulting guidance in the psychological therapies has the potential to become one of the most significant revolutions in mental health care. It is incumbent on the consumers of research and clinical guidance – purchasers, practitioners, managers and clients – to ensure that it is used appropriately. In the end it will be its *utility* in routine care that will be the criterion of success for EBHC.

ACKNOWLEDGEMENTS

We would like to acknowledge the contributions of Steve Page and Gladeana McMahon in preparing material on practitioner research, some of which has been included in this chapter.

REFERENCES

Baker, M., Maskrey, N. and Kirk, S. (1997) *Clinical Effectiveness and Primary Care*. Abingdon: Radcliffe Medical Press.

Bergin, A.E. and Garfield, S.L. (1994) Overview, trends and future issues, in A.E. Bergin and S.L Garfield (eds) *Handbook of Psychotherapy and Behaviour Change*. New York: Wiley.

Beutler, L.E. (1991) Have all won and must all have prizes? Reviewing Luborsky et al.'s verdict. *Journal of Consulting and Clinical Psychology*, 59: 226–232.

Bohart, A.C., O'Hara, M. and Leitner, L.M. (1998) Empirically violated treatments: disenfranchisement of humanistic and other psychotherapies. *Psychological Research*, 8(2): 141–157.

Bond, T. (1993) *Standards and Ethics for Counselling in Action*. London: Sage.

Bryman, A. (1984) The debate about quantitative and qualitative research: a question of method or epistemology? *British Journal of Sociology*, 235 (1): 75–92.

Bryman, A. (1992) Quantitative and qualitative research: further reflections on their integration, in J. Brammen (ed.) *Mixing Methods: Qualitative and Quantitative Research*. Aldershot: Avebury.

Clarkson, P. (ed.) (1998) *Counselling Psychology: Integrating Theory, Research and Supervised Practice*. London: Routledge.

Dale, F. (1997) Stress and the personality of the psychotherapist, in V. Varma (ed.) *Stress in Psychotherapists*. London: Routledge.

Dryden, W. (1994) Possible future trends in Counselling and Counsellor Training: a personal view. *Counselling, Journal of the British Association for Counselling*, 5 (3): 194–197.

Duffy, M.E. (1987) 'Methodological triangulation: a vehicle for merging quantitative and qualitative research methods' in *IMAGE: Journal of Nursing Scholarship*, 19(3): 130–133.

Etherington, K. (1996) The counsellor as researcher: boundary issues and critical dilemmas. *British Journal of Guidance and Counselling*, 24 (3): 339–346.

Goss, S.P. and Mearns, D. (1997) A call for a pluralist epistemological understanding in the assessment and evaluation of counselling. *British Journal of Guidance and Counselling*, 25 (2): 189–198.

Goss, S.P. and Baldry, S. (1999) Information technology – effects and consequences for counselling. Presentation at the fifth BAC Research Conference, Leeds.

Greenhalgh, T. (1999) Narrative based medicine in an evidence based world. *British Medical Journal*, 318: 323–325.

Howard, G.S. (1983) Toward methodological pluralism. *Journal of Counselling Psychology*, 30, (1): 19–21, cited in McLeod (1994).

Jenkinson, C. (1997) Assessment and evaluation of health and medical care: an introduction and overview, in C. Jenkinson, *Assessment and Evaluation of Health and Medical Care*. Buckingham: Open University Press.

Jick, T.D. (1979) Mixing qualitative and quantitative methods: triangulation in action. *Administrative Science Quarterly*, 4: 602–611.

Kazdin, A.E. (1994) Methodology, design and evaluation, in A.E. Bergin and S.L Garfield (eds) *Handbook of Psychotherapy and Behavior Change*. New York: Wiley.

Luborsky, L., Diguer, L., Schweizer, E. and Johnson, S. (1996) The researchers therapeutic allegiance as a 'wildcard' in studies comparing the outcomes of treatments. Presentation at the 27th Annual Meeting of the Society for Psychotherapy Research, Amelia Island, Florida.

McLeod, J. (1994) *Doing Counselling Research*. London: Sage.

Mearns, D. and McLeod, J. (1984) A person-centered approach to research, in R.F. Levant and J.M. Schlien, *Client Centered Therapy and the Person Centered Approach*. New York: Praeger.

Miles, M.B. and Huberman, A.M. (1984) Drawing valid meaning from qualitative data: toward a shared craft. *Educational Researcher*, May: 20–30.

Morrow-Bradley, C. and Elliott, R. (1986) Utilisation of psychotherapy research by practising psychotherapists. *American Psychologist*, 41 (2): 188–197.

Muir-Gray, J. (1997) *Evidence Based Health Care*. London: Churchill Livingstone.

Parker, M. (1995) Practical approaches: case study writing. *Counselling, Journal of the British Association for Counselling*, 6 (1): 19–21.

Rescher, N. (1977) *Methodological Pragmatism*. Oxford: Clarendon Press.

Rescher, N. (1993) *Pluralism Against the Demand for Consensus*. Oxford: Clarendon Press.

Richards, P.S. and Longborn, S.D. (1996) Development of a method for studying thematic content of psychotherapy sessions. *Journal of Consulting and Clinical Psychology*, 64 (4): 701–711.

Rosen, L.D. and Weil, M.M. (1998) *The Mental Health Technology Bible*. London: John Wiley & Sons.

Tolley, K. and Rowland, N. (1995) *Evaluating the Cost-Effectiveness of Counselling in Healthcare*. London: Routledge.

Sackett, D.L., Rosenberg, W.M.C., Grey, J.A.M., Haynes, R.B. and Richardson, W.S. (1996) Evidence based medicine: what it is and what it isn't. *British Medical Journal*, 312: 71–72.

Shafi, S. (1998) A study of Muslim Asian women's experiences of counselling and the necessity for a racially similar counsellor. *Counselling Psychology Quarterly*, 11 (3): 301–314.

WHO Regional Office for Europe Working Group (1981) *The Assessment of Competence of Students in the Health Field*. Varna: World Health Organization.

Wheeler, S. and Hicks, C. (1996) The role of research in the professional development of counselling, in S. Palmer, S. Dainow and P. Milner (eds) *Counselling: The BAC Counselling Reader*. London: Sage.

Index